KEEP SCROLLING TILL YOU FEEL SOMETHING

McSWEENEY'S
SAN FRANCISCO

www.mcsweeneys.net

Copyright © 2019

Cover art by Anna Lakisova.

Back-cover warnings by Alex Baia.

McSweeney's and colophon are registered trademarks of McSweeney's,
a privately held company with wildly fluctuating resources.

ISBN: 978-1-944211-72-1

Printed in China

KEEP SCROLLING
TILL YOU
FEEL SOMETHING

TWENTY-ONE YEARS OF HUMOR FROM
McSWEENEY'S INTERNET TENDENCY

Edited by SAM RILEY *and* CHRIS MONKS

II. CHILDHOOD: 2005–2010

A MCSWEENEY'S INTERNET TENDENCY ORIGIN STORY

A MCSWEENEY'S INTERNET TENDENCY ORIGIN STORY

III. ADOLESCENCE: 2011–2015

A McSWEENEY'S INTERNET TENDENCY ORIGIN STORY

IV. EMERGING ADULTHOOD: 2016–2019

WENDY MOLYNEUX'S EXCERPTS FROM POPULAR
MCSWEENEY'S INTERNET TENDENCY LISTS THROUGHOUT HISTORY:

WENDY MOLYNEUX'S EXCERPTS FROM POPULAR
MCSWEENEY'S INTERNET TENDENCY LISTS THROUGHOUT HISTORY:

V. APPENDIX

EDITORS' NOTE

W E SHOULD HAVE CLOSED up shop back in '09 after we helped cure bird flu. We know, *we know*. How else could an internet comedy site with a couple thousand unique pageviews a day (slightly less on weekends and federal holidays) top itself? We saved millions of human lives, and restored the quiet dignity of birds. All thanks, of course, to a ridiculous yet historically profound list we published ("Hot New Styles in Face Masks") by Walter Carson. Shout out to that now famous team of teenaged cryptology interns from the CDC (we see you Mary, Todd, and Tater!) who cracked its code and discovered the formula for the bird flu vaccine embedded within its text. They may have been unpaid, but their work will never go unseen.

So, that should have been it. We should have gone out while we were at the height of our humor and public health games, before we completely bungled the TV and film rights to "Hot New Styles in Face Masks" and lost out on any money from what eventually (after numerous rewrites and litigation) became Netflix's hit reboot *Fuller House*.

But, no, we didn't end the Tendency and instead continued posting daily humor almost every day. Why? Well, we had already paid for the URL, but more importantly because fine, good-humored writers kept sending us their writing. We received dozens upon dozens of submissions a day, and sure, half of them were riding on the coattails of the groundbreaking face-mask list, but the other half were funny and silly and odd and not about face masks, and we felt compelled to share them with the world.

After twenty-one years we were still going strong, but a nagging feeling stopped us in our tracks, forcing us to reflect, regroup, and assess what we had done. You may be wondering: *Twenty-one years? What a random swath of time!* Well, perhaps twenty years is a meaningful moment of maturation in the lifetime of a website, or perhaps we were embroiled in a legal battle with Walter Carson after bungling that *Fuller House* deal. Perhaps we are not allowed to discuss this further. Thus we began scrolling back in time, way back before birds and influenzas ever dreamed of commingling, all the way to 1998, the year the site was born.

When we finally arrived back to the beginning, our minds were blown. We remembered why we got into this humor-peddling game in the first place. This wasn't another disease-ending discovery but a revelation, the perspective-shifting kind that comes from nearly thirty minutes of self-reflection. We were fucking hilarious. We'd been funny the whole time! Twenty-one years later and somehow the jokes were still fresh, even the early days when esoteric almost-literary satire was a thing. A seventeen-year-old dance lesson could make us chuckle as much as a five-year-old list of feminist humblebrags, or a recent collection of word problems for the race conscious. The Tendency is so much more than the website that ended bird flu. We were the website that invented laughter. If you don't believe us, look it up, but not before asking yourself if the truth will really make you happy.

This book is not complete by any means, but it does contain some of our favorite pieces from the twenty-one-year history of the website in something that approximates chronological order. We've included as many introductions as possible, as well as origin stories; very few people were around when the site was born, and thus there emerged competing narratives, all of which seem at least a little bit true. We've also included, here and there, reflections from some of our steady and unwavering contributors because, in the end, the site is the sum of our writers' efforts. So, reader, join us as we scroll down memory lane, rejoicing in a website that has matured before our eyes. Maybe time is made up. Maybe living in the past is just as good as living in the present. Maybe the *Fuller House* producers would at the very least put our URL in the credits.

—CHRIS MONKS & SAM RILEY

A SHORT NOTE
FROM THE FIRST EDITOR OF
McSWEENEY'S INTERNET TENDENCY*

E DITING THE TENDENCY IS one of the best jobs I ever had. Basically strangers you will never meet send you funny things and you try to make them slightly funnier by cutting the unfunny parts. You laugh half the day, you post stuff for no reason, and all the while, you don't have to stand up or even move. Then you wake up and do it again. Until you stop doing it, which is what happened with me after a few years. The site needed more professional editors, and they should be acknowledged here.

Kevin Shay was the first person to masterfully edit the site, and he was a spectacular reader, editor, and human. He was in charge of the site from roughly 2000–2002.

When we moved McSweeney's to San Francisco, Lee Epstein and Gideon Lewis-Kraus took over and edited the site with great literary acumen and roguish good looks. Their tenure went from about 2002–2003.

Then, for a heroic stretch, from 2003–2007, John Warner took over and guided and expanded the site and made it dizzyingly great and multifaceted, going on to serve as editor-at-large until 2015. John is, I expect, remembered by many comedy writers who started under his tutelage. He has been a constantly encouraging force in the lives of countless writers and we all owe him a debt of gratitude.

He handed the reins to Chris Monks, coeditor of this book, and editor of the website to this day. Chris continued the growth that

John began and, like John, has been a mentor, champion and expert improver of comedy for about twelve years now. As all can attest, he is invariably polite, has an infectious laugh, and in all ways is the editor everyone wants when starting out. He's the cool babysitter you can't believe your parents are leaving you with. Chris cares deeply about all the writers who share their work on our site, and the loyalty goes both ways. Everyone we asked to help with this book readily jumped in. It's been that kind of thing from the start—scrappy, unprofitable, ridiculous, and essential to the sanity of many of us.

—DAVE EGGERS
ACTUALLY SOMEWHERE IN IDAHO
SUMMER 2019

---

* The name of the website came from early McSweeney's editor-at-large Todd Pruzan. We were looking for a way to differentiate the website from the print journal—*Timothy McSweeney's Quarterly Concern*—and Todd came up with Timothy McSweeney's Internet Tendency. With the royalties, Todd has bought multiple houses, one of them made of platinum.

WHAT MIGHT THE FIRST
EXAMPLE OF INTERNET-DELIVERED
COMEDY HAVE LOOKED LIKE?

A FOREWORD TO
THE INTRODUCTION
by JAKE TAPPER

I T WAS ARBOR DAY 1981, *and at his Pentagon cubicle, Dr. Frances Pollack-Christiansen logged onto the Advanced Research Projects Agency Network, or ARPANET, with one goal in mind: to be the first person ever to tell a joke using the technology that would ultimately become the World Wide Web.*

"What do you call someone who has no body and no head, he's just a nose?" Pollack-Christiansen typed to ARPANET's Undersecretary of Defense Geoffrey McGillicudy.

McGillicudy didn't write back; he thought the entire ARPANET project a boondoggle.

But had he written back, Pollack-Christiansen would have responded: "No-Body Nose."

And with that, the first internet joke would have been made. Save for the revelation that roughly seven terabytes' worth of jokes were shared in the 1970s on the French research network CYCLADES, though they were all X-rated or anti-Semitic or both.

- - -

Okay, none of that was true. But what is true: In 1995, two employees of *Wired* magazine's online, less-respected little brother, HotWired.com, decided to go guerilla. Joey Anuff and Carl Steadman, using pseudonyms, furtively created the website Suck.com to offer biting and hilarious commentary on Silicon Valley and beyond.

Anuff and Steadman were soon discovered. Oddly enough, their editors allowed them to continue the site, which quickly became supported by ad revenue. They were among the first on the web to achieve such status.

Anuff and Steadman did it, in part, to vent.

The Onion soon got into the internet act for a different reason: pride.

The satiric newspaper, then based in Madison, Wisconsin, had been around since 1988. Seven years later, its story "CLINTON DEPLOYS VOWELS TO BOSNIA: Cities of Sjlbvdnzv, Grzny to Be First Recipients" began bouncing around on list-serves across the country, completely free of attribution. The hosts of NPR's *Car Talk* even read it on the air. As *Wired* noted in 1999, "Nobody credited The Onion, because nobody knew The Onion was the original source."

By May 1996, the web-skeptical editor had been convinced that going online was the best way to assure The Onion got credit for its work. Later that year, Chevy Chase read the same story aloud at a DNC fundraiser to President Clinton—this time with attribution. Chase told *Wired* that Clinton laughed heartily and called it "the funniest thing he'd ever heard."

And then there came *Timothy McSweeney's Quarterly Concern*, which contained a great number of rejections from the *New Yorker*'s Shouts & Murmurs section. Besieged with countless rejections after that publication hit bookstores, Timothy McSweeney's Internet Tendency was launched in 1998 to ensure that each of these rejected offerings had a home. McSweeney's thus became dedicated to the imperative of quantity over quality.

Then did they flock: CollegeHumor, launched at Wake Forest University in 1999; Modern Humorist, created by humorists Michael Colton and John Aboud in 2000; and Cracked.com, which in 2015 became its own original humor site instead of just the loser cousin of *MAD*. The tradition continued through the early part of the century with other legendary sites such as Yankee Pot Roast, Haypenny, The Toast, Reductress, and Very Smart Brothas.

By 2007, there was enough humor thriving online for academics to study. Writing in the Univeristy of Southern California's Annenberg School for Communication & Journalism's International Journal of Communication, Limor Shifman, in "Humor in the Age of Digital Reproduction: Continuity and Change in Internet-Based Comic Texts," noted that, "A content analysis of 400 humorous texts from eight salient humorous websites shows that the internet functions both as a 'carrier' of old humor types such as jokes and cartoons and as a 'generator' of new humor types." Indeed.

That same year Will Ferrell and Adam McKay birthed *Funny or Die*. It was clear that there was gold in them thar hills, but only if you had money to burn or very low overhead.

In my younger days, I contributed to Suck.com (my *nom de plume* was James Bong), Modern Humorist (a series of covers for the Hergé-esque "Adventures of Clintin"), and *McSweeney's*, which is how this entry came to be. It is, I admit, odd for people to read my (attempts at) humor and fiction as I am known for humorless nonfiction. For this reason, my 1999 spoof of men's magazine profiles of young actresses—"Though I Can't Be Certain, I Suspect That This Hollywood Actress I'm Interviewing May Be Entertaining Thoughts of Having Sex with Me"—is often misinterpreted as a confession. Likewise, my recent attempt to spoof the more weak-kneed profiles of the alt-righters among us, titled, "I Am the Melted Skull of Nazi Major Arnold Toht, the Ruthless Gestapo Agent with the Burned Hand in Raiders of the Lost Ark, and I Appreciate Your Sudden Interest in My Thoughts and Feelings," did not receive as many clicks as I had hoped, but it did help me get something off my chest.

You won't find those trifling offerings inside this volume, but you will find some of the legendary masterworks that have made McSweeney's Internet Tendency such a great and long-lasting site. This includes "The Talent Competition," by Tim Carvell, who went on to become head writer at *The Daily Show with Jon Stewart* and the showrunner for *Last Week Tonight with John Oliver.* And inside are classics of the genre such as "*Maxim* Does the Classics," by Wendy Molyneux of *Bob's Burgers*; and "A Guest Columnist Still Getting the Hang of It," by Ellie Kemper of *The Office* and *Unbreakable Kimmy Schmidt.*

I could go on and on because so many *McSweeney's* alumni make you laugh, whether in the pages of the *New Yorker* or on Netflix or at that dive bar in Brooklyn. It is cliché to observe that if we weren't laughing, we'd be weeping, so I shall avoid that note, except to say I hope you find joy in this book that is tantamount to its authors' despair.

AN INTRODUCTION BEFORE
YET ANOTHER FOREWORD
by DAN KENNEDY

Y OU HOLD IN YOUR hands a powerful manual which, if misused properly, can fortify your spirit and serve as a sturdy shield with which to deflect the joyless, the self-flagellating martyrs, mean-spirited wine heads, strung-out status fiends and ego junkies—all of whom life will hurl at you with frightening competency as the years go by. Life is full of square haircuts and dream vampires who are only going to get angrier and suck harder as you stay your path and hold fast to the magic contained within your heart and within this book. Twenty-one years ago, this magic would be the sort of thing you'd bestow upon the energized and urbane; semi-showered city-dwelling outliers who carried canvas and leather messenger bags, even though they weren't sure if they were a messenger, or what the message was. Those were halcyon days. But these are desperate times: we're up against a bulkhead of terrible men on their last stand, forging their own signatures on scorched earth manifestos, wearing cheap ties and herky-jerky middling jackets above semen-encrusted slacks and the kind of shoes angry stepfathers stomp around in. This is why the volume you hold in your hands is a portable collection. It's the kind of thing that can be lashed to a 650cc dirt bike and taken with you on the escape route from the urban and cultural apocalypse. You hold the book, but the rest is up to you—steer clear of humorless zealots! Run your life like a tight ship crewed by a few misfits with good hearts! Keep spirits high while navigating dark and narrow straits to wherever we're all headed!

Personally, after twenty-one years of living in the middle of New York City, I set a course for the mountains that loom over Manhattan, up a labyrinth of bear-infested dirt trails, to a modest fortress on the side of one of the mountains, guarded, buttressed. Up here, I'm by David Bowie's ashes, and the road where Dylan crashed his motorcycle while hiding out from sudden fame, a stone's throw from where Spalding Gray found his terrors of pleasure, and a couple hollows over from Donald Fagen's steely compound. If you have small pieces of iron in your forehead, it means you've already homed in on my exact location. It also means you're a pigeon, and how are you even reading this? I don't have the answers. None of us do, but together, we will.

A couple nights ago, we were awakened here by a pack of coyotes taking something down in the tree line; bloody screams, weird yippy battle cries, mongrel growls, howling—all maybe ten or twenty yards away from the bedroom window in the dark forest. The one thing I'd like to tell you from up here in deep snow under a beautiful full moon: wild animals are assholes. Years of Disney and Pixar and Henson have programmed our hearts not to think so, but wild animals can be selfish jerkoffs with bloody short-sighted agendas, trust me. You spend enough time in cities and you think people are the problem, and they are, but let me assure you: animals can be real dickheads to each other, too. I digress, this is shaping up like a TED talk on mushrooms and no sleep, delivered under duress by a speaker who is highly disoriented. I guess all I'm trying to say here is that the world today is a glacier on fire, full of cruel animals, controlled by broken sociopaths and former reality television hosts—and you're going to need someone on your side like never before. That's where this book comes in. Biting satire and humor, to be sure, but on a more pragmatic level, it's reasonably thick, of decent weight, and serves as a blunt instrument to emphasize your point, or conk out the advancing adversary.

Over the last twenty-one years, I've been lucky enough to meet some of the smartest people in the world—astronauts, diplomats, neuroscientists, Pulitzer and Nobel Prize winners, various white-collar criminals, tax dodgers working in the fashion industry, and a guy named Gary who stole my glasses right out from under me like a Las Vegas illusionist. And I can tell you this: They're no smarter than you, especially now that you're armed with this book. I mean, I can't be certain of this, not having met you... but it doesn't pack the same punch to end on that note, does it? So let me just say: They are probably no smarter than you. Or, you know what? Never mind the joke, this is the truth: they're no smarter than you as long as you have this book in your heart, by your side, or strapped to your trusted dirt bike as you move forward through this polite and ominous world. I believe in every one of you. Except Gary, until he's willing to change.

"I'M A FOREWORD TO A McSWEENEY'S INTERNET TENDENCY ANTHOLOGY"

by TEDDY WAYNE

HERE I AM, A FOREWORD to a McSweeney's Internet Tendency anthology! I'm telling you this in the first person, even though I'm not technically a person. (If you want to send me an open letter, I'm also unlikely to respond.) Gosh, it feels great to break the fourth wall and get all meta. Wait, do people still use "meta" on its own? It feels sort of late '90s. And now I'm dating myself. And no, I don't mean I'm taking myself out to dinner and a movie! Jesus, that joke's dated, too—people just "Netflix and chill" now, right?

Now that I've established my anthropomorphic premise in the opening sentence, is there anything to me after that initial setup? I sometimes worry that I'm just all, what-if-this-thing-we're-used-to-was-transposed-onto-a-radically-incongruous-context flashy conceit with no substance, a vehicle for the same conceptual joke repeated a dozen times with slight variations and the barest of narrative progressions. I need to tell some kind of story, don't I? People want to see how the main character has changed. They want to believe that life has meaning, that our time here isn't irrelevant—that tomorrow will be measurably different from today.

Or do they? I don't really know, to be honest. I'm just an inanimate foreword; I've never seen life outside of this book. I haven't frolicked in the grass with a loved one or ridden a Ferris wheel on a warm summer evening while licking an ice cream cone. I haven't vulgarly described my love for hard-skinned, fleshy fruits typically eaten in the autumn. I haven't juxtaposed a hostile tone with a pedestrian sans serif font. Huh, it seems like you get a lot of comic mileage by ending things on a cursed insult—doesn't it, you blowhard?

I can't even do that well.

Sorry, that was really serious. I forgot I'm supposed to be funny, especially in the middle, when people's attention sags and they scroll down to see how much is left. I didn't even get the comedic Rule of Three right—when you list two things that are normal and the third goes zanily off the rails. No wonder I'm just a foreword and not a real humor piece. Should I throw in a string of academic jargon and complaints about teaching that adjunct professors will smilingly nod at and post on social media? What other niche subjects do underemployed creative-class people love? Hemingway imitations in decidedly non-Hemingway situations? Varieties of green tea? Whole Foods and Trader Joe's? How hard it is to take care of kids? Prestige-cable shows? Mocking the dystopian White House? Parodies of prestige-cable shows set in the dystopian White House? Sometimes I think I should just change myself from a foreword to a list of items that are all alike with a last thing that is completely different.

Well, I'm at paragraph five, typically where you might find the conclusion in a short foreword. To recap, I created a premise, questioned the premise itself, changed gears for a sober-minded digression in which I got kind of deep, threw a bunch of shit at the wall to see what stuck, and now I have to wrap things up in a way that reminds readers of the original conceit while commenting on it from a new angle. But, honestly, I don't know what that new angle is, or how to express it, or how to do much of anything anymore. I've been racked with self-doubt ever since that lame "dating myself" joke.

Maybe I'll just end myself on one punchy sentence, dickheads.

TABLE OF CONTENTS

AN APOLOGY FROM THE PUBLISHER: Regarding this table of contents, it's come to our attention that our intrepid copyeditor Alexander could not resist the temptation to see his own writing in print. We apologize for the error, which we had time to fix but didn't. The fantasy novel to which this TOC belongs has some character development issues, but otherwise it's not bad, and it will be self-published by Amazon in the fall. — RIVER CLEGG AND EVAN WAITE

I.
INFANCY/EARLY CHILDHOOD
1998–2004

THE TALENT COMPETITION

by TIM CARVELL

The talent portion of the Miss America pageant got off to a rousing start last night when Miss Alabama annexed the Sudetenland. The applause was deafening.

Her turn was followed by Miss Alaska's bravura performance as Jake LaMotta in her stage adaptation of *Raging Bull*, supported by Miss North Dakota as Vickie and Miss South Dakota as Joey. The judges, impressed, granted Miss Alaska a perfect score, which nearly compensated for the fact that, in gaining forty pounds for the role, she had pretty much ceded the swimsuit competition.

Miss Arizona, who was pre-med at her junior college, then removed Miss Arkansas's kidney, using her bare hands. For her part, Miss Arkansas attempted to survive despite the removal of said kidney. She received a warm ovation.

In an unusual departure from form, Miss California gave birth to a litter of beagles, which Miss Colorado then suckled. Miss Connecticut—whose platform is the need to have pets spayed or neutered—then euthanized the pups, amid general outcry.

Miss Delaware—as have all Miss Delawares before her—pointed out the state of Delaware on a map. Miss District of Columbia granted Miss Puerto Rico statehood, amid much crying and hugging.

Ever topical, Miss Florida re-enacted Section II, portions (B) through (E), of the Starr Report to Congress, leaving several of the judges impressed and visibly flushed.

Miss Georgia recited "The Love Song of J. Alfred Prufrock," then dared to eat a peach.

Miss Hawaii presented her cure for polio. Upon being informed that polio had already been cured, she burst into tears.

In a feat both impressive and stultifying, Miss Idaho sat alone onstage for three hours and took the SAT, as the audience fidgeted. Later in the evening, it was announced that she had received 690 in the verbal portion, and 730 in the math, to scattered applause.

Miss Maine made a mockery of the Holocaust, and received seven Academy Award nominations.

Miss Maryland got her groove back.

Miss Michigan assisted an elderly woman's suicide, although it was later disclosed that the woman was in perfect health and had not requested the service.

Miss Minnesota blamed Ted Hughes for everything.

Miss Missouri, with the help of Miss Montana and Miss New York, re-enacted the assassination of Archduke Ferdinand. (Miss Montana's performance as the carriage received particularly high marks.)

In the competition's most dramatic moment, Miss Iowa attempted to escape from handcuffs and a straitjacket while chained underwater. She failed, and was awarded the Miss Congeniality title.

Miss New Hampshire built a life-size replica of herself out of suet. Miss New Jersey ate said replica.

Miss New Mexico told the old chestnut about the priest, the rabbi, the minister, and the syphilitic prostitute, which is not fit to be shared in mixed company, but which, rest assured, brought down the house.

Miss Ohio devised a fair and equitable partition of Bosnia, while Miss Oklahoma blew saliva bubbles until she was forced to stop.

As the competition entered its sixth hour, Miss Pennsylvania, who is Amish, churned butter, and Miss Rhode Island hit sixty-two home runs in a row. In rapid succession, Miss South Carolina disclosed which of her fellow contestants had "had work done," and where; Miss Utah ate five pounds of raw veal in under five minutes; Miss Vermont bought Dell when it was at 12½.

Through a prior arrangement with the New Jersey courts, Miss Louisiana, Miss Indiana, Miss Kansas, Miss Texas, Miss Nebraska, Miss Nevada, Miss Washington, Miss Tennessee, Miss Mississippi, Miss Iowa, Miss North Carolina, and Miss Oregon served as the jury for a capital-murder case. They voted for conviction, and the death penalty.

Later, with the help of a group of students from Northwestern University, Miss Illinois proved the executed man's innocence. Muted applause ensued.

Lending a brief moment of levity to the proceedings, Miss Virginia impersonated Miss West Virginia. And vice versa.

And finally, Miss Wyoming sprouted pink furry wings and flew around the arena. The other contestants quickly followed suit, creating a thunderous noise as they flapped away and shed their sashes, which fell like streamers upon the amazed audience. They were last seen above the Atlantic Ocean, flying in formation, slowly receding into the sunset, until they disappeared entirely.

I AM MICHIKO KAKUTANI

by COLIN MCENROE

What started as a basically innocent college prank has gotten seriously out of hand, and, at the urging of the small group of people who know the truth, I have decided to come forward and admit it.

I am Michiko Kakutani.

Many people will have a hard time accepting the idea that an essentially undistinguished middle-aged white man living in Hartford, Connecticut, is actually the brilliant, acerbic, reclusive, rarely photographed, lynx-like *New York Times* book critic and Pulitzer winner.

But I am.

The recent disclosure that Riley Weston changed her name and adjusted her age from thirty-two to nineteen in order to continue writing and acting in network television persuaded me that America is ready to hear my story.

Also, I'm tired of being the skunk at the American literary garden party. Do you know what it took out of me to grab a whip and a chair, to go into a steel cage and get this whole Toni Morrison tiger under control?

It's not as if I've been able to call in to my regular job at the insurance company and say, "Look, I've been up all night poking holes in the windy, specious, New Age utopian blather of some author you probably never heard of in my capacity as Michiko Kakutani. I'm going to be in a little late."

The whole thing started at Yale in the winter of 1972 when my roommates and I made up the name as an all-purpose coinage.

We'd answer the phone: "Kevin? No, he's not here. This is his roommate Michiko Kakutani."

We'd use it as a catch-all for any nameless, broken part of our stereo: "Aha! The problem's with the Michiko Kakutani."

We'd use it, I'm embarrassed to say, as a metaphor for onanism.

"What'd you do last night?"

"Had a big date with Michiko Kakutani."

In my junior year, my friend Scott had a job in the registrar's office, so we enrolled Michiko Kakutani in a bunch of classes. I got her through Constitutional Law. Steve took African Art for her. Fred got her an A in Biology.

We also got her into a seminar on Marxist Themes in the Work of the Lake Poets, because it seemed like something she'd like, but then nobody could stand the thought of going, so she took an incomplete.

But Michiko Kakutani was always fundamentally my baby. I thought her up. I gave her life.

One night, Fred asked me if I was coming out with him and Peter for late-night hot tuna grinders.

"I'd like to, but Michiko Kakutani has had a long day. She wants to turn in."

There was a long pause.

"Colin," Fred began gingerly, "there is no Michiko Kakutani."

I blew up.

"There is! She's got more guts and brains than all of you jerks put together. And one of these days, she's going to expose American culture for the simpering, self-referential, pretentious fraud that it is!"

After that, my friends started giving me a little more space.

The next semester, Michiko Kakutani's folklore professor abruptly announced the final exams would be oral.

I didn't have to think about what I was going to do. I bought a wig, a pretty silk blouse, and lots of makeup. I was thin already, but I dieted and wore a girdle. I caused a lot of trouble when I characterized Zora Neale Hurston's work as "an overrated hodgepodge exalted by three generations of self-hating, guilt-ridden white men," but I got an A.

After that, I was Michiko Kakutani whenever I needed to be.

I can hear the reader saying, "Oh Jesus, here comes some kind of weird bend-over *Madame Butterfly* scene."

The reader is wrong. Readers, I have noted, are frequently wrong.

I did not begin leading a secret personal life as Michiko Kakutani, nor did I find it more and more difficult to do the writing required for Michiko Kakutani's life without dressing up as her.

One thing I'm kind of proud of, in fact, is how professionally I handled the Michiko Kakutani side of my life. Once I grasped the fact that she was a serious intellectual force urging the reinstitution of craft and the repudiation of sterile, nihilistic culture, I rid myself of lark and caprice and went at it straight ahead.

I have not dressed up as her more than fifty times in my life. To be brutally frank, one reason I've come forward now is that I'm forty-four and my body is thickening, my metabolism slowing, and getting ready to be Michiko Kakutani now requires three weeks of obsessive exercise, diuretics, and amphetamines.

The last time I did it, for a function at the New York Public Library, I arrived in a state of speed-fueled psychosis, which caused me to wait until Dale Peck was walking down a shadowy corridor and cold-cock him. Just turned his fucking lights out.

Looking back, I'm sorry I did that.

But, well, it was Dale Peck. Can I be blamed?

There were mornings when I lay exhausted in my bed, and Alice Shaughnessy, the Sligo-bred housekeeper I inexplicably have, would tiptoe in with coddled eggs and toast points.

"Sure and you've been at it again, sir," she'd gasp. "Herself came out again last night?"

"She reviewed Norman Mailer's silly, self-important, inadvertently comical Jesus novel," I'd groan. "Somebody had to knock that fat bastard down, Alice. Michiko Kakutani was the only one with the spine for the job."

"Sir, it's not my place to say," Alice would falter, "but I worry, sir. I fear you're consorting with dark forces beyond your control, sir."

"Alice, it's a 'zacked-out, feel-good literary culture of mutually masturbatory blurb-writers. Nobody wants to be the turd in the punchbowl. Only Michiko tells the tough truth."

Do I feel bad about the deception? Not really. There's more of this stuff going on than you might suspect. When I interviewed Gore Vidal, he kept peering strangely and fidgeting unhappily, and I began to think he saw through my disguise.

I found out later Gore Vidal regularly sends a body double to interviews. The guy was actually nervous that I might see through his disguise.

I also met, through one of the places that sells me supplies, a woman who did three weeks as Robert James Waller. That one, I hear, is a deal where they rotate new people through at intervals, like Menudo.

Believe me, I know what comes next. Every puny author who ever got his ass kicked by yours truly scuttles out of the woodwork and demands to know how I can make writing with conviction the litmus test when *I was a fake.*

If they were better writers, they would know I was never a fake. That's like saying Batman was a fake (within the reality of the comic, I mean). I mean, is Bruce Wayne more real than Batman?

Somebody else will have to decide. I have a ton of lawn work to do, and I want to get it done before the news breaks because my neighbor Charlie is the kind of guy who will spend the whole day yelling, "Don't worry, Michi! My wife Claire is actually James Wolcott."

The main thing to remember is this: you won't have Michiko Kakutani to kick you around anymore. I'm shutting her down, like Hal in *2001*. Actually, I'd like to write a bunch of reviews pointing out that most human characters in current American fiction are not as fully drawn, as warm-blooded, as humanity-laden as Hal. I want to, but you know what would happen? People would say, "There goes Michi again."

But it doesn't seem to matter what I say, and that's why I'm quitting. That and the fact that Dirk Bikkembergs no longer has the brushed-on liquid eyeliner I liked. It was very notice-me.

SOMETREE/ANYTREE?

by BEN GREENMAN

Say I am a tree and there is another tree next to me.

We don't talk at first. That's how trees are: cautious.

But then one afternoon it's nice in the forest, not too warm, not too cold, squirrels and birds present in plentiful but hardly worrisome numbers, and I decide to say hello, and the other tree says hello in return, and that's when it begins.

That first day, it's a long conversation. Have you ever noticed the way the wind comes through here at night? Why are there so many kinds of airborne seeds? Isn't bark weird? By the end of that conversation, I'm pretty sure that the other tree is not just an interesting and intelligent tree, but a fascinating tree, a lovely tree, a wonderful and great tree, one of the best trees I have ever had the pleasure of meeting. I am thrilled to have the other tree next to me, and a little bit embarrassed that I didn't notice the other tree until now. Sometimes those things escape you: there is a sheet of sky to look at, and the purling of a nearby stream.

The next day the other tree and I talk again, all day long, and it's as if that second day, too, is the first day. Every bit of the discussion shines like a particularly smooth, flat stone after a rainstorm.

But it's not nearly as beautiful as the other tree, which I realize the third day, which is spent primarily in contemplation of the tree's charms. Sometimes a trunk is just a trunk, and branches are just branches, but sometimes a trunk has a perfect thickness, and branches taper just right, and then there are the leaves, so exquisitely arranged along each branchlet, with such lovely fall coloration, that it makes me want to hire someone to come out with an axe and chop me down so I can fall near the roots of the other tree and lay there forever. This is the romantic fantasy that I entertain as I talk to the other tree that third day. My conversation is somewhat distracted, but I come out of my fog long enough to see that the other tree's conversation is distracted as well, and that's when it occurs to me that maybe the other tree, too, is dreaming of being chopped down and falling near my roots and lying there forever.

The fourth day I discover that I have a tiny wire-like twig that almost reaches one of the other tree's twigs, and I concentrate on growing that twig, and while the fifth day is frustrating, the sixth day is far less so, and the seventh and the eighth days are spent in bliss, twigs entwined. "Or is it entwigged?" the other tree says, and this strikes me as the one of the most appealing things I have ever heard, witty and poignant and critical and bewitching all at the same time.

The morning of the ninth day, we discover that we're entwigged at a second point, this one a bit closer to the trunk.

On the tenth day, the other tree loses some leaves, and I offer comforting words, and even point out that a few of my own leaves are falling, that it's a natural process, happens every year, nothing to worry about. The other tree doesn't say anything, but there's a small reward in the form of pressure at that first entwigging point, and that's enough for me.

The eleventh day is like the twelfth, and the thirteenth, and the fourteenth, and the fifteenth. I only know that time is passing because the sun rises and sets.

Then, on the sixteenth day, I notice something strange. A few of the knots of twigs have undone themselves. I ask the other tree about it, and the answer is vague, something about cold air coming up from the other side of the forest. This isn't how it works with twigs, and I know it, and I know that the other tree knows it, but I don't make a big deal about it.

The seventeenth day, more entwiggings disappear, and on the eighteenth, only the original one is left.

By now, I can't keep quiet any longer, and I ask the other tree a series of questions, trying to keep my tone level and calm but, I'm sure, betraying my anxiety and anger and desire and, above all, my sadness. That's when the other tree tries to fend me off with a metaphor. "Assume," the other tree says, "that there are two trees next to one another, and they grow closer, sometimes by almost imperceptible degrees. But then assume that there is a countermovement, and they grow more distant, sometimes by almost imperceptible degrees. It doesn't mean that the trees are less beautiful to one another, or even less close to one another. It is difficult to move a trunk. It just means that sometimes twigs will do what twigs will do."

"There are other trees on the other side of me," the other tree says. "They have twigs, too." I explain that I don't care about that, and at that moment I don't. Trees have hundreds of twigs. I know that. I'm not an idiot. I just know what I like—what I need—and that's the feeling of some of the other tree's twigs entwined with my twigs. The other tree tells me I'm yelling, and I realize I am, and that's when I go dead silent.

The nineteenth day is a wintry day, the first really unpleasant weather of the year, and I spend most of the morning feeling one of my own leaves working itself free from a branch. Finally, a small blast of icy wind dislodges it, and it falls, slowly, with a side-to-side motion, and for a moment it looks as if the leaf might come to rest on one of the other tree's branches before sliding off and disappearing against the carpet of leaves, the gold, the red, the orange, the brown. I want the leaf to brush across the other tree's branch on its way down, to serve as a reminder, if only for a moment, of the feeling of twig on twig. I don't want the other tree to feel guilty. It's only the fact of my devotion that I want the other tree to feel, and not even all of it, just a bit of it, which is powerful, which is enough. But to feel the fact of a devotion that is, for the moment, detained, this is a form of melancholy, much like the fact that a leaf will fall and lay motionless before sinking into the earth and disappearing forever. The leaf bounces on an updraft. I look away.

The twentieth day I stop looking away. Who has time for petulance? The other tree is just as lovely as ever. The way the lowest, largest branches flow out of the trunk breaks my heart.

A LOGIC PUZZLE AND A HANGOVER CURE

by JOHN HODGMAN

I.

There is a room with seven chairs in it.

Eight people are standing in the room.

Some of them are Vampires.

Some of them are Normals.

Vampires always lie.

Normals always tell the truth.

The room has three enormous windows in it, all facing west.

It is six o'clock on an October evening.

Sunset may be seen through the westward windows. It is magnificent.

(By the way, the Vampires have been awake all day. The sun does not kill them. They're not that type of Vampire.)

The Vampires are very handsome and very beautiful at the same time.

They only tell handsome and beautiful lies.

The Normals are wandering around the room, spreading vicious truths wherever they go.

There are two large bottles of inexpensive wine on the table, one of which is poisoned, one of which is not.

Also, you are ruinously drunk.

Either a Vampire or a Normal touches your shoulder and suggests something that surprises you.

It begins as a statement and ends as a question.

Without feeling for fangs, and lying or telling the truth as you see fit, what three questions and two statements do you pose in order to determine whether you are standing or sitting down?

HINT: The wine is rosé.

2.

Combine the yolk of 1 egg with 4 ounces of flat club soda.

Add milk and vodka (warm) to taste.

Rent *Seven Samurai* and begin watching it.

Drink the yolk/soda/milk/vodka combination while watching Tape 1 of *Seven Samurai*, rubbing bare feet on the carpet.

Upon conclusion of Tape 1, decide to take a shower, then change your mind.

Prepare a box of instant mashed potatoes as directed. Add 1 whole bottle of Tabasco and the juice of 1 lemon.

While mixing, remember high school until it becomes too painful to continue.

While sucking on 1 ice cube, watch Tape 2 of *Seven Samurai* until conclusion.

Reaffirm your faith that any effort to save a village of peasants from marauding bandits will always end in tragedy.

Sleep for ten hours.

Awaken at sunset and suddenly realize: EVERYONE is standing, including yourself.

Attempt to explain this to your wife.

If you do not have carpeting, substitute a bathmat or an old coat.

BAD NAMES FOR PROFESSIONAL WRESTLERS

by JEFF JOHNSON

Linus

The Spiller

Lace

The Soup-Eater

Stilts

The Tailor

Mitochondria

Kimono Boy

The Really Tiny Moth

The Bulimic Cheerleader

Winston Churchill

Vasco da Gama, Jr.

Tickles

The Fig Wasp

Cookies 'n' Creme (tag team duo)

The Healer

El Wusso

The Precocious Feline

The Professor

Balsamic Vinegar

The Stooge

Diabetes

Warren G. Harding

The Wilting Zinnia

The School Boy

The Yearling

The Pediatrician

The Old Coward

Naomi

The Narcoleptic

Magic Realism

MORE BAD NAMES FOR PROFESSIONAL WRESTLERS

by JEFF JOHNSON

The Vegan

The Lonely Marine

Grace Kelly

Peter Billingsley

Swimmer's Itch

The Orderly

Smarty Pants

Babette

Jivamukti

Paul McCartney

The Shlub

The Shrill Housewife

The Truant Officer

The Dartmouth Grad Student

The Keokuk Optometrist

The Whispering Mime

Aaron Copeland

The Impressionist

The Phonics Expert

Nancy Walker

Hospice Boy

Noel Coward

Frondeur

The Demimonde

The Victim

The Tattletale

Truffle

Victor Kiam

The Poet Laureate

Mrs. Grundy

Burt Hooton

The Pawn

Dale

The Little Ragu

Morrissey

PERIODIC TABLE OF THE ELEMENTARY SCHOOL

by ALYSIA GRAY PAINTER

Vanadium is sitting next to Titanium—they always sit together in the same row. Vanadium had been crying near the elm tree that grows by the fence, because somebody had called it nothing but Chromium, which just isn't true. Of course, Chromium is a lustrous steel gray and is widely regarded to prevent corrosion when used in steel plating, but this didn't make Vanadium cheer up. Not even the thought that Vanadium is a helpful carbide stabilizer stopped the tears. And Titanium was no comfort. All Vanadium's rowmate could do was talk about having five stable isotopes, like that was something special.

A few rows back and over slumped Iridium, not looking so good. There were whispers that molten salts, like NaCl and NaCN, might be causing Iridium's illness. Bismuth, who everyone regarded as a showoff, thought acids might have attacked Iridium, but everyone knows that Iridium is immune to that sort of stuff, at least the nurse said so when she visited the class that one time. Bismuth just thinks it is all bad or something because it has superior electrical resistance. Like, I'm bad, I'm more diamagnetic than you, I'm all cool or something. Astatine, who sits pretty close to Bismuth (especially when Polonium stays home, faker), says that having some big electrical resistance isn't as awesome as being a halogen that is radioactive. Astatine one time promised to unleash some uranium on Bismuth's butt, but no one knew if it was kidding or not. Uranium is no joke.

Hardly anyone associates with Francium, who lurks in the corner. Francium, the heaviest of the alkali metals, thinks it is a weight thing. Radium, who sits next to Francium, sometimes lets off some radon gas, which makes Francium laugh and Radium smile. They might have a sleepover this weekend if their mothers agree.

Nearby, Hafnium spontaneously ignites. Tantalum slides over into the empty desk, because the board is easier to see without Niobium's big head always oxidizing in the way.

The bell rings and everyone wants to know what everyone else is doing for the afternoon. Some are planning to burn together, while someone else has an appointment to be excited by electrical discharge— their dad says they have to or else, bummer. A few will be melting before TV time, and a handful will solidify with some speed by dinner. One has plans to be defused by hydrogen, but everyone has homework.

A BRIEF PARODY
OF A TALK SHOW THAT
FALLS APART ABOUT
HALFWAY THROUGH

by TIM CARVELL

(*Busy music and a kaleidoscope of colorful graphics, which ultimately part to reveal an ecstatic audience consisting largely of middle-aged women, with some middle-aged men and college students thrown in. The talk show's host stands in the crowd, holding a fuzzy-headed, slightly oversized microphone.*)

HOST

Hello, and welcome back to our show. Our topic today is: "People Who Enjoy Being Verbally Abused by Talk-Show Audiences." Now, before we went to the break, we were talking to Steve.

(*CUT TO: STEVE. He is around thirty-five, about forty pounds overweight, and wearing an unflattering sweater.*)

HOST

Now, Steve: Since you were a teenager, you've fantasized about being told off by a sassy woman holding a microphone. Is that right?

STEVE
(ashamed)

Yes. That's right. It's ruined many of my relationships: I can't relate to women unless they have a microphone in their hand and are making disparaging comments about me, preferably in front of a large crowd. Some women tried to accommodate me for a while—we'd attend open-mic nights, high school football games, companies' annual meetings—any place where there was an audience and a mic, but after a while, none of them would be able to take it anymore.

HOST

Well, we have someone here who wants to comment on that.

SASSY LADY

Yeah, I just wanted to say that you're sick. *(Audience cheers.)* What kind of a man does that to a woman? You need to get yourself some help.

HOST

Steve?

(STEVE looks pleased. Then ashamed. Then pleased.)

HOST

We have someone else here who'd like to make a comment. Yes, sir?

AUTHORIAL VOICE

Yeah, I think that this is pretty much a one-joke story.

HOST

True enough.

AUTHORIAL VOICE

So, you know, perhaps it could end now.

HOST

Seems fair enough to me.

(*STEVE, HOST, SASSY LADY begin filing toward the exits of the studio, along with the rest of the audience.*)

AUTHORIAL VOICE

You know, we don't all have to get up and leave. The illusion that any of us actually exist—which was pretty shaky to begin with—has by now been fairly well destroyed. The story can now just end abruptly at any moment.

HOST

True enough. It could just end, cutting either one of us off in mid sent—

AUTHORIAL VOICE

Hm. That's odd. I thought it was going to end just then.

HOST

Yeah. Me too.

(*They stand together, uncomfortably, awaiting the end of the story. A few minutes pass. Then centuries pass. Then a few more minutes. They turn into marvelous fire-breathing dragons, then into baby chicks. They turn one another inside out. They invent time travel and prevent the assassination of Archduke Franz Ferdinand, only to discover that World War I was inevitable, and that nothing in the present day has changed. They introduce the unicorn to the rainforest. A few more centuries pass. They share a hard-boiled egg. Centuries, centuries. Millennia. The story, at long last, ends. No, wait, they also dive for undersea treasure!*)

PRANK CALLING MY MOTHER, FOUR TRANSCRIPTS

by AMIE BARRODALE

WED., NOV. 8, 2000:

[ring... ring... ring...]

Pat Barrodale: Hello?

A: (hissing)

PB: Is this Amie?

MON., DEC. 11, 2000:

[ring... ring... ring...]

PB: Hello?

A: Do I have a woman on the line?

PB: Amie. It's four in the morning.

THU., JAN. 4, 2001

[ring... ring... ring...]

PB: Hello?

A: [hangs up]

SEVERAL MINUTES LATER
[ring... ri...]
PB: Hello?
A: [hangs up]

MOMENTS LATER:
[ring...]
PB: Hello?
A: Yes, have you been calling here and hanging up?
PB: No.
A: Well, someone has.

SAT., JAN. 6, 2001
[ring... ring...]
PB: Hello?
A: Yes, we had an order for some pornos?
PB: [hangs up]

MOMENTS LATER
[ring...]
PB: What, Amie?
A: [pause] It's Grandpop.
PB: Leave me alone.
A: This is Grandpop.
PB: Amie, I mean it.
A: Grandpop speaking.

JOHN MOE'S POP SONG CORRESPONDENCES: JAMES TAYLOR ISSUES AN UPDATE ON "THE FRIENDSHIP RING"

by JOHN MOE

Dear Friends,

As you know, I've always been there for you over the years. But I regret to inform you that, as of July 1, I will no longer come running when you call out my name.

I realize this comes as a shock to some of you, especially those who seem to have had occasion to call out my name several times a day, thus forcing me to come running with all due haste. While I hope that you will still think of me as a friend, I know it will be a blow to not have me at your disposal. You might be angry. But this change in policy must take place.

When I originally recorded "You've Got a Friend," in 1971, it was meant to reach a select audience of people to whom I was actually very close. Having been endowed with certain abilities (super speed, ultra-hearing, a pleasant singing voice, and a loving nature), I decided to use my powers for good and provide assistance to others in the form of a sort of "super friendship." While other superheroes chose to fly, catch bank robbers, patch up dams, and the like, I decided that James Taylor would be the most powerful and loving friend this world had ever known. And, hopefully, maintain a successful recording career at the same time in order to pay the bills and have a creative outlet.

The plan worked well. The song became a hit, sold millions of copies, and was distributed around the world. Since it was a song from my heart (even though Carole King wrote it), I was pleased by its success and hoped that listeners would think of it as a sentiment to be shared between two friends, neither of which would necessarily be me. For the most part, that was the case. But soon there emerged a growing group that cracked my code, realizing that "You've Got a Friend" was not just a song but an implicit contract. Almost none were really my friends to begin with, but they started calling out my name. I would be in the middle of tuning my guitar or making tea in my kitchen at the Martha's Vineyard house and my ultra-hearing would pick up a desperate "James Taylor!" from someone who had just had a fight with their boyfriend, or binged on ice cream again, or lost out on a promotion, or needed someone to hold the ladder while they cleaned the gutters, or whatever. When that happened, I would dutifully come running to see them. Again.

For a while, I was fine with this. My superpowers made it all feasible, if a bit time-consuming. I was seeing the world and I really seemed to be helping people. Sure, I never knew the boss or the family member that they were complaining about, so I couldn't give advice really, but I just listened (a lot!), and that seemed to be what they needed anyway. But by the late '80s, I noticed that my recording career was tapering off. Billy Joel or Christopher Cross would call me up (using the phone, thank goodness) to record something, but I would be too busy responding to a farmer in Iowa calling out my name or a banker in Tokyo who decided to yell "James Taylor!" as loud as he could because he felt "uneasy." And boom, because I was being a friend, I lost out on the gig.

By the '90s, things were clearly out of control, but a deal was a deal. I had told people that I would be there, yes I would. But I was going days without sleeping, eating whatever food I could grab on the road, rarely seeing my family, who wondered, quite fairly, why I never seemed to be around for them. And it was always the same people calling out my name. Four or five times a day. Occasionally, in desperation, I would bring them puppies or kittens, something else to channel their love to, but they would never get the hint. Free copies of the *Sweet Baby James* album were rarely accepted enthusiastically.

Finally, after a particularly harrowing beginning of 2004, I've decided that enough is enough. Was it Mrs. S of Minneapolis who had taken to calling out "James Taylor! And grab some ice cream! Strawberry!"? Might have been. Could have been Mr. F in Melbourne who screamed my name at two in the morning and then changed his mind when I got there and told me to leave. The entire classroom of first-graders to whom Ms. W taught the "James Taylor trick" certainly didn't help matters.

But in reality, it's all of these cases. And so many more over so many years. Because while I have been a friend, I don't think most of you know the meaning of friendship. So the deal is off. As of July 1, if you call out my name, all you'll hear is the sound of your own voice. I will be taking time to work on a new album and touring some colleges in the Northeast with my good friend Art Garfunkel. Between now and June 30, however, the deal still stands, but I do ask you to use it judiciously and perhaps begin to taper off.

Thanks.

Your "friend,"
James Taylor

REFLECTIONS FROM A McSWEENEY'S INTERNET TENDENCY WRITER

by JOHN MOE

IT'S 1985 AND I'M one of four high school students piled into my friend Kris's Camaro, driving around south King County, south of Seattle, where we live. I can't say we're cruising for chicks because we don't know how. We're not going anywhere, really. We're just driving around. We might stop and get some Doritos later.

The four of us are in a kind of too-late hippy period, enjoying the odd rebellion of listening to CSN and James Taylor, enjoying the dissonance of doing so in a Camaro. "You just call out my name," James Taylor sings on the tape deck.

"JAMES TAYLOR!" I yell.

"And you know wherever I am, I'll come running to see you again," Sweet Baby James vows.

I roll down the window and look around for him, making a big show of it. "James Taylor is a fucking liar, man." I conclude. It gets laughs. We keep driving.

Then for the next several years, that joke conceit rattles around in my head. Could JT make that promise and actually fulfill it? How inconvenient that would be! How does Billy Joel's boss in "The Piano Man" feel about him saying mean things about the customers? Isn't John Fogerty far too old and unathletic to play center field?

I've had a hard time making sense of the world and my place in it but popular music has always been a safe place for me. Something about the compartmentalized structure of it all: albums, songs, videos, everyone in the band having a specific musical job, I found it reassuring. And

I become a lyric geek to match up with the comedy geek I'd always been. Thus, the idea of hyper-literalism emerges with Jon Bon Jovi riding an actual steel horse. I smile thinking about if, in ZZ Top's world, some women have no idea how to use their legs and mistakenly think they're telephones.

In 2000, I'm trying to get started as a writer so I send a list of terrible hair salon names to McSweeney's, a site full of humor that matches my own. They accept it and I'm stunned. So I write more and submit more just to see if this was a fluke. Somehow it's not. I keep going.

Finally, John Warner, the editor at the time, says, "A lot of the things you're writing seem to be about overly literal interpretations of songs. And letters. Do you think there's a thing there? A column or recurring bit?" I checked and he was right. I had taken this conceit and let it out into the world through my new trusted ally, McSweeney's.

"Yes," I replied. "And we shall call it 'Pop Song Correspondences.'" I always dug the slightly too-many-words trope associated with the site. Many such letters ensued. Then it became a staple of a radio show I did. Then a book came out.

I still think in terms of these gags when I hear music. It's a mental anomaly that found a home in my head and on your computer screen.

Thanks for getting in that car with me in 1985, McSweeney's readers.

REVISING STRUNK
AND WHITE

by DAN KENNEDY

PAGE 67 — REWRITING A FAMILIAR SENTENCE

Suppose we take, "These are the times that try men's souls." Here we have eight short, easy words forming a simple declarative sentence. Yet, in that arrangement they have shown great durability; this sentence, written by Thomas Paine in 1776, is into its third century. Now compare a few less effective variations:

These are times for soul men that are trying.

I try so that men's souls feel it these times.

It's hard out there, man… and I'm looking for some times to keep my soul trying.

PAGE 18 — USE THE ACTIVE VOICE

The active voice is usually more direct and vigorous than the passive.

I shall always remember my first visit to Boston.

This is much better than:

> There was something pathetic about visiting her
> in, uh, that city… and it will be sort of, you know,
> etched into my brain for eternity and recalled as
> this, like, basic response to anyone saying the name
> "Boston" or "Kristin." I mean, god help me if some-
> thing painfully coincidental happens, you know,
> like somebody starts raving about their favorite
> bar in Boston named Kristin's… it'll induce, like,
> a… a seizure of nervous memories and sobbing in
> me, right in the middle of whatever dinner party
> it happens at, and everyone will assume something
> terrible happened to me in a bar or something… or
> that I have something against Boston.

PAGE 79 — AN APPROACH TO STYLE: DO NOT INJECT OPINION

His writing has been largely criticized as "dull" and "humorless."
Regardless of what some critics say, he is a popular contributor to
several journals and weeklies.

This is better than:

> Jesus, there's nothing Strunk and I hate more than
> the high-horse that whiny little leftist collegians

rest on so confidently when they further ruin their typically dull and humorless writing by garnishing contributions with the crap they actually believe in. I swear to everyone in hell and heaven, if there is such a thing (who would know if it's still around with all of the freaks giving whatever higher power resides there a bad name these days?) that I will refuse to pick up another one of those stupid-ass (always free, you'll notice) weeklies as long as I have blood in my body and breath in my lungs. I'm serious. Drop the opinions, ass-bites. Don't push me, because you have no idea how close to the edge I am, you weak and empty also-rans. You little twenty-eight-year-old journal junkies that still take rides home from lectures and taverns courtesy of your moms and girlfriends.

WENDY MOLYNEUX'S EXCERPTS FROM POPULAR McSWEENEY'S INTERNET TENDENCY LISTS THROUGHOUT HISTORY: 1607

LIST

101 NEW NAMES FOR THE JAMESTOWN SETTLEMENT

by ELDREDGE SWIFTMAN

98. No-food-opolis

99. Please Send Assistance City

100. Seriously, If You Are Reading This, Please Send Help, This Isn't a Submission

101. JimmyVille

THE DANCE LESSON

by TIM CARVELL

1. Listen to the beat of the music.

2. Oh, for god's sake. Then turn some music on, will you? You were going to try to dance without any music playing? What's wrong with you?

3. I don't know. Something lively. Something with a beat to it. No, not that. Not that either. Fine, that'll do.

4. Okay, now listen to the beat of the music. Clap along to it. No, that's not it—you're going too fast. No, now you're going too slowly. That's it, you've got—no, you've lost it again.

5. How about this: Instead of clapping, just try to move your feet a

bit to the music. Just shuffle them at a pace that seems right to you. Good, good, you've got it. That looks nice.

6. Let's take this up a notch now. Start moving your arms around to the music.

7. OH MY GOD. STOP MOVING YOUR ARMS THIS INSTANT. What was that? What were you doing? What the fuck was that supposed to be? I told you to move your arms, not flap them. You looked like a total dork.

8. First things first: when you move your arms, bend your elbows a bit. You don't have to hold them perfectly straight when you move them. Just bend your elbows a little. Bend them. You can bend your elbows, can't you? There.

9. No, you're not supposed to lock your elbows at a perfect right angle, either. You look like an organ grinder's monkey. Just relax a bit. Relax. RELAX!

10. So it's my fault that you can't relax? I don't think I've been "screaming at" you. I think I may have gotten a little *agitated*. I may have *raised my voice* a bit. But that doesn't constitute screaming.

11. Look, I'm sorry. I'm sorry. You're right. I was wrong, you were right. I know that teaching you to dance was my idea, and you've been a really good sport. I'm a jerk. I admit it. But I only yell at you because I want so badly to see you succeed—you *know* that. C'mon. Let's start over. Let's go back to where you were just shuffling your feet to the music.

12. Good, good, good. You're doing great. Just great. You look terrific. Now, let's try moving your arms a little to the music—just sway them back and forth a bit.

13. Um, okay, okay, that's... *nice*. That's really *nice*. But, you know, like I said before, you're allowed to bend your elbows just a bit.

14. That's *super*. Just super. You keep this up, and you'll be dancing great in no time. Now, try and vary your movements just a bit. Just go with the flow of the music. Improvise a little. You know, do what feels natural.

15. I'm sorry. I didn't mean to laugh. It's just that, when I told you do what felt natural, I had no idea that what felt natural to you would be looking like... this.

16. Why are you crying? Oh, for Christ's sake, it's always like this with you, isn't it? I try and do something nice for you, and all of a sudden, you're all in tears because it hasn't turned out the way you planned. This is the thanks I get? Look: I'm trying to help you. I knew you'd have more fun if you knew how to dance, and so I agreed to take the time to teach you—time that I could have spent somewhere else, somewhere *fun*, hanging out with people who don't burst into tears for no reason. People who know how to take a fucking joke. I had other plans for today, but instead, here I am, being guilt-tripped by you for, like, the millionth time. You *know* I don't need this. You *know* I've got trust issues I've been working through. But don't let that stop you. No—you go right on ahead. Keep on crying, making me feel like a heel for trying to help you.

17. You're damn right, you're sorry.

18. Because I don't want to teach you, that's why.

19. Now you're going to dance? Without any input from me? Go ahead. Dance. I don't care.

20. I'm not watching you.

21. Okay, one quick pointer: You're still not bending your arms. Just a little. Just bend them a little. No, that's a jig. You're doing a jig. Oh, for god's sake…

---

* Read an interview with Tim Carvell about this piece on page 637.

UNUSED AUDIO COMMENTARY BY HOWARD ZINN AND NOAM CHOMSKY, RECORDED SUMMER 2002 FOR *THE FELLOWSHIP OF THE RING* (PLATINUM SERIES EXTENDED EDITION) DVD, PART ONE

by TOM BISSELL AND JEFF ALEXANDER

CHOMSKY: The film opens with Galadriel speaking. "The world has changed," she tells us, "I can feel it in the water." She's actually stealing a line from the non-human Treebeard. He says this to Merry and Pippin in *The Two Towers*, the novel. Already we can see who is going to be privileged by this narrative and who is not.

ZINN: Of course. "The world has changed." I would argue that the main thing one learns when one watches this film is that the world hasn't changed. Not at all.

CHOMSKY: We should examine carefully what's being established here in the prologue. For one, the point is clearly made that the "master ring," the so-called "one ring to rule them all," is actually a rather elaborate justification for preemptive war on Mordor.

ZINN: I think that's correct. Tolkien makes no attempt to hide the fact that rings are wielded by every other ethnic enclave in Middle Earth. The Dwarves have seven rings, the Elves have three. The race of Man has nine rings, for god's sake. There are at least nineteen rings floating around out there in Middle Earth, and yet Sauron's ring is supposedly so terrible that no one can be allowed wield it. Why?

CHOMSKY: Notice too that the "war" being waged here is, evidently, in the land of Mordor itself—at the very base of Mount Doom. These terrible armies of Sauron, these dreadful demonized Orcs, have not proved successful at conquering the neighboring realms—if that is even what Sauron was seeking to do. It seems fairly far-fetched.

ZINN: And observe the map device here—how the map is itself completely Gondor-centric. Rohan and Gondor are treated as though they are the literal center of Middle Earth. Obviously this is because they have men living there. What of places such as Anfalas and Forlindon or Near Harad? One never really hears anything about places like that. And this so-called map casually reveals other places—the Lost Realm, the Northern Waste (lost to whom? wasted how? I ask)—but tells us nothing about them. It is as though the people who live in these places are despicable, and unworthy of mention. Who is producing this tale? What is their agenda? What are their interests and how are those interests being served by this portrayal? Questions we need to ask repeatedly.

CHOMSKY: And here comes Bilbo Baggins. Now, this is, to my mind, where the story begins to reveal its deeper truths. In the books we learn that Saruman was spying on Gandalf for years. And he wondered why Gandalf was traveling so incessantly to the Shire. As Tolkien later establishes, the Shire's surfeit of pipe-weed is one of the major reasons for Gandalf's continued visits.

ZINN: You view the conflict as being primarily about pipe-weed, do you not?

CHOMSKY: Well, what we see here, in Hobbiton, are farmers tilling crops. The thing to remember is that the crop they are tilling is, in fact, pipe-weed, an addictive drug transported and sold throughout Middle Earth for great profit.

ZINN: This is absolutely established in the books. Pipe-weed is something all the Hobbits abuse. Gandalf is smoking it constantly. You are correct when you point out that Middle Earth depends on pipe-weed in some crucial sense, but I think you may be overstating its importance. Clearly the war is not based only on the Shire's pipe-weed. Rohan and Gondor's unceasing hunger for war is a larger culprit, I would say.

CHOMSKY: But without the pipe-weed, Middle Earth would fall apart. Saruman is trying to break up Gandalf's pipe-weed ring. He's trying to divert it.

ZINN: Well, you know, it would be manifestly difficult to believe in magic rings unless everyone was high on pipe-weed. So it is in Gandalf's interest to keep Middle Earth hooked.

CHOMSKY: How do you think these wizards build gigantic towers and mighty fortresses? Where do they get the money? Keep in mind that I do not especially regard anyone, Saruman included, as an agent for progressivism. But obviously the pipe-weed operation that exists

TOM BISSELL AND JEFF ALEXANDER

is the dominant influence in Middle Earth. It's not some ludicrous magical ring.

ZINN: You've mentioned in the past the various flavors of pipe-weed that Hobbits have cultivated: Gold Leaf, Old Toby, etc.

CHOMSKY: Nothing better illustrates the sophistication of the smuggling ring than the fact that there are different brand names associated with the pipe-weed. Ah, here we have Gandalf smoking a pipe in his wagon—the first of many clues that link us to the hidden undercurrents of power.

ZINN: Gandalf is deeply implicated. That's true. And of course the ring lore begins with him. He's the one who leaks this news of the supposed evil ring.

CHOMSKY: Now here, just before Bilbo's eleventy-first birthday party, we can see some of the symptoms of addiction. We are supposed to attribute Bilbo's tiredness, his sensation of feeling like too-little butter spread out on a piece of bread, to this magical ring he supposedly has. It's clear something else may be at work, here.

ZINN: And soon Gandalf is delighting the Hobbits with his magic. Sauron's magic is somehow terrible but Gandalf's, you'll notice, is wonderful.

CHOMSKY: And note how Gandalf's magic is based on gunpowder, on explosions.

ZINN: Right.

CHOMSKY: And it is interesting, too, that Gandalf's so-called magic is technological, and yet somehow technology seems to be what condemns Saruman's enterprises, as well as those of the Orcs.

ZINN: Exactly.

CHOMSKY: But we will address that later. Here we have Pippin and Merry stealing a bunch of fireworks and setting them off. This might be closer to the true heart of the Hobbits.

ZINN: You mean the Hobbits' natural inclination?

CHOMSKY: I think the Hobbits are criminals, essentially.

ZINN: It also seems incredibly irresponsible for Gandalf to have a firework that powerful just sitting in the back of his wagon.

CHOMSKY: More of his smoke and mirrors, yes? Gandalf conjures the dragon Smaug to scare the people.

ZINN: One can always delight the little people with explosions.

CHOMSKY: As long as they're blowing up somewhere else. Now we come to Bilbo's disappearance. Again, we have to question the validity of the ring, and the magic powers attributed to it. Did Bilbo Baggins really disappear at his party, or is this some kind of mass hallucination attributable to a group of intoxicated Hobbits? When forced to consider so-called magic compared to the hallucinatory properties of a known narcotic, Occam's Razor would indicate the latter as a far more plausible explanation.

ZINN: I also think it is a spectacular display of bad manners to disappear at your own birthday party. And here, for the first time, Gandalf speaks to Bilbo about magic rings. Still, it is never clearly established why this one ring is so powerful. Everything used to justify that belief is legendary.

CHOMSKY: Gandalf is clearly wondering if it's time to invoke his plan for the supposed revelation concerning the secret magic ring. Why now? Well, I think it's because the people in Mordor—the Orcs, I'm speaking of—are starting to obtain some power, are starting to ask a little bit more from Middle Earth than Middle Earth has ever seen fit to give to them. And I don't think it's unreasonable for them to expect something back from Middle Earth. Of course, if that happened, the entire economy would be disrupted.

ZINN: The pipe-weed-based economy.

CHOMSKY: And, as you pointed out earlier, the military-industrial-complex that exists in Gondor. This constant state of alertness. This constant state of fear. And here Gandalf reveals his true nature.

ZINN: Indeed. Gandalf darkens the room and yells at poor Bilbo for rightfully accusing him of trying to steal his ring. It is abundantly obvious that Gandalf wants to steal the ring. But if he is caught with the ring himself, his pretext will dissolve. He needs to throw as much plausible deniability into his scheme as possible, which is why, later, he has Frodo carry the ring for him.

CHOMSKY: Gandalf knows the ring is powerless. It's interesting that he attaches so much importance to it and yet will not pick it up himself.

This is because he knows that merely possessing the worthless ring will not help his cause. It's important to keep others thinking that it can. If Gandalf held the ring, he might be asked to do something with it. But its magic is nonexistent.

ZINN: Well, power needs to have its proxies. That way the damage is always deniable. As long as the Hobbits have the ring, no one will ever question the plot Gandalf has hatched. So here is the big scary ring, and all that happens when Gandalf moves to touch it is that he sees a big flaming eye. And notice it is a... different kind of eye—not like our eye.

CHOMSKY: Almost a cat-like eye.

ZINN: It's on fire. Somehow being an on-fire eye is this terrible thing in the minds of those in Middle Earth. I think this is a way of telling others in Middle Earth to be ashamed of their eyes. And, of course, you see the Orcs' eyes are all messed up, too. They're this terrible color. And what does Gandalf tell Frodo about the ring? "Keep it secret. Keep it safe."

CHOMSKY: "Let's leave the most powerful object in all of Middle Earth with a weak little Hobbit, a race known for its chattering and intoxication, and tell him to keep it a secret."

ZINN: Right. And here we receive our first glimpse of the supposedly dreadful Mordor, which actually looks like a fairly functioning place.

CHOMSKY: This type of city is most likely the best the Orcs can do if all they have are cliffs to grow on. It's very impressive, in that sense.

ZINN: Especially considering the economic sanctions no doubt faced by Mordor. They must be dreadful. We see now that the Black Riders have been released, and they're going after Frodo. The *Black Riders.* Of course they're black. Everything evil is always black. And later Gandalf the Grey becomes Gandalf the White. Have you noticed that?

CHOMSKY: The most simplistic color symbolism.

ZINN: And the writing on the ring, we learn here, is Orcish—the so-called "black speech." Orcish is evidently some spoliation of the language spoken in Rohan. This is what Tolkien says.

CHOMSKY: From what I understand, Orcish is a patois that the Orcs developed during their enslavement by Rohan, before they rebelled and left.

ZINN: Well, supposedly the Orcs were first bred by "the dark power of the north in the elder days." Tolkien says that "Orc" comes from the Mannish word *tark*, which means "man of Gondor."

CHOMSKY: Shameless really.

ZINN: Gandalf mentions the evil stirring in Mordor. That's all he has to say. "It's evil." He doesn't elaborate on what's going on in Mordor, what the people are going through. They're evil because they're there.

CHOMSKY: I think the fact that we never actually see the enemy is quite damning. Then again, Gandalf is the greatest storyteller of all. He weaves the tales that strand Middle Earth in this state of perpetual conflict.

ZINN: He is celebrated on one hand as a great statesman, a wise man, and viewed by the people who understand the role that he actually plays as a dangerous lunatic and a war criminal. And you will notice that Gandalf's war pitch hits its highest note when the Black Riders arrive in Hobbiton. I don't think that's a coincidence.

CHOMSKY: This is *The Triumph of the Will*.

ZINN: And now Frodo and Sam are joined by Merry and Pippin, as they finally escape the Shire. They're being chased by the Black Riders. Again, if these Black Riders are so fearsome, and they can smell the ring so lividly, why don't they ever seem able to find the Hobbits when they're standing right next to them?

CHOMSKY: Well, they're on horseback.

ZINN: Right.

CHOMSKY: This episode in Bree should cause us to ask, too, how much Frodo knows about the conspiracy. He seems to be piecing it together a little bit. I think at first he's an unwitting participant, fooled by Gandalf's propaganda.

ZINN: I'm much more suspicious of Frodo than you are. I've always viewed him as one of the most malevolent actors in this drama, precisely because of how he abets people like Gandalf. He uses a fake name, Mr. Underhill, just as Gandalf goes by several names: Mithrandir, the Grey Pilgrim, the White Rider. Strider is also Aragorn, is also Estel, is also Elessar, is also Dunadan. He has all these identities.

CHOMSKY: We call those aliases today.

ZINN: But is Sauron ever anything but Sauron? Is Saruman ever anything but Saruman?

CHOMSKY: And now, with Frodo in the midst of a hallucinogenic, paranoid state, we meet Strider.

ZINN: Note that the first thing he starts talking about is the ring. "That is no trinket you carry." A very telling irony, that. It is the kind of irony that Shakespeare would use. It is something Iago might say. And did you hear that? "Sauron the Deceiver." That is what Strider, the ranger with multiple names, calls Sauron. A ranger. I believe today we call them serial killers.

CHOMSKY: Or drug smugglers.

ZINN: And notice how Strider characterizes the Black Riders. "Neither living nor dead." Why, that's a really useful enemy to have.

CHOMSKY: Yes. In this way you can never verify their existence, and yet they're horribly terrifying. We should not overlook the fact that Middle Earth is in a cold war at this moment, locked in perpetual conflict. Strider's rhetoric serves to keep fear alive.

ZINN: You've spoken to me before about Mordor's lack of access to the mineral wealth that the Dwarves control.

CHOMSKY: If we're going to get into the socio-economic reasons why certain structures develop in certain cultures... it's mainly geographical. We have Orcs in Mordor—trapped, with no mineral resources—hemmed in by the Ash Mountains, where the "free peoples" of Middle Earth can put a city, like Osgiliath, and effectively keep the border closed.

ZINN: Don't forget the Black Gate. The Black Gate, which, as Tolkien points out, was built by Gondor. And now we jump to the Orcs chopping down the trees in Isengard.

CHOMSKY: A terrible thing the Orcs do here, isn't it? They destroy nature. But again, what have we seen, time and time again?

ZINN: The Orcs have no resources. They're desperate.

CHOMSKY: Desperate people driven to do desperate things.

ZINN: Desperate to compete with the economic powerhouses of Rohan and Gondor.

CHOMSKY: Who really knows their motive? Maybe this is a means to an end. And while that might not be the best philosophy in the world, it makes the race of Man in no way superior. They're going to great lengths to hold onto their power. Two cultures locked in conflict over power, with one culture clearly suffering a great deal. I think sharing power and resources would have been the wisest approach, but Rohan and Gondor have shown no interest in doing so. Sometimes, revolution must be—

ZINN: Mistakes are often—

CHOMSKY: Blood must be shed. I forget what Thomas Jefferson—

ZINN: He said that blood was the—

CHOMSKY: The blood of tyrants—

ZINN: The blood of tyrants—

CHOMSKY: —waters the tree of—

ZINN: —revolution.

CHOMSKY: —freedom. Or revolution. Something like that.

ZINN: I think that's actually very, very close.

ON THE IMPLAUSIBILITY OF THE DEATH STAR'S TRASH COMPACTOR

by J.M. TYREE

I maintain that the trash compactor onboard the Death Star in *Star Wars* is implausible, unworkable, and moreover, inefficient.

The Trash Compactor Debate hinges on whether the Death Star ejects its trash into space. I, for one, believe it does. Though we never see the Death Star ejecting its trash, we do see another Empire ship, the so-called Star Destroyer, ejecting its trash into space. Therefore, I see no reason to suspect that Empire protocol dictating that trash be ejected into space would not apply equally to all Empire spacecraft, including the Death Star.

The Death Star clearly has a garbage-disposal problem. Given its size and massive personnel, the amount of waste it generates—discarded food, broken equipment, excrement, and the like—boggles the imagination. That said, I just cannot fathom how an organization as ruthless and efficiently run as the Empire would have signed off on such a dangerous, unsanitary, and shoddy garbage-disposal system as the one depicted in the movie.

Here are the problems, as I can ascertain them, with the Death Star's garbage-disposal system

1. Ignoring the question of how Princess Leia could possibly know where the trash compactor is, or that the vent she blasts open leads to a good hiding place for the rescue crew, why are there vents leading down there at all? Would not vents leading into any garbage-disposal system allow the fetid smell of rotting garbage, spores, molds, etc., to seep up into the rest of the Death Star? Would not it have been more prudent for the designers of the Death Star to opt for a closed system, like a septic tank?

2. Why do both walls of the trash compactor move towards each other, rather than employing a one-movable-wall system that would thus rely on the anchored stability, to say nothing of the strength, of the other, non-moving wall, to crush trash more effectively?

3. Why does the trash compactor compact trash so slowly, and with such difficulty, once the resistance of a thin metal rod is introduced? Surely metal Death Star pieces are one of the main items of trash in need of compacting. It thus stands to reason that the trash compactor should have been better designed to handle the problem of a skinny piece of metal. (And while I hate to be the sort of person who says I told you so, I'd be remiss if I didn't point out that a one-movable-wall system would have improved performance.)

4. Why does the trash compactor only compact trash sideways? Once ejected into space, wouldn't the flattened, living-room-sized, and

extremely solid panes of trash that result from such a primitive, unidirectional trash compactor pose serious hazards for Empire starships in the vicinity?

5. And what of the creature that lives in the trash compactor? Presumably, the creature survives because the moving walls do not extend all the way to the floor of the room, where the liquid is. After all, if the walls reached the floor, the creature would be killed each time trash is compacted. The design employed on the Death Star must allow the organic trash to filter down to the bottom, where the parasitic worm-creature devours it. But what happens when heavier pieces of non-organic trash fall down there? Would such trash not get wedged under the doors, causing them to malfunction? Do stormtroopers have to confront the creature each time they retrieve pieces of un-compacted trash?

6. Why not have separate systems for organic and inorganic waste, thus allowing full compaction of the inorganics and a closed sanitary system for the organics?

7. Why does the Empire care, anyway, about reducing its organic garbage output? Are we to believe that the architects of the Death Star, a group of individuals bent on controlling the entire known universe, are also concerned about environmental issues? Would organic garbage rot in space? So what? Furthermore, why has the Empire gone to the trouble of acquiring a frightening parasitic worm-creature and having it eat all organic trash, especially given the aforementioned flaws in the design of the compactor and overall maintenance hassles?

8. Personally, were it up to me, I would have designed special garbage ships instead of employing a crude, cumbersome, and inefficient (to say nothing of unsanitary) compactor-worm combo to deal with the trash.

9. If the Empire insists on ejecting trash into space, why do they bother compacting it? Space is infinite, is it not? In such an environment, it hardly matters what size the trash is. In fact, a persuasive argument can be made that it's actually better for the trash to take up more space, so that it appears on radar systems as something for Empire ships to avoid. Compacted trash creates smaller chunks of harder trash that would undoubtedly cause serious damage to Empire starships. And needless to say, damage to starships would, in turn, create yet more hassles and headaches for the Empire.

Please understand, gentle reader, I am all for creating hassles and headaches for the Empire. I just doubt that the Empire would have created so many for itself. Q.E.D.

E-MAIL ADDRESSES IT WOULD BE REALLY ANNOYING TO GIVE OUT OVER THE PHONE

by MICHAEL WARD

MikeUnderscore2004@yahoo.com

MikeAtYahooDotCom@hotmail.com

Mike_WardAllOneWord@yahoo.com

AAAAAThatsSixAs@yahoo.com

One1TheFirstJustTheNumberTheSecondSpelledOut@hotmail.com

BUTTERBALL HELPLINE HELPLINE

by ALYSIA GRAY PAINTER

Q: A caller just said she forgot to baste every ten minutes. I advised her to serve the turkey anyway. Was I correct?

A: Not at all. The turkey is merely the vehicle for the basting. In a recent poll, nine out of ten people would rather sit down at the table and suck on the end of a baster full of buttery juices than gnaw at some dry old wing. Bad call.

- - -

Q: I just overheard my coworker advising a home cook to truss the bird. I arrived late at the "Talk Turkey" seminar last week and missed the trussing segment. Can you advise?

A: Trussing, while not the chef's best friend, is that pleasant acquaintance you see about once a year and always have a compliment for. Trussing is legal in every state. Trussing comes from the word *truss*, which means "to truss," or tie string, or put pins in a turkey to help it stay in a pretty poultry-like shape that is pleasing to the eye. Cooks must remove pins and string before consuming. If a caller wants to know if she should truss, you should tell her you only go around this crazy world once. Trust truss.

- - -

Q: Cinnamon or nutmeg?

A: Cinnamon is a nice spice people are comfortable consuming throughout the year, sprinkled either on toast or in a delicious coffee beverage. Nutmeg is a nasty, gritty substance that wants nothing to do with us in the spring or summer but demands our favor come November, only to disappear to the back of the shelf for another year. Why do we continue to accommodate this so-called seasoning? Nutmeg is a stupid jerk.

- - -

Q: I just hung up with a caller with the words "gobble, gobble" instead of "goodbye"—was this appropriate?

A: No. Make sure you note that in your report to your supervisor on Monday.

- - -

Q: The vending machine on the second floor is broken and we're starved. Should we call maintenance?

A: Maintenance is home eating a proper dinner with family and friends. Go to the office kitchen and look in the cupboard behind the fridge. There will be a half-eaten box of Triscuits there, because every office kitchen in existence contains a half-eaten box of Triscuits in the cupboard behind the fridge. Triscuit dust is an acceptable snack when poured into a small paper cup and drunk in the manner of water. Do not use a straw.

- - -

Q: My boyfriend didn't care if I worked the holiday. Is our relationship in trouble?

A: Perhaps your boyfriend wanted to watch football unencumbered and without you fussing around with gravy boats and miniature marshmallows. If your boyfriend is a fresh-faced soap star who wants to move up to Broadway, look for him tap dancing his heart out in front of Macy's around 10:35 a.m.

- - -

Q: I've been answering calls from perplexed home cooks all day and I still don't know why we bother, really.

A: Everyone talks about the bickering relatives and the burnt yams, but few talk about taking a weekday to eat and nap and gossip with a sibling about another sibling. No one owns it. No focus group studies it. Just you and a mostly empty bowl of stuffing and no clean utensils, so use your fingers already.

WINNIE-THE-POOH IS MY COWORKER

by JOHN MOE

MARCH 5

Maureen brought the new guy around who's going to be working in our group. After the Jason fiasco, we really could use someone with a little bit of a brain who can keep up on things. This guy's named Winnie and, I don't know, I just have a bad feeling.

MARCH 9

I've been training Winnie for three days now and I'm ready to kill him. I showed him how the spreadsheets are updated on the network, and he just stared at me with this blank expression. I tried to demonstrate the copy machine, but he somehow got his head stuck in one of the slots. I heard his muffled cry of "Oh, bother!" as five of us worked on getting him out. Honestly, is this the best that recruiting could do?

Kirk thinks Winnie might be someone's cousin or something. Not a bad explanation, except that we don't have any other yellow bears working here.

MARCH 11

Although he's worthless, everyone loves Winnie. The girls from marketing come by at least a couple of times a day to hang around his cubicle and talk to him. It's not like they respect his work, since he doesn't do any. And I don't think they even respect him. They're just there to be, like, amused. If he were to make a move on one of them, they'd shoot him down so fast. I mean, I don't respect Winnie, either, but at least I keep my distance.

MARCH 15

I gave Winnie this file of research material on Crawford & Horowitz because I thought he might want to read up on it before the group meeting tomorrow. I'm doing him a favor, right? So I go to get it back from him after lunch and find Winnie sitting on the floor, his hand in a honey jar, and all this paperwork, including the file I need, smeared with thick honey. It's unusable now. I might as well throw it away. Trying not to just go off on the bear, I asked him what the hell happened. He looked all confused and mumbled something about needing "a little post-lunch snack." Jesus. Have a freakin' apple, dude.

MARCH 16

Turns out Winnie got honey all over his keyboard as well. So what happens? They bring him a whole new computer. Top of the line machine, too. Here I've been pounding away on this ancient piece of crap for years, and Mr. Honeypot gets a whole new setup. The tech guy who came by said it looked like Winnie had never even turned the old machine on.

MARCH 19

Winnie's friends came by to take him out for lunch today: a little pig, a pissed-off-looking rabbit, an adolescent kangaroo, and a tiger that had to be on coke. Kirk said he saw them at Sbarro eating their slices and looking scared out of their minds. I guess they live way out in the country or something, so I bet the big city blew their minds. Winnie was really happy around them, though. I guess that's good, since he's just been sitting around here moping all the time and staring out the window. He should just leave and spend *all* his time with them.

MARCH 26

Three times this week, Winnie's asked if I want to join him for a picnic or maybe an adventure. No thanks, I tell him very pointedly, I have a lot of work to do. He just sighs and walks off on his own. Silly old bear.

MARCH 30

It's Robin. Walt Robin, the V.P. of finance. That's how Winnie got the job. Apparently, Winnie has some sort of relationship with Robin's grandson or nephew or something. That's what Kirk told me, and he knows someone in H.R. Frankly, I wonder if that's going to be enough to let Winnie stick around. He showed up three hours late today and gave this long story about being chased by bees. Then he brought out another honey pot (his cubicle is covered with empty ones), ate the honey with his hands for a while, and passed out on his desk. I mean, it's so far beyond just not contributing to the workload at this point. It's unhygienic for us and he's so clearly not healthy. Someone should do something. The little bitch Tami from marketing came by to rub his tummy. Unbelievable.

APRIL 6

Winnie hasn't shown up in three days. I figured he called in sick, but I guess no one's heard anything. He has no phone, so no one's been able to reach him.

APRIL 7

H.R. asked me to drive out to Winnie's house, since I'm his best friend at the company (sad). I followed the directions and found him in this hollowed-out tree where he apparently lives. He must have offered me honey like twelve times. I have to admit, he looked happier than he ever did at work. I asked if he was planning on coming back to work, but he just said that the office was "quite an adventure" but that he was "glad to be home." He really is a nice guy, but I think it's better for everyone that it's over. He told me to come back and visit sometime and I lied and said I would.

GOOFUS, GALLANT, RASHOMON

by JIM STALLARD

TED, COWORKER OF GALLANT:
That freak belonged to the cult of manners. Talk about a true believer. I rode on an airplane with him once, and he wouldn't start eating his meal until everyone was served.

SHEILA, GOOFUS'S HIGH-SCHOOL CLASSMATE:
My memory of Goofus is that people saw what they wanted to. I was drawn to him because I sensed he was hurting inside. That's why he put up that wall and was "rude," but who's to say which way is right? It's just a social construct. Is there some cosmic, universal book of manners? I knew they'd find a way to make him pay, though. They always do.

RONALD, MIDDLE-SCHOOL CLASSMATE OF BOTH:
It was weird; they started at our school at the exact same time. Eighth grade. Everyone thought they were brothers, but it turns out their fathers were just transferred at the same time to the cereal plant in town. Gallant sits down in the front row and starts sucking up to Mr. Anderson, the English teacher. Volunteers for everything, like our literary journal, *Chrysalis*—all that gay stuff.

SHAWN, HIGH-SCHOOL CLASSMATE OF GOOFUS:
Goofus—my god, what a bad-boy poseur. I could tell he had picked up his Nietzscheism from a comic book. He would talk about the "Will to Power." But there was also some G. Gordon Liddy mixed in there. He loved doing the candle trick, moving his hand through the flame and pretending he didn't mind the pain. Then I did the same thing with my finger, showing him how full of shit he was.

NATALIE, GALLANT'S HIGH-SCHOOL FRIEND:
Gallant was one of the few mature guys in our high school. Sensitive. We used to talk about James Taylor during lunch. I thought him the perfect gentleman, and of course my parents loved him. But when someone is polite to the point of having that Moonie quality, it gets to you. Finally, it dawned on me that he used that politeness as a way of controlling me. That was what it was all about—he followed the rules because it gave him the advantage.

ALEX, HIGH-SCHOOL TEACHER OF GOOFUS:
Goofus had a top-notch bullshit detector. Most teenagers think they

have one, but his was the real thing, and I'm one of the few teachers who can relate to it. I introduced him to Kerouac, Bukowski, Burroughs. He acted enthusiastic about writing a paper in which they interacted. But it turned out to be seven pages of... Well, I was one of the characters in the scene, which was extremely graphic and not what we agreed on.

PAUL, GALLANT'S COLLEGE ACQUAINTANCE:

Gallant just didn't get it when it came to relating to people. He would say words the "proper" way that no one normal ever does—you know, "Don't act immatoor." Always the authority. One night, I'm walking to dinner with him and another student, a friend from England, and we're ragging on each other—he's calling me Yank and I'm calling him Limey. Gallant breaks in to inform us that "Limey" comes from the British navy, eating limes to avoid scurvy, blah, blah, blah. Gee, thanks, Gallant. Dork.

BRANDON, JUNIOR-COLLEGE CLASSMATE OF GOOFUS:

Was Goofus a rebel? He sure liked to think so. He cultivated that tousled-hair thing. He wouldn't go out unless he thought it was prominent enough. I sat in his living room for forty-five minutes once waiting for him to sculpt it into the perfect unkempt shape. But that roughness was skin deep. I knew he'd be easy pickings in a real fight.

DAN, GALLANT'S COLLEGE ACQUAINTANCE:

Gallant would walk into a party and suck all the air out of the room. He would pretend not to be disapproving but he always made a point of commenting on what you were drinking, or how many you had. "You must really like that kind of beer"—until you edged away.

DARLENE, EX-WIFE OF GOOFUS:

I thought I could change Goofus. Remember, I'm a town girl who's never gone anywhere, and I was looking for some excitement. I had a lot to learn about men. With that electronic ankle bracelet, he couldn't leave the house after dark, so it was always me doing the shopping and running last-minute errands. And through all that he was always talking about how oppressed he was. Try raising three kids when your husband won't get off his ass.

STEVE, GALLANT'S COLLEGE ACQUAINTANCE:

Gallant's attempts to seem cool were just painful. One time after making some incredibly lame joke he said, "I'm just breaking your balls," and the rest of us almost died laughing.

SHANE, GOOFUS'S ARMY BUDDY:

Goofus loved Jack Daniels. And Yukon Jack. He always wanted to do snakebites even though I don't think he liked them—just the name. He would do two and then switch to something else.

BRAD, GALLANT'S COWORKER:

Gallant was the total company man. There's not a buzzword he didn't use to death. We're at a strategy meeting one day and he actually says, "If you *fail to plan you plan to fail.*" I had to avoid making eye contact with Tony, another coworker, because I knew we would both lose it and get in trouble.

REVEREND JOHN SWAFFORD, GALLANT'S MINISTER:
Gallant was a wonderful addition to our church. He always showed tremendous concern for the members, making inquiries and then letting me know which ones seemed to be having personal problems. If he had just had a little more concern for himself, things would not have turned out the way they did.

HAROLD, CHARITY-EVENT ORGANIZER:
What happened was a disgrace. I put together nice events with the right kinds of people attending. I don't need this kind of publicity.

DAVID, GALLANT'S COWORKER:
I don't really understand what pushed Gallant over the edge. Serving from the right rather than the left—who even pays attention to that stuff? Especially at a fundraiser. I think Gallant must have been on something. There's a side of him nobody knows. It's weird how everything came full circle, though. It was fate Goofus got assigned to serve that table.

DEAN, FELLOW WAITER WITH GOOFUS:
Goofus told me in the kitchen he had a bad feeling about that night. It was weird because he's not usually superstitious. I was still in there putting garnishes on the plates when I heard the altercation—I just thought someone was getting chewed out for dropping a tray.

DAVID, DEPUTY MAYOR:
I was at the next table. Everything is normal. The waiters are bringing

the entrees out and whisking the salads away. Suddenly, this nice-looking man at their table explodes in rage. He screams out, "Right is wrong!" several times at this poor server who's looking at him in shock. Before anyone can move he puts one hand on top of the server's head, the other on his jaw, and just snaps his neck, Delta Force-style. Then he sat back down and put his napkin in his lap.

EVAN, GALLANT'S COWORKER:

I was sitting across from Gallant. Goofus was baiting him—he was looking right at me with this smirk on his face while he set the plate down. Well, he got a reaction all right. I hope Goofus is happy wherever he is—where exactly do scum go when they die?

GEORGE, GALLANT'S COWORKER:

Wow—a life sentence. Normally, I'd say Gallant won't last a week on the inside. But I can definitely imagine him being very helpful to some inmate, if you get me.

HAROLD, CEMETERY CUSTODIAN:

Goofus's tombstone is not marked well and is hard to find, but the teenage kids have started making pilgrimages to it. They go there and get drunk and weepy. I find their beer cans and wine bottles along with flowers and notes saying stuff like, "You spoke the truth and they killed you for it." I'm thinking: You want to make him out to be your hero? Go crazy, I don't care. Just don't leave your crap all over the ground for me to clean up. Didn't anybody ever teach these kids manners?

A BRIEF AUTOBIOGRAPHY OF CAMILLE PAGLIA, AS TOLD THROUGH INTRODUCTORY APPOSITIVE PHRASES FROM HER ONLINE COLUMN

by LISA WHIPPLE

All the phrases below are real, and appeared in Camille Paglia's regular column on Salon.com.

"As a native of the snow belt of upstate New York, I..."

"As the product of an immigrant family (my mother and all four grandparents were born in Italy), I..."

"As someone only one generation (on my mother's side) and two generations (on my father's side) removed from the Italian countryside, I..."

"As an archaeology fan from childhood, I..."

"As someone whose childhood idol was Amelia Earhart, I..."

"As a scruffy tomboy, I…"

"As a tomboy whose Amazonian craze was always for swords and spears, I…"

"As a refugee from Roman Catholic 'Religious Ed.' (which we public-school students were sent off to once a week), I…"

"As a lapsed Catholic who grew up under the gigantic bat-wings of the Legion of Decency (America's anti-Hollywood Inquisition), I…"

"As a student in the 1960s, I…"

"As a 1960s pop Warholite and rock fan, I…"

"As a pop Warholite and pornographic apostle of the 1960s sexual revolution, I…"

"As a faithful Warholite since college, I…"

"As a fan of Erving Goffman from my college days, I…"

"As a grad student then systematically searching the university libraries for changing definitions of male and female in world history, I…"

"As a pop acolyte of Marshall McLuhan and Andy Warhol, I…"

"As a '60s zealot of the mystic sciences (astrology, palmistry, I Ching, Tarot, et al.), I…"

"As a teacher, I…"

"As a teacher still animated by 1960s ideals, I…"

"As a proponent of Egyptian and Greco-Roman studies, I…"

"As a scholar of sexual history and culture, I…"

"As an arts educator, I…"

"As a feminist and career teacher, I…"

"As an equity feminist, I…"

"As a reform feminist, I…"

"As a dissident feminist and football fanatic, I…"

"As an equity feminist, as well as an open lesbian, I…"

"As a lesbian, I…"

"As an open lesbian, I…"

"As an open lesbian, first of all, I…"

"As a lesbian with a male brain, I…"

"As an Amazon feminist, I…"

"As an Amazon feminist, inspired by masculine achievements, I…"

"As an Amazon with the brain of a pre-Stonewall gay man, I…"

"As a pugnacious Amazon, I…"

"As a superstitious Italian, I…"

"As a libertarian, I…"

"As a strict libertarian, I…"

"As a capitalist libertarian, I…"

"As a civil libertarian, I…"

"As a vigilant civil libertarian, I…"

"As a libertarian Democrat, I…"

"As a libertarian Democrat who cast my primary ballot for Bill Bradley, I…"

"As a longtime supporter of Geraldine Ferraro, I…"

"As a Democrat who voted for Jesse Jackson in the 1988 presidential primary, I…"

"As someone who voted for Jesse Jackson in the 1988 Democratic primary (yes, I know he's morphed into a pampered Vernon Jordan-style socialite and stagey race-baiter), I…"

"As a Clinton Democrat, I…"

"As someone who voted for Clinton twice—and would vote for him a third time because I support most of his policies—I…"

"As a now-disillusioned early admirer of the Clintons, I…"

"As an ex-Catholic (like Hitchcock) and as an admirer of canonical Western art (like Hitchcock), I…"

"As a lapsed Catholic and professed atheist, I…"

"As an atheist, I…"

"As a disciple of Oscar Wilde, I…"

"As a disciple of the Cambridge School of Anthropology (Sir James George Frazer, Jane Harrison, et al.), I…"

"As a worshipper of Sweden's national treasure, Ingmar Bergman, I…"

"As a supporter of capital punishment, I…"

"As an advocate of capital punishment, I…"

"As a longtime proponent of capital punishment, I…"

"As a free speech advocate, I…"

"As a militant free-speech advocate, I…"

"As a culture warrior, I..."

"As a biology-minded social analyst, I..."

"As a devotee of Glennda Orgasm (Glenn Belverio's immortal drag alter ego), I..."

"As a Hellenophile, I..."

"As a theorist of sex, I..."

"As a notoriously gender-dysfunctional, mental teenager myself, I..."

"As a teacher who's been marking papers for 26 years, I..."

"As a teacher for 27 years, I..."

"As someone who has devoted her career (at great cost) to arts education, I..."

"As a football fan, I..."

"As a committed television enthusiast, I..."

"As a television watcher, I..."

"As a resident of one of the southeastern Pennsylvania counties declared a disaster zone last week by the federal government, I..."

BONUS: A DEMOGRAPHIC ANALYSIS OF CAMILLE PAGLIA'S READER-
SHIP, AS TOLD THROUGH INTRODUCTORY APPOSITIVE PHRASES IN
THEIR LETTERS TO HER ON SALON.COM.

"As a young journalist, I..."

"As a student of American politics, I..."

"As a retired veteran New York City police officer with over 20 years
in the streets, I..."

"As an owner of three 'assault' weapons, I..."

"As a clinical psychologist, I..."

"As the product of a mother from a fairly traditional Lebanese-Amer-
ican family and a father of skinny hard-drinking Scots-Irish farmers
and lawyers (all from Meridian, Miss. ... think about that!), I..."

"As someone who really hopes the Green Party will get off the ground
in the United States (and who plans to vote for Nader if he happens
to appear on my state ballot), I.. ."

"As a New Yorker in self-imposed exile, I..."

"As a gay male who would like to become a good thinker, I..."

"As a junior wonkette and history buff, I..."

"As an Englishman last year resident in Canada, I..."

"As a tubby Midwesterner, I..."

CORRECTION: The phrase "As a tubby Midwesterner, I..." was mistakenly attributed to Paglia, rather than to one of her readers, when this piece originally ran. McSweeney's regrets the error.

MAXIM DOES THE CLASSICS

by WENDY MOLYNEUX

THE GREAT GATSBY

Gatsby follows this chick Daisy to South Padre Island for spring break. While jet-skiing, he finds out that she has already hooked up with his buddy Tom. So he hooks up with this other girl, Mabel. When Mabel's husband finds out, he suggests a three-way.

HAMLET

Got MILF? A wealthy bachelor falls for an older lady named Gertrude. Then he finds out that his buddy's sister Ophelia has got the hots for him. Who should he choose? Are you kidding me? *Why* should he choose?

A TALE OF TWO CITIES

Two identical dudes fall for the same chick. The chick is none the wiser that there are two dudes, so they can both get the chick and get a little action on the side. Was it the worst of times? No way, it was the best of times, dog.

LITTLE WOMEN

Four young ladies living in the middle of nowhere. When one of them dies, the other three have to comfort each other. They start with hugging and kissing each others' tears away. I think you know what happens next, friend.

THE GRAPES OF WRATH

A bunch of guys get together to ride their motocross bikes across the country to California to find girls. When one of them gets hurt, they stop in wine country and meet girls named Rose and Sharon who agree to "nurse" the injured guy back to health.

THE LOVE SONG OF J. ALFRED PRUFROCK

A long poem which neatly captures the dilemma of the modern man: plagued by indecision, bewildered by women, wondering how to connect with others. The poet asserts that all men must ask themselves, finally, the heart-rending questions "Do I dare disturb the universe?" and "Do I dare to eat a peach?"

If by "peach" you mean "pussy," *Maxim* says belly up to the bar, J-Man.

HOW PAST
GIRLFRIENDS COULD
HAVE CHANGED HISTORY

by BRIAN SACK

ADOLF HITLER

Tammy wouldn't like Hitler's sense of humor and would give him a frowny face every time he told a joke. He would invite her to his parades and she'd tell him the goose-stepping looked "gay" and that she "didn't get" the swastika. This would undermine his confidence and make it harder for him to retain an iron grip on power. "I don't know what you see in that Goebbels," she'd say. "He seems like kind of a loser." Her constant criticisms would result in Hitler and Goebbels not hanging out as much. As a result, Nazi propaganda would suffer. Tammy would also insist that they forgo his favorite watering holes and instead go to places she likes. The putsch would then happen at a tacky folk-music bar with her ex-boyfriend playing guitar. Most of Hitler's friends wouldn't have shown up, because they couldn't stand the constant arguing. In the middle of their relationship, Tammy would tell Hitler she was going on a trip with some coworker. With Hitler's self-esteem in the gutter, he'd lack the support and influence necessary to invade Poland and start World War II. Eventually, he'd break up with Tammy and call Himmler, whom he'd blown off for two years.

THE TITANIC

Sharon would go into the captain's quarters and refuse to leave. "I just want to talk," she'd say, "I just want to talk." He'd beg her to leave, but she would just keep telling the captain she loved him and wanted to talk. "I don't want to talk," he'd say, "I don't want anything to do with you." Sharon would tell him that's not true and that she knew he loved her. She'd say she wouldn't let him break up with her anyway. The captain would threaten to call the police. "Go ahead," she'd say, "I'm not leaving." Frustrated and desperate to get away from her, he'd flee his quarters and run on deck, where he'd spot the giant iceberg. "Goodness! Go a few degrees port-ish," he'd tell the folks piloting the ship—averting potential disaster. Sharon would be unaware that she saved so many lives, as she would be busy trying to feed the captain's cat a tomato—because she thinks cats can eat them. After finally exiting the captain's quarters for good, she'd leave a long message on his voice mail telling him he was an ugly loser and everyone hated him. Then she'd make out with his first mate.

SEPTEMBER 11

In the middle of planning a surprise attack on civilians, Osama bin Laden would be invited to meet Anna's family in rural Pennsylvania over Christmas break. Osama would get along fine with the overbearing mom and timid dad until the mom went through his bags and found

Anna's marijuana and birth control pills. With her mother's dormant psychosis triggered, Anna would then be dragged upstairs for six hours of being called a whore. This would be discomforting to Osama, who would sit in the living room freaking out. When Mohammed Atta called to check in, Osama would be totally frazzled. "Hold off on the martyrdom ops, dude. I'm up to my ears in shit," he'd say. Anna and Osama would decide to cut the trip short and leave the next day. The following morning, Osama would sit in the freezing car for another three hours while the mom wrapped up calling her daughter a whore and drug addict. While her dad remained in the house peering from behind the curtains, Anna's mom would come out to curse at Osama for ruining their daughter's "white wedding." Osama would be forced to spend the next year dealing with Anna's being disowned. While tending to her subsequent nervous breakdown, he'd neglect his evil endeavor, which would give a vigilant INS the chance to notice that several pilots-in-training had no interest in flaps or landing gear.

CUBAN MISSILE CRISIS

Maggie would regularly call Castro "Mr. Poops," which he'd find endearing but, at the same time, childish. Though she's an extremely beautiful and sweet girl, Castro would have a hard time finding her sexy because of the childlike demeanor. Every time he said, "So...," she'd finish with "... buttons on your fanny." Again, something he'd find cute but weird. Castro would find it very hard to stay threatening on the phone with Kennedy, because she would make puckered-up fish faces as he talked. She would only communicate with him in baby-speak, which he would accidentally carry over into his conversations with the Soviets. After hearing Castro say, "Toodles, my noodle," Khrushchev would call a little powwow at the Kremlin. The Politburo would decide that Mr. Poops wasn't the best person to mind their nuclear weapons. There would be no missile crisis. A few weeks later, Castro would call the relationship quits when he hears Maggie pee.

WACO

Kelly would keep trying to get David Koresh to have sex in the shower. "C'mon, baby doll," she'd say in a Southern twang. "C'mon, baby doll." He would be very concerned about the FBI/ATF forces amassed outside his compound, but she would only talk about sex. She'd tell him to try some ecstasy because the sex would be great when on ecstasy. About twelve minutes later he'd realize he was chemically impotent, but that would be okay with him. He'd just smile. "What's the matter, baby doll?" she'd ask. "You gay, baby doll?" He'd take deep breaths and sink into the bed as his pupils dilated to maximum. Having discovered the remarkable texture of Kelly's fake breasts, he'd start rubbing them lovingly and telling her how fantastic they were. The warmth of her skin would resonate as awesome ATF agents beautifully entered his wonderful bedroom and fired two gorgeous rounds into his eye.

II.
CHILDHOOD
2005–2010

A McSWEENEY'S INTERNET
TENDENCY ORIGIN STORY

WHEN WE RULED THE WORLD
by BEN GREENMAN

"What best represents the human mind?
Is experience itself a text? Where are my shoes?"

I AM SITTING IN THE present, here in 2030, remembering the past. I am sitting in a car that may well be mine. The meter is running out of money, in the sense that it is running out of time. I can't find any more money, so instead I will run backwards in time, back to 2001, when I sat in the basement of a Brooklyn brownstone, surrounded by discarded Ikea furniture and the unmistakable smell of Thai food edged with pizza from the restaurants at street level. There was a third smell, as well: the eternally humble arrogance of human creativity.

It was midnight, or four in the morning, or noon. We had no clocks. Or rather, we were the clocks: me and Lawrence Krauser and Amy Fusselman and some others. That was the core group, the nucleus, the creamy center of the golden sponge cake of literary thought. There were others. Dave Eggers dropped by now and again, as did Sarah Min. I remember even more occasional visitors named William and James and Jane and another Jane and "Gator" and "Dead Zone." Entering that basement space meant elevating your thinking. This was the central paradox. "Isn't everything a paradox?" Lawrence said.

WELCOME TO PAGE 127

"A small medical practice is," I said.

We all fell out laughing. We were bracing ourselves for the difficult task ahead, which involved drafting a charter. We began to take
notes on the chalkboard that covered one of the walls of the basement.
Amy had a box of chalk that she had purchased at a drugstore. It was
brittle and broke if you were too rough with it. "Fascinating," I said.
"It's almost as if our ideas are too strong for the physical materials with
which we are trying to express them."

"Chalk's always like that," Amy said. I thought I heard her sigh.
I know she rolled her eyes in exasperation.

We began to pepper Amy with questions. What best represents
the human mind? Is experience itself a text? Where are my shoes? She
wrote them down and then furnished the answers: a map; no; under the
bench. That's when Lawrence made his remark about a paradox, and
when I made my joke. Or had that preceded our chalkboard charter?
Now I have lost the thread of the chronology. Time is an abstraction,
at any rate. I remember mostly being hungry and feeling that I had
only two choices, Thai and pizza. I ran upstairs, got slices for everyone, and came back down, thinking elevated, where I used a copy of
In Watermelon Sugar as a plate.

We fell asleep. We woke up. The chalkboard was empty. The chalkboard was full. Existence was impenetrable. Existence was transparent.
We knew nothing except one thing, which is that we had a real chance
at knowing everything. That's how things were back then, in the literary hotbed of early *McSweeney's*. Were we writing humorous pieces?
Perhaps we were, but only in the sense that the world was in pieces,
and we humored it. Go, lightning, and sear the sky! Go, thunder, and
shake the trees! Go, rain, and drench the previous two sentences!

One morning, I stumbled into the room. Everyone was there. Lawrence was standing. Amy was sitting. Some others were leaning on

the wall. I was there, too. I had stumbled into the room. Remember? They were all pointing to a door drawn on the chalkboard. "Open it," Lawrence said. I laughed. How could you open a drawing? But then it opened on its own, and I saw the future. I saw how we would perfect and then destroy irony; how we would forever alter the landscape of American letters; how life would descend on us in all its metallic gray; how we would go on to become adults, husband and wives, lawyers, doctors, and in one case even the president of the United States. But that was still decades away.

"What the hell are you talking about?" Dead Zone said. I had not realized that I was speaking out loud. I was suddenly mortified to be stuck in the past. I recalled myself to the present and put more money in the meter. I am not sure where I found it. A pocket, probably.

FOLLOWING MY CREATIVE WRITING TEACHER'S ADVICE TO WRITE "LIKE MY PARENTS ARE DEAD"

by ELLIE KEMPER

FROM "AUTUMN DAYS ARE FLEETING"

There was a slight nip in the air, and I pulled my anorak closer. The leaves were beginning to turn. Orange, brown, bright yellow. Autumn, I thought. I inhaled deeply, imagining the crisp air filling my lungs. Oh, God. I miss Mom. Why did you take her from me, God? Why did she have to die? She is gone.

FROM "SEVEN DAYS, FIVE OF THEM WORKING"

I agreed with Cynthia. I did. Four hours would never be enough time to prepare the presentation. There was too much data. There were too many bar graphs. It wasn't our fault. We were told the meeting would be on Thursday; it got bumped back to Wednesday. Oh, God.

Wednesday. My dad's favorite day. What was it that he used to call it again? Oh, yeah: Hump Day. I miss Dad so much.

FROM "REFLECTIONS ON A LAKE"

"You guys go ahead," I told Timothy. "I'll wait for you at the dock." Timothy nodded. Really, what was the point of my going out on the sailboat, feeling like this? I would bring down the entire party. After all, that's how both of my parents died. On a sailboat. Lakes aren't always as placid as you might think. Lakes kill. A lake killed my parents. Five months ago today. That's when they died. That's why they're gone.

FROM "COMAS AND SHIT"

Sometimes I wonder if my mother is ever coming out of this coma. This is horrible, just sitting here and watching her. This chair is so uncomfortable. It's like she isn't even here. It's like she isn't even alive. It's as though she were just—what's that sound? What does that sound mean? Nurse. Nurse! I think we've lost her. I think we just lost my mom to death.

FROM "ON DEATH"

Death is inevitable and everywhere. It will happen to all of us. Just like how it already happened to my parents. I would like to write about something else, but it is nearly impossible. Death fills my every thought. It's not fun to go on living when both of your parents are dead. Especially when you got along really well with both of them, like I did. Sure, we had our tiffs here and there, but, on the whole, we were really polite to one another. How can I write about something as inconsequential as winter snow when I have no parents? It is horrible to live with parents who are dead.

FROM "WEDDING DAY"

"He's not here," I told the priest. "My father is not here to give me away." The priest gave me a dirty look. I could feel my face redden with ire. "He's not here," I growled, "because he's *dead*."

FROM "TELLING CHILDREN ABOUT GRANDPARENTS"

"You don't have any," I told Allison for the fourth time that day. "You don't have any grandparents. Your father died before ever introducing me to his parents, and both of my parents are dead. You don't have a grandparent in the world. Because they are either dead or unknown. In my case, they are dead." Allison began to cry, for the fourth time that day.

FROM "ME"

It was back to that nagging question: what exactly am I? A mess of bone and flesh. A clump of nails and hair. I am all of those things. But isn't there something more? Hidden in this cage of ribs, deep within these layers of tissue, lurking in these strands of sinew, isn't there a soul? I would like to think so. Otherwise, my parents are just straight-up dead. Deep in the ground, down in the dirt, just... dead. Dead as doornails. Oh, sweet Lord. Please let there be a soul. Please, God. Please don't let my parents just be *dead*.

FEEDBACK FROM JAMES JOYCE'S SUBMISSION OF *ULYSSES* TO HIS CREATIVE WRITING WORKSHOP

by TEDDY WAYNE

Great opening hook, but do you need 96-point Garamond for the S? Kind of feels like you're padding the page count.

Truly felt I got to know Leopold (Poldy?). Nitpicky, logistical question: Is this really how people think?

"Snotgreen" = hyphenated.

Show us how these characters process memory, language, abstractions, and the urban landscape through stream of consciousness, don't just *tell* us.

More commas, please.

Stephen comes off a little unsympathetic. I remember you used him in a previous story—maybe you could integrate some of that material here?

Unclear where and when this is set.

Caught some allusions to *The Odyssey*. Nice.

Proper punctuation for dialogue is double quotes, not em dashes.

Balked a bit at some of Molly's "sexier" thoughts, which read like male fantasy. You can do better than this, Jim.

Think you accidentally stapled in something from your playwriting workshop for chapter 15.

The voice reminds me of the story "Which Is More Than I Can Say About Some People" from Lorrie Moore's *Birds of America*. Read it?

"History is a nightmare from which I am trying to awake." *So* true.

Everything Buck said had me LOL—hilarious character! Where do you come up with this stuff?

Kick-ass work, JJ, but *way* too long. Have you considered turning this into a short-short?

Noticed schematic chapter variations in literary technique, bodily organ, artistic subject, color, and symbol—really complex stuff. It's obvious you spent a while on this one.

I normally appreciate your extravagant wordsmithing, but got the sense here that you wore out the Shift+F7 keys (i.e., thesaurus). "Honorificabilitudinitatibus"? What, are you trying to impress that girl Nora?

I think you can push the experimentation even further in your next piece. Remember last week after workshop, when we got trashed on Guinness and came up with the ludicrous idea of a 700-page novel that puns every few words on the name of a river? Maybe there's something to that.

Typo: last word capitalized.

THE ONLY THING THAT CAN STOP THIS ASTEROID IS YOUR LIBERAL ARTS DEGREE

by MIKE LACHER

By now you're probably wondering what this is all about, why FBI agents pulled you out of your barista job, threw you on a helicopter, and brought you to NASA headquarters. There's no time, so I'll shoot it to you straight. You've seen the news reports. What hit New York wasn't some debris from an old satellite. There's an asteroid the size of Montana heading toward Earth and if it hits us, the planet is over. But we've got one last-ditch plan. We need a team to land on the surface of the asteroid, drill a nuclear warhead one mile into its core, and get out before it explodes. And you're just the liberal arts major we need to lead that team.

Sure, we've got dozens of astronauts, physicists, and demolitions experts. I'll be damned if we didn't try to train our best men for this mission. But just because they can fly a shuttle and understand higher-level astrophysics doesn't mean they can execute a unique mission like this. Anyone can learn how to land a spacecraft on a rocky asteroid flying through space at twelve miles per second. I don't need some pencilneck with four PhD's, one-thousand hours of simulator time, and the ability to operate a robot crane in low-Earth orbit. I need someone with four years of broad-but-humanities-focused studies, three subsequent years in temp jobs, and the ability to reason across multiple areas of study. I need someone who can read *The Bell Jar* and make strong observations about its representations of mental health and the repression of women. Sure, you've never even flown a plane before, but with only ten days until the asteroid hits, there's no one better to nuke an asteroid.

I've seen your work and it's damn impressive. Your midterm paper on the semiotics of *Band of Outsiders* turned a lot of heads at mission control. Your performance in Biology for Non-Science Majors was impressive, matched only by your mastery of second-year Portuguese. And a lot of the research we do here couldn't have happened without your groundbreaking work on suburban malaise and its representation and repression in John Hughes' films. I hope you're still that good, because when you're lowering a hydrogen bomb into a craggy mass of flying astronomic death with barely any gravity, you're going to need to draw on all the multidisciplinary reason and analysis you've got.

Don't think I don't have my misgivings about sending some hotshot Asian Studies minor into space for the first time. This is NASA, not Grinnell. I don't have the time or patience for your renegade attitude and macho bravado. I can't believe the fate of mankind rests on some roughneck bachelor of the arts. I know your type. You feed off the thrill of inference and small, instructor-led discussion. You think you're some kind of invincible god just because you have cursory understandings of Buddhism, classical literature, and introductory linguistics. Well listen up, cowboy. You make one false move up there, be it a clumsy thesis statement, poorly reasoned argument, or glib analysis, and your team is dead, along with this whole sorry planet.

I've wasted enough time with chatter. Let's get you over to mission control. Our avionics team needs your help getting their paper on gender politics in *The Matrix* properly cited in MLA format.

COVERING TEEN WOLF: ONE COACH'S GUIDE

by PASHA MALLA

Used to be, the key to beating Teen Wolf's Beavers was just to play them on any night there wasn't a full moon. We were unlucky one season in that we met them twenty-eight days apart, both times in their barn, and Teen Wolf destroyed us—64 points in the first game, then a quadruple-double in the second, with fourteen blocked shots and twenty-five steals. Our third matchup, though, we were fortunate enough to have a 76 percent waxing gibbous, so it was regular Scott Howard, who turned the ball over twice before fouling out, scoreless, in eight minutes of play. These days, however, it seems the guy can change over whenever he wants, which poses a real problem to opposing coaches. What follows is the best strategy my staff and I have come up with to limit Teen Wolf's effectiveness on the court. While admittedly far from foolproof, it will, hopefully, prove useful to your team. We're all in this together, folks.

To begin, you're going to have to resign yourself to the fact that Teen Wolf is probably going to drop at least fifty points. That might seem like a lot, but, unfortunately, it's just the way the ball bounces. As coach, you need to recognize that your job isn't to do the impossible; you're not going to stop Teen Wolf entirely, but you *can* try to contain him by making him play your team's style of basketball. Discipline and defensive fundamentals help: nose on the ball, feet moving, channeling him into traps—careful with those, though. Soon as Teen Wolf gets two guys on him, he tends to find the open man. He's a heads-up ballplayer with great court sense, so if you're going to bring a trapping zone against Teen Wolf, make sure you have solid weak-side rotation and your defenders are communicating.

Of course, that's only if he feels like passing. Teen Wolf gets scrappy once you put the pressure on, and he's a great ball handler with a low-to-the-ground style reminiscent of Pistol Pete or a young Isiah Thomas. Add to his skill and quickness those gigantic, hirsute paws, and you're up against one hell of a dribbler. We've tried giving Teen Wolf a step, respecting his speed, but we've found that if our guys slack off him, he'll generally hit the open jumper—or else take off from wherever he's standing on the court, sail over everyone's heads, and finish with one of those dunks where he ends up sitting on the top of the backboard, howling, feet dangling down through the hoop.

While you're welcome to try it, my feeling is that man-to-man defense simply isn't an option. Some teams like to play a box-and-one, which generally works well against most lycanthropes. With Teen Wolf, though, you have to be careful. He'll just stand baying by the sideline while the rest of the Beavers run four-on-four. Then, at a signal from Coach Finstock, Teen Wolf will come screaming down the lane, fur bristling and fangs bared, for the alley-oop. (And with him having what's rumored to be a 78-inch standing vertical leap, rest assured he's even more difficult to stop once he gets up in the air.) I've heard of coaches dealing with this by putting a sniper in the crowd with a box of silver bullets and a hunting rifle. We tried it once, back when Teen Wolf was only a freshman: the shooter missed, and when the cops showed up and cleared the gym we were forced to default.

So, I bet you're wondering, if it's impossible to cover him through conventional defenses, what can we do? Here's the key: Teen Wolf doesn't get along with his teammates. While he's certainly got the individual skills to dominate most games, I'd have to struggle to think of ever seeing a more selfish player in my twenty-eight years of coaching. He tends to alienate his fellow Beavers by doing things like stealing the ball off them, or stealing their girlfriends, and their resentment is easy for opposing teams to exploit. Sympathy seems to work well; get your players to say stuff like, "Man, sure sucks playing with Teen Wolf," or "I'd hate to have a guy like Teen Wolf on *my* team," and you'll be surprised how quickly the Beavers' team defense will start to open up.

Another trick is to keep on the officials about aggressive play. Granted, most refs are pretty scared to call anything on Teen Wolf what with the risk of being devoured in the parking lot after the game. Still, it's hard to ignore someone being gouged by lupine talons, especially if the player's entrails are exposed. Coach Finstock hates sitting Teen Wolf, but if his star picks up three fouls early, there won't be any other option. Just make sure to tell your guys to resist taunting Teen Wolf while he's on the bench; it only makes him angrier, and with that anger comes frightening strength.

Finally, keep in mind that beneath all that fur, Teen Wolf is only human—or half-human, whatever—with weaknesses, just like any of us. And as a hormonally imbalanced, eternally cursed teenager, he's particularly fragile. For one thing, at just under 70 percent, Teen

Wolf's free-throw shooting is comparatively weak; if you've got a kid on your team brave or crazy enough to knock Teen Wolf down with a hard foul, encourage it. Make him earn his points at the line. "Hack-a-Wolf" brought us within ten of the Beavers during last year's play-offs—that is, until Teen Wolf dunked eight consecutive trips down the floor from the three-point line, putting the lead out of reach.

Okay, that's pretty much all I've got. As I mentioned earlier, defending Teen Wolf isn't an exact science, and you're more than welcome to alter these tactics as befits your own ball club. I hope that between us we can keep the lines of communication open and continue to share strategies that seem to work. My feeling is that there's no team that is completely unbeatable, even if their star transforms into a werewolf before every game. Oh, and if you come up with some way of preventing Teen Wolf from jumping up and catching your team's shots, I'd be particularly interested in hearing it.

Thanks, and best of luck.

BACK FROM YET ANOTHER GLOBETROTTING ADVENTURE, INDIANA JONES CHECKS HIS MAIL AND DISCOVERS THAT HIS BID FOR TENURE HAS BEEN DENIED

by ANDY BRYAN

January 22, 1939

Assistant Professor Henry "Indiana" Jones Jr.

Department of Anthropology

Chapman Hall 227B

Marshall College

Dr. Jones:

As chairman of the Committee on Promotion and Tenure, I regret to inform you that your recent application for tenure has been denied by a vote of six to one. Following past policies and procedures, proceedings from the committee's deliberations that were pertinent to our decision have been summarized below according to the assessment criteria.

DEMONSTRATES SUITABLE EXPERIENCE
AND EXPERTISE IN CHOSEN FIELD

The committee concurred that Dr. Jones does seem to possess a nearly superhuman breadth of linguistic knowledge and an uncanny familiarity with the history and material culture of the occult. However, his understanding and practice of archaeology gave the committee the greatest cause for alarm. Criticisms of Dr. Jones ranged from "possessing a perceptible methodological deficiency" to "practicing archaeology with a complete lack of, disregard for, and colossal ignorance of current methodology, theory, and ethics" to "unabashed grave-robbing." Given such appraisals, perhaps it isn't surprising to learn that several Central and South American countries recently assembled to enact legislation aimed at permanently prohibiting his entry.

Moreover, no one on the committee can identify who or what instilled Dr. Jones with the belief that an archaeologist's tool kit should consist solely of a bullwhip and a revolver.

NATIONALLY RECOGNIZED FOR AN EFFECTUAL
PROGRAM OF SCHOLARSHIP OR RESEARCH SUPPORTED
BY PUBLICATIONS OF HIGH QUALITY

Though Dr. Jones conducts "field research" far more often than anyone else in the department, he has consistently failed to report the results of his excavations, provide any credible evidence of attending the archaeological conferences he claims to attend, or produce a single published article in any peer-reviewed journal. Someone might tell Dr. Jones that in academia "publish or perish" is the rule. Shockingly, there is little evidence to date that Dr. Jones has successfully excavated even one object since he arrived at Marshall College. Marcus Brody, curator of our natural history museum, assured me this was not so and graciously pointed out several pieces in the collection that he claimed were procured through Dr. Jones's efforts, but, quite frankly, we have not one shred of documentation that can demonstrate the provenance or legal ownership of these objects.

MEETS PROFESSIONAL STANDARDS OF CONDUCT IN RESEARCH AND PROFESSIONAL ACTIVITIES OF THE DISCIPLINE

The committee was particularly generous (and vociferous) in offering their opinions regarding this criterion. Permit me to list just a few of the more troubling accounts I was privy to during the committee's meeting. Far more times than I would care to mention, the name "Indiana Jones" (the adopted title Dr. Jones insists on being called) has appeared in governmental reports linking him to the Nazi Party, black-market antiquities dealers, underground cults, human sacrifice, Indian child slave labor, and the Chinese mafia. There is a plethora of international criminal charges against Dr. Jones. The charges include but are not limited to: bringing unregistered weapons into and out of the country; property damage; desecration of national and historical landmarks; impersonating officials; arson; grand theft (automobiles, motorcycles, aircraft, and watercraft in just a one week span last year); excavating without a permit; countless antiquities violations; public endangerment; voluntary and involuntary manslaughter; and, allegedly, murder.

Dr. Jones's interpersonal skills and relationships are no better. By Dr. Jones's own admission, he has repeatedly employed an underage Asian boy as a driver and "personal assistant" during his Far East travels. I will refrain from making any insinuations as to the nature of this relationship, but my intuition insists that it is not a healthy one, nor one to be encouraged. Though the committee may have overstepped the boundaries of its evaluation, I find it pertinent to note that Dr. Jones has been romantically linked to countless women of questionable character, an attribute very unbecoming of a Marshall College professor. One of these women was identified as a notorious nightclub singer whose heart he attempted to extract with his hands, and whom he then tried, and failed, to lower into a lake of magma. Another was a Nazi scholar he was seen courting just last year who, I'm told, plummeted into a fathomless abyss at Dr. Jones's hand. And, of course, no one can forget the slow decline and eventual death of Professor Abner Ravenwood after Dr. Jones's affair with Abner's underage daughter was made public, forcing her to emigrate to Nepal to escape the debacle.

DEMONSTRATES SUCCESSFUL RECORD IN UNDERGRADUATE AND GRADUATE TEACHING

In his nine years with the department, Dr. Jones has failed to complete even one uninterrupted semester of instruction. In fact, he hasn't been in attendance for more than four consecutive weeks since he was hired. Departmental records indicate Dr. Jones has taken more sabbaticals, sick time, personal days, conference allotments, and temporary leaves than all the other members of the department combined.

The lone student representative on the committee wished to convey that, besides being an exceptional instructor, a compassionate mentor, and an unparalleled gentleman, Dr. Jones was extraordinarily receptive to the female student body during and after the transition to a coeducational system at the college. However, his timeliness in grading and returning assignments was a concern.

ESTABLISHMENT OF AN APPROPRIATE RECORD
OF DEPARTMENTAL AND CAMPUS SERVICE

Dr. Jones's behavior on campus has led not only to disciplinary action but also to concerns as to the state of his mental health. In addition to multiple instances of public drunkenness, Dr. Jones, on three separate occasions, has attempted to set fire to the herpetology wing of the biology department. Perhaps most disturbing, however, are the statements that come directly from Dr. Jones's mouth. Several faculty members maintain that Dr. Jones informed them on multiple occasions of having discovered the Ark of the Covenant, magic diamond rocks, and the Holy Grail! When asked to provide evidence for such claims, he purportedly replied that he was "kind of immortal" and/or muttered derogatory statements about the "bureaucratic fools" running the US government. Given his history with the Nazi Party, I fear where his loyalty lies.

To summarize, the committee fails to recognize any indication that Dr. Jones is even remotely proficient when it comes to archaeological scholarship and practice. His aptitude as an instructor is questionable at best, his conduct while abroad is positively deplorable, and his behavior on campus is minimally better. Marshall College has a reputation to uphold. I need not say more.

My apologies,
Prof. G.L. Stevens
Chairman

CINEMATIC EXPRESSIONS OF INNER SELF-LOATHING IF THERE WERE NO MIRRORS TO SMASH

by ROSS MURRAY

Junkie jazz singer sees self in back of spoon; uses clairvoyant powers to bend it out of shape.

Actress who clawed her way to the top catches reflection in pond; uses nearby backhoe to drain pond.

Woman who married for wealth rather than love looks at photo on driver's license; goes to DMV to ask for new photo.

Politician who has forsaken his grassroots values discovers potato in shape of own head; mashes it.

Burnt-out rock star looks down at himself during out-of-body experience; refuses to go back in body "until we start seeing some changes around here, mister."

Aging supermodel has plaster cast made of face; backs over it in SUV.

Alcoholic author looks at reflection in a tumbler of scotch; drinks scotch; pours another to see if he looks any better in this one.

SO YOU'VE KNOCKED OVER A ROW OF A MOTORCYCLE GANG'S MOTORCYCLES

by SARAH WALKER

First, don't panic. Although they appear to be enraged, you would not believe how many times this has happened to the motorcycle gang. At least once a week, a tourist comes seeking directions at the lonely roadside diner the motorcycle gang frequents, and tips over all of their motorcycles, usually by accidentally walking backward into the first of the row. The motorcycle gang actually has domino-effect-tipping insurance from Allstate, but you can be sure they won't tell you that. They want you to think you must pay (and they don't mean with money) for the damage you've caused through your clumsiness. No, what this motorcycle gang wants to see is the unbridled horror that spreads across your face as you realize what you've done and you stand helplessly by as not one, not five, but twenty motorcycles topple over, one by one. The process is almost excruciatingly long, just long enough that it seems you should do something to stop the chain of events, so you run to the end of the line to try and halt the tipping process by exerting your full body weight against the last motorcycle, but the combined force of the twenty bikes proves to be too much, and you become pinned under the last enormous bike. You really should not have done that, because now you are in a very vulnerable position, and the motorcycle gang can now do what they enjoy doing most in the world: form a circle around you that blocks out the sun, look down upon you as they punch their fists together, and slowly chuckle or growl.

Again, don't panic. You must try and muster all of your strength and roll out from under the bike. The motorcycle gang will actually allow you to stand up, as this lets them do what they enjoy doing second most in the world: slowly walk toward you as a group while you edge backward, stammering apologies and telling them to "take it easy." However, you should not be walking backward, because then you bump into a second row of motorcycles! Actually, this row happens to be a row of the motorcycle gang's girlfriends' Vespas. Now, this has never happened before, and it genuinely upsets the motorcycle gang, as their insurance does not cover their girlfriends' Vespas. Although considered gifts and tax-deductible, they are not covered under their Allstate plan as, again, they are not motorcycles but Vespas.

Now maybe you should panic because, honestly, the motorcycle gang was not prepared for this turn of events and now their girlfriends are upset. Although they actually do not want to beat you up—after all, it was clearly a mistake and they are not unreasonable men—they can't back down in front of their women. This is when you should start to run, and you now actually have an advantage as it will take the motorcycle gang a while to right all of their toppled motorcycles. You forgot that you drove here, though, and now you're sprinting down a desert highway with no idea of where you're going. After all, you did initially stop at this roadside diner to ask for directions. However, your technically flawed decision to ditch your car was actually the correct solution as it is extremely hard to engage in a low-speed chase on a motorcycle, especially when the object of pursuit is on foot, and a motorcycle gang would never chase anyone without their motorcycles. Therefore, the motorcycle gang, with their girlfriends on the back of their bikes, actually shoots by you, and when the leader realizes that they have far outstripped you, he emits a shout of rage and orders everyone to turn around, but amid the confusion of a 180-degree turn, the motorcycle gang becomes tangled, and once again their motorcycles go tumbling over. You see this, and instead of continuing to sprint toward the motorcycle gang, you quickly turn around (easy for you on foot), run back toward the diner, fumble for your keys, and triumphantly speed away in the opposite direction while the motorcycle gang shakes fists at your rapidly disappearing car.

WHOOPS!

by MIKE SACKS

To: All Staff

9:12 a.m.

Subject: Whoops, Sorry About That Last E-mail!

I'd just like to apologize for the last e-mail, which I sent to "All Staff."
I meant to send it to my friend Alex Stafford. It was a mistake. Sorry.

To: All Staff

10:14 a.m.

Subject: Clarification on Apology E-mail!

I want to apologize for not being entirely clear in my last e-mail. Let
me try to be more specific: originally, I was attempting to send my

friend Alex Stafford (not All Staff) an e-mail on horses and how I've always liked to watch horses run. I then made a leap into the realm of the imaginary. Again, I do apologize.

To: All Staff
11:01 a.m.
Subject: re: what the fuck?!

Wow. Today just ain't my day! I've been told that I have more "explaining" to do, re: "the realm of the imaginary." So here goes: I probably should have told you that for the past two years, give or take a few months, I've imagined myself as a talking horse and that, as this talking horse, I've ruled a fantasy kingdom populated by you guys, my coworkers. The twenty-seven images I included in the first e-mail are, in fact, Photoshop montages, not actual photos. Carry on!

To: All Staff
12:20 p.m.
Subject: re: You Have More Explaining to Do About Those Images!

There are days and there are days! Perhaps I'm not expressing myself as well as I should. I guess that's why I'm in accounting and not PR! OK, let's start from the very beginning. In this imaginary world I've created, I'm a talking horse. Simple. You guys are my servants. All of you have kept your real names, but your "imaginary" selves have taken on new roles in my fantasy land. A quick example:

"Mary Jenkins" from Benefits is a fair maiden who was born in a stable and grew up to fall in love with "Chris Topp" from Payroll, who works as a candlemaker and sleeps behind the bar in the tavern run by "Wayne Harris" from the mailroom, who is secretly seeing "April Kelly" from Office Services, who works as my "horse girl" and soaps me down every night before I sleep on my bed of hay. Is this making more sense? For the record, all Photoshop images are a combination of photos found on the internet and your headshots from the company directory. Steve, I'm about ready for lunch if you are.

To: All Staff
1:23 p.m.
Subject: re: I Feel Violated!!!

Imagine my surprise to return from lunch only to find hundreds of e-mails in the ol' inbox! Seems that quite a few of you have additional questions concerning the roles that each of you play within my magical fantasy land. Sigh. It's really quite simple:

"Hope Marks" from the nurse's office refuses to sleep with "Darryl Russell" from Security because Darryl is a centaur (see image #6) and Hope is a unicorn (image #3). "Kathryn Haynes" from marketing has caught wind of this because she was born with oversize ears (image #14) and can hear literally everything. She also tends to walk around the village nude (image #8) and sleep with anyone who happens to be available; in one instance, she cavorts with "Jamie Devine" from Payroll by the banks of a river, as "Betsy Schneider" and "Krista Stark" from the cafeteria look on in wonder (image #7). I also look on in wonder (images #4 and #5).

In another instance, "Katy Devine" from Special Projects climbs to the top of the bell tower that's located on my castle and makes love to "Doug Benson" from Security, as "Jessica McNally" from the nurse's office braids my tail in a most tender fashion (image #11). She is not wearing a top (image #12) or a bottom (image #13).

Meanwhile, "Alexis Weber" from the front office is an angry dwarf in need of gold. He has just taken on an assignment to kill "Bob Simmons" from Purchasing, but only after he has promised "Marina Delgado" from Human Resources that he will turn her into a good witch by way of a magical spell. This magical spell consists of having sex with a complete stranger ("Mitch Morton," also from Human Resources) while riding a white mare, ass-back and fancy-free, across a great plain (image #9). The horse, if you haven't already guessed, is me (image #1). In the background, if you look closely enough, you can just make out "Joe Griggs" from Janitorial looking on in wonder (image #2).

Whew! Done! By the way, anyone have the forms for the Milner project? I *really* need them by this afternoon. Thanks!

To: All Staff
3:12 p.m.
Subject: re: you're sick!

Holy cripes! Sometimes I wonder if anyone besides me gets any work done around here! I step away from my desk for two seconds and I come back to discover that a thousand more questions have been posed! Don't get me wrong: I think it's super that all of you are taking an active interest in my fantasy kingdom, but my goodness! So let me just tie up one loose end and let me do it real, real quick, because I've just been notified that I've been fired:

Yes, that is you, "Samantha Rymer" from Expenses, standing next to a razzleberry bush in image #15. And yes, Samantha, that is indeed a crown of doves perched atop your head, and no, Samantha, those are not your real breasts (images #16–27).

Everyone up to date? I'm really gonna miss all of you! I feel we've become especially close over these past two years! And that even goes for "Marina the Good Witch" from Human Resources! I honestly did not know that "good witches" could get so angry! LOL!

Your Imaginary Leader Who's Now Waving Goodbye as Kathy from Security Hangs on Tightly and Rides Him (please see attached image),

Mike the Talking Horse

WHEN A STRANGER EMAILS

by JASON ROEDER

February 3, 2006, 7:03 p.m.
From: *Maniac@butchermail.com*
To: *jill_w_johnson03@yahoo.com*
Subject: Children

Have you checked the children?
—Maniac

- - -

February 3, 2006, 8:40 p.m.
From: *Maniac@butchermail.com*
To: *jill_w_johnson03@yahoo.com*
Subject: Children (follow-up)

Seriously. This is not spam. You really might want to check the children. :(
Maniac

- - -

February 3, 2006, 9:15 p.m.
From: *Maniac@butchermail.com*
To: *jill_w_johnson03@yahoo.com*
Subject: Quickie confirmation?

Sorry if you were put off by my tone in the last message. Could you just verify that you received this message so I know I haven't been keying in the wrong e-mail address? I'm not the greatest typist in the world. Feel free to check on the children at your earliest convenience. I eagerly await your feedback.

Best,
M

- - -

February 3, 2006, 10:48 p.m.
From: *Maniac@butchermail.com*
To: *jill_w_johnson03@yahoo.com*
Subject: Um...

I know you're not getting a lot of cash for this job and that much of your compensation is taking the form of pizza rolls the parents left in the freezer. But I should think it would occur to you to check on the children at least once over the course of an evening without having to be prompted by the crazy man with the nail gun. I'm telling you, sister, this message was flagged "Urgent" for a reason.

—M

- - -

February 3, 2006, 11:20 p.m.
From: *Maniac@butchermail.com*
To: *jill_w_johnson03@yahoo.com*
Subject: Un-friggin'-believable

What kind of bored teenage babysitter doesn't check her e-mail? I bet you won't touch the liquor cabinet, either. I mean, Jesus. Okay, don't bother calling the cops: in case you haven't figured it out, I'm in the house. I'm the guy upstairs with the iBook and blood on his boots. You know what? I just have to take another peek at what you're doing down there... Okay, I am now looking at you and—are you kidding me? Are you actually reading *A Farewell to Arms*? Catherine dies, okay? Like you didn't see that coming.

- - -

February 3, 2006, 11:52 p.m.
From: *Maniac@butchermail.com*
To: *jill_w_johnson03@yahoo.com*
Subject: I give up

So, I found your MySpace page. I was going to contact you that way, but then I'd have to register and all that. For what it's worth, I found the Hello Kitty wallpaper startling.

I think I'm just gonna leave. Sorry about the—well, someone will check the children eventually, right?

Man, I miss the '70s.

TRIPADVISOR.COM REVIEWS: JEKYLL & HYDE B&B

by KATE HAHN

"A REAL GEM"

Five out of five stars! Host Jekyll so friendly and accommodating. (Did not meet partner Hyde.) Highly recommended. Just what a British B&B should be! Jekyll showed us charming basement laboratory (yes—pronounced it that oh-so-English way!), where he's working on "experiments." Cute! Probably where he cooks up the amazing homemade jam. Three kinds at breakfast. One was quince!

"ALMOST PERFECT"

Agree, Jekyll stellar. But be aware: delicate situation with Hyde due to physical handicaps—limping, speech impediment. But loved his enthusiasm when it came to killing spider in our room at midnight! Not to mention brute strength with luggage. Only two kinds of jam (black currant, gooseberry) but tasty.

"GEM? NOT EVEN JAM!"

Did we stay at same place as above posters? Did not meet Jekyll, only Hyde. Limp and slur, probably from drinking! Actually leered at my wife and played grabby hands. No vacancy elsewhere or would have left. Lots of noise—walls paper thin... Heard moaning and groaning coming from downstairs all night... Jam sounds nice. Barely had toast.

"HIGHS, BUT MORE LOWS"

Earlier post made us slightly apprehensive, since we had already made our reservations and sent deposit... Relieved when met at front door by Jekyll. Polite but pale and shaking visibly. Why didn't anyone mention his smoking? Place reeked and he lit one after the other. Kindly set up croquet wickets for us in garden, then went off into woods—minutes later, Hyde loped out of the trees with rabbit that he had obviously killed with bare hands. Could not finish croquet game after that. Is this the famous British eccentricity? Checked out before breakfast, so not sure of jam situation.

"WON'T GO BACK"

Stayed on a whim—wish I had read posts before. Not his fault, but Jekyll had really bad back spasm while pouring tea in morning. Suddenly hunched forward and could not stand up again. Bared teeth in pained grimace. Hands frozen in claw-like shape. He kept calling "Hyde!" who never showed up to help. Awkward when we tried to check out, because Jekyll could not run our credit card with fingers stuck in claw position.

"SCARY DUDE"

Hyde answered door, eating jam (brambleberry?) straight from the jar with his fingers. Said Jekyll was "gone forever." Dirty dishes on table. Broken glass beaker on floor. We are two girls traveling alone. Felt uncomfortable. Did not check in.

"HEP ME"

Writing from compter at b&b. RUN. DO NOT OCME he... hep...

"CLOSED"

Not sure about above post. Flag? Curious, so walked past one evening on way back to our B&B. Met guy on porch who said he was Jekyll's lawyer, and that B&B closed indefinitely and no one home. But, as walking away, we saw light in basement window and hunched figure moving around. Maybe exterminators? Or Jekyll getting back in swing of things to make more jam? I'll put in a request for some damson plum!

NFL PLAYERS WHOSE NAMES SOUND VAGUELY DICKENSIAN, AND THE CHARACTERS THEY WOULD BE IN AN ACTUAL DICKENS NOVEL (2007–2008 REGULAR SEASON EDITION)

by SUSAN SCHORN

ETHAN ALBRIGHT

Honest and upright youngest son of the dissolute Lord Albright. Childhood favorite of his deceased mother, Lady Alicia Albright, and said to resemble her most uncannily. He comes to grief attempting to foil his father's plot against the innocent Jeremy Trueblood.

MARCUS MAXWELL

Dodgy owner of the disreputable Circus Marcus. Suspected by Magistrate Petitgout of feeding the circus's performing tigers upon surplus orphans.

DARNELL DINKINS

Ticket-taker at Marcus Maxwell's Circus Marcus. Testifies against his employer before the Queen's Bench, though he knows it may well cost him his life.

LUKE PETITGOUT

Energetic city magistrate who appears, early in the story, to be integral to the plot, but spends the last two-thirds of the novel on injured reserve.

CHANNING CROWDER

Disreputable eldest son of the hidebound and sanctimonious banker Mr. Epaphroditus Crowder. Employed by Marcus Maxwell on an unsavory bit of business, he returns home transformed in a truly startling fashion.

REX HADNOT

Orphan.

JAMES DEARTH

Orphan.

WILL WITHERSPOON

Dead orphan.

LANGSTON WALKER

Grim and grasping orphanage director of dubious honor and doubtful motives. Views his tender young charges as a tradable commodity and actively seeks out new markets of exchange. Also, weighs 366 pounds (26 stone).

CHRIS SNEE

Body found in river.

OTIS GRIGSBY

Ship's doctor on the Adelaide, possessing a unique and gruesome collection of South Sea island curiosities. He maintains a cheerful outlook on life despite being much afflicted by gout, baldness, and an old harpoon injury. Has a remarkable talent for gleaning information from waterlogged corpses.

ALGE CRUMPLER

An ancient and comically deaf farmer residing on the Albright estate. Catch phrase: "Speak up! Lord Cardigan stole me ears!" Quite possibly insane.

JEREMY TRUEBLOOD

Ward and protégé of the kindly Magistrate Petitgout, he is forced to flee London when Petitgout's sworn enemy, Lord Albright, falsely implicates him in a shady land deal so complicated Dickens eventually gives up trying and changes the crime to attempted arson, mid-novel, without explanation. Marries Jenny Applegate.

ELLIS HOBBS

An honest barrister who continually loses his court cases, but can run the 40 in 4.3. Defends Jeremy Trueblood on charges of fraud (chapters 27 to 42) and arson (chapters 43 to 65).

JAMAAL FUDGE

Criminal-court judge with a pronounced distaste for cats. Even Dickens cannot sustain the utterly preposterous title "Judge Fudge," and writes him out of the story in the eighth installment.

DERRICK DOCKERY

A clockmaker who's always about to wind, or has just wound, a clock. Miraculously escapes the conflagration in his shop by riding an over-sized pendulum bob to safety on the next rooftop. Known for his fabulous mustaches, which Dickens originally intended to compare to the hands on a clock face but somehow never got around to doing so.

DARNELL DOCKETT

Senior partner in the clockmaking firm of Dockett and Dockery. His testimony on the accurate timing of sprint races, the periodicity of 26-stone pendulums, and the combustibility of pinchbeck secures the acquittal of Jeremy Trueblood, and the convictions of Messrs. Maxwell and Walker. Takes the disowned, destitute Ethan Albright as his apprentice at novel's end, to the general satisfaction of all.

HAMLET (FACEBOOK NEWSFEED EDITION)

by SARAH SCHMELLING

Horatio thinks he saw a ghost.

Hamlet thinks it's annoying when your uncle marries your mother right after your dad dies.

The king thinks Hamlet's annoying.

Laertes thinks Ophelia can do better.

Hamlet's father is now a zombie.

- - -

The king poked the queen.

The queen poked the king back.

Hamlet and the queen are no longer friends.

Marcellus is pretty sure something's rotten around here.

Hamlet became a fan of daggers.

- - -

Polonius says Hamlet's crazy—crazy in love!

Rosencrantz, Guildenstern, and Hamlet are now friends.

Hamlet wonders if he should continue to exist. Or not.

Hamlet thinks Ophelia might be happier in a convent.

Ophelia removed "moody princes" from her interests.

Hamlet posted an event: "A Play That's Totally Fictional and In No Way About My Family."

The king commented on Hamlet's play: "What is wrong with you?"

Polonius thinks this curtain looks like a good thing to hide behind.

Polonius is no longer online.

- - -

Hamlet added England to the Places I've Been application.

The queen is worried about Ophelia.

Ophelia loves flowers. Flowers flowers flowers flowers flowers. Oh, look, a river.

Ophelia joined the group Maidens Who Don't Float.

Laertes wonders what the hell happened while he was gone.

- - -

The king sent Hamlet a goblet of wine.

The queen likes wine!

The king likes… oh crap.

The queen, the king, Laertes, and Hamlet are now zombies.

Horatio says, "Well, that was tragic."

Fortinbras, Prince of Norway, says, "Yes, tragic. We'll take it from here."

Denmark is now Norwegian.

MACBETH AND MACDUFF GET INTO AN ARGUMENT OVER SEMANTICS

by RAPHAEL BOB-WAKSBERG

(Macbeth and Macduff are fencing in front of a castle.)

MACBETH: Macduff! Let fall thy blade on vulnerable crests. I bear a charmed life, which must not yield to one of woman born.

MACDUFF: Despair thy charm! Macduff was from his mother's womb untimely ripped.

(They stop sword fighting.)

MACBETH: Pardon?

MACDUFF: I was extracted surgically, in an operation.

MACBETH: Okay, but thou wast still born, right?

MACDUFF: No. Untimely ripped.

MACBETH: Okay, but after thou wast ripped, thou wast of woman born.

MACDUFF: I don't know…

MACBETH: Wast thou ripped from a man?

MACDUFF: No…

MACBETH: Then thou wast of woman born, what's the problem?

MACDUFF: I think, technically, to be "born" you need to pass through the birth canal.

MACBETH: No. If you exist, then you were born.

MACDUFF: I grant you it's a bit of a gray area.

MACBETH: No! Any sane definition of the word "born" would also house the subcategory of Cesarean sections.

MACDUFF: Okay, thou hast no need to get snippy.

MACBETH: I'm not snippy.

MACDUFF: Thou ist. A little bit.

MACBETH: Well I'm a little stressed out right now. They said, "No man of woman born—"

MACDUFF: Who said?

MACBETH: The old ladies. By the side of the road.

MACDUFF: Uh… huh.

(*CUT TO: Macduff and Macbeth by the side of the road, looking at three old dancing witches.*)

WITCH: Dibble dabble dribble doo. Put a monkey in a stew.

MACBETH: Okay, well, now they're just talking gibberish but before they said, "Fear not till Birnam wood do come to Dunsinane," and —

MACDUFF: Which it did.

MACBETH: No! You dressed up like the wood. That's not the same thing at all.

MACDUFF: Look. I'm just going to kill thee, okay?

MACBETH: No! Thou canst! Because thou wast of woman born!

MACDUFF: Okay, seriously though, thou needst to chill out, a little bit, with the "of woman born" stuff. Have you consulted a physician about this, or did you just declare yourself the expert on the differences between "born" and "not born"?

MACBETH: You want to consult a physician? Because honestly I would LOVE to consult a physician about this.

MACDUFF: Let's go.

MACBETH: Let's go right now, I'm not doing anything.

(CUT TO: *Macduff and Macbeth in a doctor's hut.*)

DOCTOR: All right, explain it to me again?

MACBETH: Okay, Macduff—who is standing before you right here!—was he born? Or was he—and remember, we're talking about this guy, who exists!—not born?

MACDUFF: Don't forget, I was from my mother's womb untimely ripped!

MACBETH: Yes, mother's womb! MOTHER. OF WOMAN BORN.

MACDUFF: Doctor?

DOCTOR: Yeah, I don't know. This is like the thirteenth century. Medical science isn't really... I mean, if you're feeling sick, maybe you have a demon inside you and you could swallow a snake to find the demon and then the snake will eat the demon and you won't be sick anymore, but then, yeah, how do we get the snake out, right?

MACBETH: Well, thank you very much; you were of no help at all.

MACDUFF: Look, I didn't want to get into a whole THING with this... Yeah, I'm just gonna kill you now.

MACBETH: No! Thou ist of woman—I mean, is everyone else crazy here, or is it me?

(*Macduff stabs Macbeth in the heart.*)

MACBETH: Ow!

(*Macduff shrugs. Macbeth dies. Then Macduff puts Macbeth's head on a stick, of all things. Audience applauds politely, but secretly thinks maybe this Shakespeare guy is kind of losing it.*)

CHAUCER TWEETS THE SOUTH BY SOUTHWEST FESTIVAL

by KARI ANNE HOLT

#SXSW hath begunne. Felawshipe is wrot amongst many fyne hypster pilgrimes. The pathwayes overflowe with dangley baddges.

As the evenning aproacheth, hypsters hath desended upon our towne, drinnking our wyne as unikornes feast upon rayes of the sonne.

O that marche daye wan the sonne shone so bryte, vishones of glorye from hypsters' mirrored sonneglasses stabbeth at myne fase.

Crulle lokkes shoote fromme the eyes of thyne bartender. Typ welle, mashine minion. Else you shall earn a boote in youre arse.

The prys paide by a lustye bacheler is this: hypster femayles groupe
like flockes of paynted chikennes. Cocques are foresaken. #sadcocques

Flocke of hypsters mightily roarred past my hoarse-carte, stampeed-
ding olde menne offreing free memorees on stix.

Hoarse-carte dryvers watcheth mappyng devises, forsayking welffayre
of inosents. Dangere hydes betwixt all lyte polles.

A nobil armye of gentil knyghts appeare to vommit in thyne alley. Alas,
they forsayke cleen chin stubbel to partee forthwith. #boot&ralleye

Wat ho, goatee'd man? Thy skinnee jenes hath byrn'd my corneyas.

Fye the dregs who weareth blootooth sets upon theyr heds. Do you
speeketh to me or to demones wither sleepe tween your eares?

IT'S DECORATIVE GOURD SEASON, MOTHERFUCKERS

by COLIN NISSAN

I don't know about you, but I can't wait to get my hands on some fucking gourds and arrange them in a horn-shaped basket on my dining room table. That shit is going to look so seasonal. I'm about to head up to the attic right now to find that wicker fucker, dust it off, and jam it with an insanely ornate assortment of shellacked vegetables. When my guests come over it's gonna be like, BLAMMO! Check out my shellacked decorative vegetables, assholes. Guess what season it is—fucking fall. There's a nip in the air and my house is full of mutant fucking squash.

I may even throw some multi-colored leaves into the mix, all haphazard like a crisp October breeze just blew through and fucked that shit up. Then I'm going to get to work on making a beautiful fucking gourd necklace for myself. People are going to be like, "Aren't those gourds straining your neck?" And I'm just going to thread another gourd onto my necklace without breaking their gaze and quietly reply, "It's fall, fuckfaces. You're either ready to reap this freaky-assed harvest or you're not."

Carving orange pumpkins sounds like a pretty fitting way to ring in the season. You know what else does? Performing an all-gourd reenactment of an episode of *Diff'rent Strokes*—specifically the one when Arnold and Dudley experience a disturbing brush with sexual molestation. Well, this shit just got real, didn't it? Felonies and gourds have one very important commonality: they're both extremely fucking real. Sorry if that's upsetting, but I'm not doing you any favors by shielding you from this anymore.

The next thing I'm going to do is carve one of the longer gourds into a perfect replica of the Mayflower as a shout-out to our Pilgrim forefathers. Then I'm going to do lines of blow off its hull with a hooker. Why? Because it's not summer, it's not winter, and it's not spring. Grab a calendar and pull your fucking heads out of your asses: it's fall, fuckers.

Have you ever been in an Italian deli with salamis hanging from their ceiling? Well then, you're going to fucking love my house. Just look where you're walking or you'll get KO'd by the gauntlet of misshapen, zucchini-descendant bastards swinging from above. And when you do, you're going to hear a very loud, very stereotypical Italian laugh coming from me. Consider yourself warned.

For now, all I plan to do is to throw on a flannel shirt, some tattered overalls, and a floppy fucking hat and stand in the middle of a cornfield for a few days. The first crow that tries to land on me is going to get his avian ass bitch-slapped all the way back to summer.

Welcome to autumn, fuckheads!

EYEWITNESS NEWS, WITH TOM DENARDO AND CHERYL CLAYBURN

by SETH REISS

… All those stories and more on tonight's Eyewitness Newscast. Good evening, I'm Jarrod Palmer. Tom Denardo is off tonight.

Dana Gibson is also off tonight. Mark Batista is off tonight. Paula Winston is off tonight. James Hastings, Carol Montgomery, and Kevin Bosley are off tonight. David Lennox is off tonight. Molly Hutchins is off tonight. Amanda Carlson is either sick or on vacation or she's off tonight. I think she's off tonight.

Adam Stapelton is off tonight. James McGrath is off tonight. Nancy Oliver is off tonight. Jason Nardozi is off tonight because this is the week he switches days with Pete Lipton. Pete Lipton, however, is sick. Trevor Einhorn is sick. Paul Granger is sick. I saw Paul the other day and he looked terrible. So did Lorraine Jacobs, who is not only sick, but is also off tonight. She's not off tomorrow night though so we'll see what happens with that. Caroline Davis is currently filling in for

Wes Shumar on the morning show. Wes Shumar is filing in for Heidi Witt on the afternoon broadcast, and Heidi Witt is off tonight.

Elizabeth Sherman is off tonight. Glenn Daniels is off tonight. Several people are currently looking for Chloe Hillman, but it doesn't matter because she's off tonight. Miranda and Tony are off tonight. Naomi Martin is here but is refusing to go on air. The same goes for Mark Reynolds, Pauline Robinson, and Kurt, whose last name escapes me at the moment. Nobody knows where the hell Fran Irving is.

I'm now getting word that Fran Irving is in fact off tonight. Thanks, David. Sorry, Steve, you sound like David. David is off tonight.

We got a call this morning from Bob Clement. He said he is sick, but might be in later, whatever that means. Kelly Damico is off tonight because she just had a baby. Congratulations to Kelly and her husband Aaron, who I've actually never met, and have only seen in pictures. Zack Corkman is off tonight. Last time I saw Pam Greenberg she was in the hallway on her way here, so I don't know where she went. Steve Jepson might know. Steve is off tonight. Bill Statsky doesn't work here anymore. Jane Burton is off tonight, but no one's too upset about that. She's sort of a divisive figure around here.

Vince Basinger is the weatherman, and he's here. Sam Kemmis is also here, but he's just an old college friend of mine visiting for the weekend and wanted to see me do my thing. He is off tonight but from a job that isn't this one. Trisha Ross is sick. The new guy, the one who sometimes fills in for Betty, that's me. I'm here. Betty is off tonight. Jenny Halfhill is currently on assignment, but works for another network so why bring her up, you know? David Stanton is not here. He should be, but he's not.

Nathan Alford is off tonight. Harold Foreman is off tonight. Sarah Utley passed away last night in her sleep. She was forty-two. Ben Benzio is off tonight. His brother Stan Benzio is also off tonight. Kind of neat that two brothers are anchors at the same network, huh?

Well, I think it's kind of neat. Bryce Fox is a kid I played little league baseball with.

Bosley Mackelfresh is here but Bosley Mackelfresh is a dog. The following pet animals, however, are sick: Clover, Mr. Oscar, and Flash. Jasper the Bloodhound is off tonight. Janet Ginsburg is sick. Rachel Koval is sick. Those last two are people, not animals. Natalie Maida is somebody I just made up. Lorrie Alster is real. She's off tonight.

Chuck Kellog is off tonight and would have been coming to you live. That would have been exciting. Chuck's the best. Erin Swink is not off tonight, but she's also not here. Personal day? Russell Crowe is off tonight. Yes, *that* Russell Crowe. Doug McConnell is off tonight. Yes, *that* Doug McConnell. Former Pittsburgh Pirates pitcher Doug Drabek is here and will have the latest from City Hall after the weather. It's odd that he doesn't do sports. We all think that. Tara Morrow is off tonight.

And sitting next to me is Lynn Grimaldi, who is filling in for Cheryl Clayburn.

WENDY MOLYNEUX'S EXCERPTS FROM POPULAR McSWEENEY'S INTERNET TENDENCY LISTS THROUGHOUT HISTORY: 1692

LIST

LESSER KNOWN WITCHCRAFT TESTS

by GOODY SMALLES

13. Ability to sit through entirety of the 2005 film *Bewitched* without shouting corrections at the screen.

14. In-line skating.

15. The Deez Test: The examiner asks the witch or warlock if he or she is familiar with the spirit Deez. When the witch or warlock replies "Deez who?" the examiner replies, "Deez nuts."

WRITING YOUR FIRST NOVEL SHOULD HAPPEN ONLY AFTER YOU'VE WRITTEN A TOME ON BUSINESS STRATEGY

by JANET MANLEY

You've got the next Great American Novel inside of you, I know. The themes accost you daily in every moment of social interaction; the transparency of the world is wrenching; you can see the strings from which reality dangles in gifted moments of illumination; there is so much beauty in decay; the umbilical cord is severed, child abandons parent; the Voice speaks to itself, is at once issued and received; the novel will be a little bit meta, but willing to expound audience expectations of a well-trodden genre; there will be an alpaca; sandwiches eat sandwich artists; it will revolutionize literature and explode the industrial author complex.

But wait, don't write the book yet. Write a book about post-acquisition integration strategy first.

Who am I to be giving advice? I've twenty-five years' experience offering consulting services to companies that don't know any better, who take my interlocking-circle diagrams gratefully and apply them to the bones of their value missions, constructing emphatic new strategic statements of intent. I've written fifty-three books on the topic (all self-published) and am currently working on the 54th.

You've probably met me before. We became isolated from the core of a barbecue assemblage once after making the decision to return to the cooler and dig, really dig, to see if another beer had been hidden under the ice and soda. It was a painful party. We got talking about what each of us "did." I gave you some twaddle about my former career as a mid-level analyst and love of recumbent bicycles, and you, wearing your self-doubt like an emblem, mentioned that you were pursuing an MFA, amidst staffing a rainforest-friendly coffee shop. I then brightened, and announced that I, too, was a writer. You asked what I had written, and I told you that I had written fifty-two books on corporate strategy and leadership during my summers in Mexico, in a writer's community near Oaxaca. I was at that time working on the fifty-third. I asked you what you had written, and you mumbled something about some short experimental fiction and unpublished poetry and essay. I responded with a limerick.

Or we could have met at the Open University open day, where people like myself peddled classes for such intangibles as, "The Art of Conversation" and, "Computer-Aided Pottery." We were overwhelmingly in the presence of people in need of editors for their memoirs, their unanchored, unexamined lives crowding the hall for prominence—you shied away from the sign-up sheet for the "getting a literary agent" night course, fully convinced by now that bullshit of all shapes and sizes was being peddled to the public, and that you had the stench of bullshit on your breath.

You've a deft hand for character treatment; lines are sung and whispered, and never spoken. Your plotlines are open-ended and hopeful yet nihilistic. You pack volumes into a single line of dialogue, but allow settings to establish themselves through prolific descriptions of wallpaper, skirting boards and the color of air moving round the characters. You offer unique insight into calots. Your imagery would be lauded by critics if anyone had actually sampled it, but you are incapable of finishing a novel. Whenever the novel begins to acquire a shape, you determine that it is too bulky, and the metaphors too clunky, or not meaty enough, or have a funny smell. Each page written is a page between yourself and literary satisfaction; sandwiched together you lose all sight.

That is why you, my dear, need to write a book on the tenets of post-gender management theory. There you can practice your metaphoric allusions to man's frontiers, to the hollowing of character, to the slow devouring of the land by the ocean and inland [moral!] salination. Simply tie them to organizational structure. Then you can structure your novel under chapter headings like "Breaking the Chain" and "Feeding the Feedback Loop." Upon such modular shelves you can plonk thoughts like cereal boxes, preconstructed kernels of composition, and thwack your bio on the back inside flap. Then, you will be. A writer.

A GUEST COLUMNIST STILL GETTING THE HANG OF IT

by ELLIE KEMPER

Four hundred thousand deaths every year—and growing. From smoking, I mean. Deaths from smoking. Nearly half a million people are dying from smoking-related things every year. Americans, that is. I'm talking about half a million Americans. I don't have the numbers of smoking-related deaths in other countries. But 400,000 Americans dying from smoking every year: that's bad. And I am not exactly sure what we should do about it.

Global warming is the biggest threat facing the globe today. Second-biggest threat. Terrorism, then global warming. Or maybe the reverse. At any rate, I will mention that teen pregnancy is also on the rise. Some people consider that a threat. Me, I'm not so sure that's a threat. My mother had me when she was nineteen, and on purpose. So that was not such a bad thing. Make love, not war, right? To an extent.

The point is: the globe is heating up, terrorists are trying to rule the world, and babies keep popping out of teenage girls. All of these things should be addressed. At some point, we will also need to figure out what to do about DVD pirating.

Christina Williams is a typical high school freshman on the outskirts of Pittsburgh. She is captain of the cheerleading squad, an active member of the French Club, and just beginning to learn tae kwon do. Christina has a steady boyfriend who loves her, for the most part, and a weekend job serving ice cream at the local Scoops. She hopes to go into law or real estate when she grows up, and recently organized a highly successful bake sale to raise awareness of France.

Christina Williams doesn't have health insurance.

As for Iraq: I must say I'm a little torn on this issue. I can sort of see all sides of the argument. Do we increase troops or begin to withdraw? Do we set a deadline or play it by ear? I don't really have an answer. If we increase troops, then that equals more Americans fighting what some might consider a hopeless war. If we withdraw now, then we will leave an extraordinary mess behind us. Setting a deadline seems pretty pointless. But if we play it by ear, then we might not feel any sense of urgency.

The whole thing is nothing short of a complete disaster. Yikes!!

When exactly did the Catholic Church become such an enormous institution? Don't get me wrong. I admire religion, but this particular one seems a tad too organized—and large. That being said, I will admit that I sort of like this current pope. Having said that, I should mention that I don't like him very much. He tends to say some pretty outrageous things. Though I do admire his chutzpah.

Dolphins keep getting snared in nets meant for tuna, but I wouldn't exactly advise a ban on tuna. There is no point in throwing out the baby with the bathwater—although maybe there is. However, a tuna ban seems pretty implausible. A lot of people really enjoy tuna fish.

What is the deal with these immigrants?

I would love to hear my readers' feedback. Most of what I write depends on what inspires me. And you, the readership, inspire me. So please send any comments, thoughts, questions, or concerns my way. I look forward to reading them.

Please send only positive feedback. I get anxious.

I PROBABLY SHOULDN'T HAVE OPTED FOR THE CHEAPEST HMO

by JIM STALLARD

THE DERMATOLOGIST

"All right, Jim, let's take a look at you here and see what you got going... Oh my god." (Vomits into wastebasket.)

"The reason I didn't say anything to you before, smart guy, is that melanoma isn't contagious. Now are you going to let me be the doctor?"

THE PRIMARY-CARE PHYSICIAN

"I didn't mean to laugh. I've just never seen this kind of muscle tone on a man before."

"The treatment won't work unless you're diligent about taking it. Did you hold the crystals in each hand for twenty minutes a day while facing north?"

THE RADIOLOGIST

"Let me show you what we're up against. See the outline of this shadow in the upper right quadrant of your lung? Ethically, I can't prescribe any treatment that would destroy the Virgin Mary."

"You don't have any metal in your body, do you? We just spent three hours cleaning out the MRI machine from our last patient."

THE UROLOGIST

"Wow, your prostate feels exactly like mine. Here, check it out."

"This has me stumped. Have you tried urinating just every other day? It's worth a shot."

THE GASTROENTEROLOGIST

"Put the earplugs in now, because I'm really gonna blast this. Tapeworms can't stand reggae."

"We need to boost your black bile so it's up to the level of your other three humors. Let me thread this doohickey up through your nostril."

THE SURGEON

"We're going to put you under now, but you'll enjoy it. Once you get a whiff of this ether, you can't get enough—take it from me."

"The cone is just to make sure you don't bite at your suture and pull out the stitches. Nobody is going to notice it, I guarantee you."

A SUBTEXTUAL READING OF YOUR HIGH SCHOOL FRENCH TEXTBOOK

by SARAH SMALLWOOD

CHAPTER I

INTRODUCTIONS

Je suis Monsieur Troucher. Je suis le père de la famille.
I am Mr. Troucher. I am the father. I am quite manly.

Je suis Jean-Paul. Je suis le fils de la famille.
I am Jean-Paul. I am also a man, therefore I come before my sister.

Je suis Marie. Je suis la soeur de Jean-Paul.
I am Jean-Paul's sister, Marie. I am being groomed to marry well.

Je suis Madame Troucher. Je suis la mère de Jean-Paul.
I am the wife. I have no first name. I am disappointed that I have a daughter instead of two sons.

Je suis Tutu. Je suis le chien de la famille Troucher.

I am Tutu the dog. I am a male dog for no foreseeable reason. Apparently, I can talk.

CHAPTER 2
WHERE DO YOU LIVE?

M. TROUCHER: Nous habitons à la capitale.

Like all French people, we live in Paris.

MME. TROUCHER: J'aime Paris! La ville d'amour!

I obviously wear my heart on my age-inappropriate cap sleeve.

MARIE: Le ville de la culture et les chefs de cuisine!

Mom, does Dad ever hurt you? Smile if the answer's yes.

JEAN-PAUL: J'aime la Tour Eiffel! C'est magnifique!

Why can we see the Eiffel Tower from, like, every window?

TUTU: J'aime les touristes et je mange leurs croissants!

I'm a poodle? I don't feel like a poodle. I bet I'm really a German shepherd.

CHAPTER 3
AT THE SUPERMARKET

M. TROUCHER: Je vais faire des courses maintenant.

I alone will buy the groceries. Stay here in the small car with the windows up.

MARIE: *J'espère qu'il achète des chocolates.*
He's gone. We could run away.

MME. TROUCHER: *Je voudrais des fleurs pour le jardin.*
He would find us, Marie. He always does.

JEAN-PAUL: *J'espère qu'il m'achète un nouveau ballon de football!*
Hey! The only things in this bag are wine and a baguette! I'm hungry!

TUTU: *Je voudrais du rosbif, s'il vous plaît.*
Why the hell did you need to bring me shopping?

CHAPTER 4
GOING OUT

M. TROUCHER: *Ce restaurant, c'est tres couteux!*
I don't like spending money. Is it still legal for me to hit you?

MME. TROUCHER: *Oui, c'est tres couteux!*
I share your opinion so completely, I do not even need to reword it.
Also, I wonder what an orgasm feels like.

JEAN-PAUL: *Marie, voulez-vous de la brioche et du fromage?*
Mom and Dad are lame. Wanna smoke a bowl in the bathroom?

MARIE: *Mais oui!*
Fuck yes.

TUTU: *N'oubliez-pas le rosbif pour le chien!*
Guess I'll just stay tied to this pole while you eat, then.

CHAPTER 5
WHAT'S HAPPENING TOMORROW?

M. TROUCHER: Je pense faire laver ma voiture demain.
I plan to wash the car. Apparently, I'll need all three of these verbs.

JEAN-PAUL: Je vais aux grands magasins avec mon ami François.
François and I are going to sell handbags out of the back of the neighbor's van for cash, which we'll spend on X. Afterward, while stoned, we'll hold each other and cry, which will lead to some awkward, life-changing sexual experimentation.

MARIE: Je prépare une tarte des pommes.
Mom, I got pregnant just so you would look at me. Mom?

MME. TROUCHER: Je vais au cinema.
Do you need a ride, Jean-Paul?

TUTU: Je pense faire une petite sieste.
If I'm not in the next chapter, it's because I died of starvation.

A McSWEENEY'S INTERNET
TENDENCY ORIGIN STORY

IT'S TWINS!
by AMY FUSSELMAN

I REMEMBER WHEN THERE WAS no McSweeney's Internet Tendency. It wasn't one of those things that suddenly came and made us all go, "Wow! Where did this amazing thing come from?!" No. Something was missing and we knew it. We went to restaurants and ordered what we thought was McSweeney's Internet Tendency and what came was always disappointing and left a sour taste. Or we waited at the bus stop for McSweeney's Internet Tendency and what came was the M86 bus and it was late and crowded and we were cold.

The funny thing was, we longed for McSweeney's Internet Tendency but when she finally arrived, we didn't notice. Because McSweeney's Internet Tendency was a twin. And she was the runty twin—the one nobody thought would make it, so we didn't focus on her at all. Instead, we set our sights on her sister, Fran, who was shiny and engaging and sang songs from *Oklahoma!* and got good grades. She later went on to start an artisanal ice cream parlor in Santa Fe, and had the enviable job of tasting ice cream flavors before they were made public.

Meanwhile, McSweeney's Internet Tendency survived. She was quiet, and left home early. She called her sister on their twenty-first birthday.

"Can you believe that people do not like 'Oh What a Beautiful Fudge Coffee Fantasia?!'" Fran complained to her twin.

"There's no accounting for taste," McSweeney's Internet Tendency replied, serenely.

WELCOME TO PAGE 209

The twins went on like that until this day, one known and one unknown—or both known, really, but in different ways—and both giving joy to people everywhere. Only Fran still does not really know what McSweeney's Internet Tendency does. She knows her favorite ice cream flavor, though: pistachio.

CONVERSATIONS MY PARENTS MUST HAVE HAD WHILE PLANNING TO RAISE A CHILD

by JEN STATSKY

DAD: I don't think we should ever talk about feelings.

MOM: Never.

- - -

DAD: I'll take the greatest number of photographs of her when she's in her most awkward stage, right in the depths of puberty.

MOM: Good idea. I'll make sure to send them to all our immediate and all our somewhat distant family and friends. Oh, and make sure you forget your camera the one night in her life that Billy Sherman talks to her, so that no proof exists of said event.

DAD: Got it.

- - -

DAD: We should talk very loudly about the truth about Santa Claus.

MOM: Yes, and let's not make any attempt whatsoever to disguise Santa's handwriting from our own.

- - -

MOM: Let's make sure we avoid the topic of sex so masterfully and so consistently that she begins to wonder if it's something made up by people on TV.

DAD: Good idea. Let's also ignore the existence of any of her long-term boyfriends, no matter how harmless, awkward, and acne-prone they are.

- - -

MOM: She should never have to worry about money, especially when she's young.

DAD: I agree. That way, she can spend all her time worrying about us getting a divorce.

- - -

DAD: When I teach her to ride a bike, I will tell her that my hand is on the seat, but then I will take it away just as she is getting the hang of it.

MOM: That will not turn out well.

DAD: No.

- - -

MOM: I'll make sure to give her a haircut that matches mine. Mine in 1972, that is.

DAD: Great. I'll wear an awkward comb-over.

- - -

DAD: I think I'll always be a little bit weirder than necessary around her friends. Especially the "cool" ones who are just over to copy notes for Ms. Reardon's AP Physics midterm.

MOM: Sounds good. I'll always talk one decibel louder than a normal person.

- - -

DAD: She will beg us to get a dog for many, many years.

MOM: And I will repeatedly tell her how I am allergic to animal hair.

DAD: You will wear a fur coat.

- - -

MOM: Whenever she does something that really upsets me, I'll always make sure to tell her that "her grandmother is rolling over in her grave."

DAD: Even though we will cremate her.

- - -

DAD: I will demonstrate a total lack of understanding of the proper grammatical way to use quotation marks, and sign every birthday card with "Love."

MOM: That will keep her on her toes.

- - -

MOM: I think the most important thing is that we will criticize her, no matter what she does or who she becomes.

DAD: And that she knows we criticize her just as much as we criticize each other.

- - -

DAD: Let's not give her a little brother or sister.

MOM: No. That might function as some sort of coping mechanism.

- - -

MOM: We can't take her on those classic-but-trite kid vacations that every other child in the Western world gets to experience, like trips to Disneyland.

DAD: No, for she will gain great popularity and respect from her second-grade classmates when she wears her I WENT TO VERMONT AND ALL I GOT WAS THIS LOUSY T-SHIRT MADE FROM 100% RECYCLED COMPOST-HEAP MATERIALS T-shirt.

- - -

DAD: We should always give her what she wants.

MOM: That way, we can hold it against her when she's older and can finally provide for herself.

THE MAGIC 8 BALL AMENDED BY MY MOTHER FOR MY MIDDLE-SCHOOL YEARS

by KATE HAHN

Very doubtful. But you brought that on yourself.

- - -

As I see it, yes. But when was the last time you cared what I thought?

- - -

My sources say yes. And they have no reason to lie about seeing you at the mall in the middle of a school day.

- - -

It is decidedly so. I just know.

- - -

Outlook good. Let's see how long that lasts.

- - -

Outlook not so good. See?

- - -

Better not tell you now. You seem upset and I'm afraid you might do something irrational. At least that's what *Time* magazine says about teenagers.

- - -

Signs point to yes. The incense, for one. How stupid do you think I am?

- - -

Don't count on it. Or on much else if you keep going the way you're going.

- - -

Yes—definitely. Oh wait, I thought that was your sister holding the ball. For you, no.

- - -

Reply hazy. Try again when I'm off the phone with my boyfriend.

- - -

Concentrate and ask again. I can't abide poor grammar.

- - -

My reply is no. Crying won't change things.

- - -

Ask again later. Maybe in twenty years, when you'll understand what you put me through.

- - -

You may rely on it. Let's just hope "it" can rely on you, too. Poor "it."

- - -

Yes. As long as an adult is present and your grades are good. So, I guess it's actually no.

- - -

Most likely. Especially if your friends are already doing it.

- - -

Cannot predict now. But, if your past behavior is any indication, the results will include my picking you up at the police station at 4 a.m.

- - -

It is certain. Everyone blames the mother.

WE ARE THE FAMILY IN THE PHOTO THAT CAME WITH YOUR NEW PICTURE FRAME

by COLIN NISSAN

Before you remove us from this frame and replace us with a picture of yourselves, I want you to take a nice, long look at us. We're gorgeous. What are the chances that your family is as happy and aesthetically pleasing as us? I'd have to say 4 percent, tops.

Do you like our sweaters? They're shearling. That means they're made from lambs. Specifically, lambs from the lamb farm we own. The same one where every summer we invite underprivileged kids to feel temporarily privileged. Does your family own a lamb farm and invite underprivileged kids there?

How rude of me, we haven't even introduced ourselves. We're the Andersons. I'm Evan. The lovely size-zero lass in the floppy sun hat is my wife Amy, and these are our best friends/children, Evan and Amy Jr. As you can see, we're very fit and active. You know what our family's average percentage of body fat is? Three. Yes, really. We got it tested last year when we all became organ donors.

You may have noticed that I'm carrying Amy on my back. We do that a lot. At least once a day, and not just when we're in fields like this; we do it on beaches and in urban environments as well. That's what happens when your love is deep and playful like ours. You should also know that we dab frosting on each other's noses every single time we eat cupcakes, which is both mischievous and very us. Do you guys even eat cupcakes?

Amy and I continue to reach new heights of sexual satisfaction fifteen years into our marriage. While you guys are sitting around in your sweatsuits fighting over who forgot to pay the gas bill, we're smiling exactly like this through hours of mind-boggling tantric intercourse.

You're probably wondering about the vintage jeep and hot air balloon in the background of our picture. That's our jeep. I restored it myself. You'd think I'd be tired of working with my hands after fixing brains as a neurosurgeon all day, but I'm not. We're about to enjoy a beautiful scenic float over the countryside—a little something we do every Saturday. Why? Because we crave adventure and have zero fear of heights, that's why. What's your idea of adventure? Let me guess, a frantic trip to Bed Bath & Beyond a half-hour before closing?

Does your family sing barbershop? Ours does. A baritone, a soprano, and our two little Mensa tenors. We even have a name for ourselves: "The Andertones." I'm looking forward to busting out one of our signature medleys on the ride of home from ballooning.

You may have noticed that Evan Jr. is the only one of us who's Asian. That's because we adopted him from China—not because we have reproductive issues of any kind, in fact Amy's doctor referred to my sperm as "troops" and her eggs as "Normandy," so our genitals are working very, very well. We simply felt that adopting was the right thing to do because we have a lot of love to give, probably two to three times more than you do.

There's Nippers, our purebred lab, running around in the distance. I love that old gal, had her since I was a little boy. I know that may sound like a physical impossibility but it isn't. Not in this family.

What's your picture of, by the way? I'm dying to know what you're so anxious to replace us with, and please don't tell me it's a shot of you guys bowling. You know the last time Amy and the kids and I bowled? Never. Because it's pathetic and dull and not representative of the enviable lifestyle we've chosen for ourselves.

Let's get real here. It's time to place your picture next to ours and ask yourself an important question. Who's better? Then put your little bowling picture back in the drawer and let the Andersons turn this house into a home.

A PERSONAL ESSAY BY A PERSONAL ESSAY

by CHRISTY VANNOY

I am a Personal Essay and I was born with a port wine stain and beaten by my mother. A brief affair with a second cousin produced my first and only developmentally disabled child. Years of painful infertility would lead me straight into menopause and the hysterectomy I almost didn't survive.

I recently enrolled in a clinic led by the article's director and editor for a national women's magazine. Technically, we were there to work-shop and polish ourselves into submission. Secretly, though, we each hoped to out-devastate the other and nail ourselves a freelance contract.

I wasn't there to learn. I've been published as many times as I've been brutally sodomized, but I need to stay at the top of my game. Everyone thinks they have a story these days, and as soon as they let women in the Middle East start talking, you'll have to hold an editor hostage to get a response. Mark my words.

There were ten of us in the room. The Essay Without Arms worried me at first, but she had great bone structure and a wedding ring dangled from a chain on her neck, so I doubted her life has been all that hard.

Two male essays wandered in late. They were Homosexual Essays, a dime a dozen, and publishers aren't buying their battle with low self-esteem anymore. Even if their parents had kicked them out, I'd put money on a kind relative taking them in. It wasn't as if they'd landed in state care, like I had, and been delivered straight into the wandering hands of recently paroled foster parents. Being gay is about as tragic as a stray cuticle, and I wasn't born a Jehovah's Witness yesterday.

I presented my essay first, and tried not to look smug as I returned to my seat. The article's director let out a satisfied sigh and said, "I see someone's done this before." Yes, someone had. I've developed something of a reputation in the industry for taking meticulous notes on my suffering. It was a lesson learned the hard way after my year in sex slavery was rendered useless from the effects of crank on my long-term memory.

The third essay that read absolutely killed. She'd endured a series of miscarriages and narcoleptic seizures living in a work camp during her youth in communist China. Initially, I was worried, but then I thought, whatever, good for her. There are twelve months in the year, and if Refugee Camp walked away with January, the April swimwear issue would be the perfect platform for my struggles with Exercise Bulimia. I don't mean to sound overly confident, but much of the unmitigated misfortune that has been my day-to-day life has taught me the importance of believing in myself.

Next up were two Divorce Essays, which came and went, forgettable at best. The editor's critique suggested as much. Alopecia followed. She had promise, but was still clearly struggling for a hook. Every essay who's been through chemo or tried lesbianism ends up bald. Bald isn't the story. Alopecia was heading in the right direction, loving herself, but she was getting there all wrong. I think she needed to focus on not having eyelashes or pubic hair. Now that's interesting. *That's* an essay.

The last kid was unpublished and new on the circuit. It was hard to figure out what we were up against with this one. He walked up to the podium unassisted, bearing no visible signs of physical or mental retardation. Maybe it was something systemic, or worse still, the latest wave of competition to hit the market: a slow-to-diagnose mental illness. I tried to relax. It was hard to build story arcs off problems cured by pills. Problems caused by pills, on the other hand, sold on query alone. Shit. Maybe he was an addict.

His essay was weird. I think he was about a Tuesday. Not the Tuesday of an amputation, just a regular any old Tuesday. He persisted on beginning sentences without the personal pronoun "I" and comparing one thing to another instead of just out and out saying what happened. I was trying to track his word count but lost myself momentarily as he described the veins in a cashier's hands. It reminded me of my grandmother, her rough physical topography a testament to a life of hard work. We all leaned in during one of his especially long pauses, only to realize he wasn't pausing, he was done.

The Refugee Essay applauded loudly, but quite honestly, I think her tepid grip on English and admitted narcolepsy barred her from being a qualified judge. The Gay Essays joined in too, but they'll clap for anything with a penis and a Michelangelo jawline.

My ovations, on the other hand, are earned, and this essay never once told me how he felt about himself. Although, I have to admit, if I'd been him during that section where his father didn't even open the gift, I'd have been devastated by the rejection. Not of the thing itself, but of what it represented. Like it wasn't a gift so much as it was longing in the shape of a box, wrapped up in a bow.

Look, it wasn't like this essay didn't have potential. I think everyone in that room agreed he had a certain something. But talent takes time. Inoperable tumors just don't sprout up overnight, and psychotic breaks are nothing if not slow to boil.

The article's director didn't bother to give him any feedback. One of the Divorce Essays tried to pipe in about the unsatisfying ending, but the editor silenced her with the stop sign of her raised palm. Wordlessly, she stared at this essay with a sorrow that reminded me of the last look the man I believed to be my father gave me before heading to Vietnam, only later to return a person wholly different from the one who left. "You deserve something better than this" the editor said. "Yet for rules I follow, but did not create, I can't help you."

I thought about this essay a lot over the next few days, like he was beside me, equal parts familiar and strange. But the thing about life is that you simply cannot settle for melancholy, even when it's true. You are a not a tragedy, you are a personal essay. You must rise above and you must do it in the last paragraph with basic grammar and easily recognized words.

Anyway, come November I will be buying every copy of *Marie Claire* I can get my one good hand on! You'll find me on page 124. If you haven't looked death straight in the eye or been sued by a sister wife, you won't see yourself in my story. But you will find solace in knowing your own problems are petty and banal. I have ascended victorious from the ashes of immeasurable self-doubt and pain. And I have not simply survived, I have flourished.

FAQ: THE "SNAKE FIGHT" PORTION OF YOUR THESIS DEFENSE

by LUKE BURNS

Q: Do I have to kill the snake?

A: University guidelines state that you have to "defeat" the snake. There are many ways to accomplish this. Lots of students choose to wrestle the snake. Some construct decoys and elaborate traps to confuse and then ensnare the snake. One student brought a flute and played a song to lull the snake to sleep. Then he threw the snake out a window.

Q: Does everyone fight the same snake?

A: No. You will fight one of the many snakes that are kept on campus by the facilities department.

Q: Are the snakes big?

A: We have lots of different snakes. The quality of your work determines which snake you will fight. The better your thesis is, the smaller the snake will be.

Q: Does my thesis adviser pick the snake?

A: No. Your adviser just tells the guy who picks the snakes how good your thesis was.

Q: What does it mean if I get a small snake that is also very strong?

A: Snake-picking is not an exact science. The size of the snake is the main factor. The snake may be very strong, or it may be very weak. It may be of Asian, African, or South American origin. It may constrict its victims and then swallow them whole, or it may use venom to blind and/or paralyze its prey. You shouldn't read too much into these other characteristics. Although, if you get a poisonous snake it often means that there was a problem with the formatting of your bibliography.

Q: When and where do I fight the snake? Does the school have some kind of pit or arena for snake fights?

A: You fight the snake in the room you have reserved for your defense. The fight generally starts after you have finished answering questions about your thesis. However, the snake will be lurking in the room the whole time and it can strike at any point. If the snake attacks prematurely, it's obviously better to defeat it and get back to the rest of your defense as quickly as possible.

Q: Would someone who wrote a bad thesis and defeated a large snake get the same grade as someone who wrote a good thesis and defeated a small snake?

A: Yes.

Q: So then couldn't you just fight a snake in lieu of actually writing a thesis?

A: Technically, yes. But in that case the snake would be very big. Very big, indeed.

Q: Could the snake kill me?

A: That almost never happens. But if you're worried, just make sure that you write a good thesis.

Q: Why do I have to do this?

A: Snake fighting is one of the great traditions of higher education. It may seem somewhat antiquated and silly, like the robes we wear at graduation, but fighting a snake is an important part of the history and culture of every reputable university. Almost everyone with an advanced degree has gone through this process. Notable figures such as John Foster Dulles, Philip Roth, and Doris Kearns Goodwin (to name but a few) have all had to defeat at least one snake in single combat.

Q: This whole snake thing is just a metaphor, right?

A: I assure you, the snakes are very real.

---

* Read an interview with Luke Burns about this piece on page 638.

THE PEOPLE IN AN OLIVE GARDEN COMMERCIAL SHARE THEIR EXISTENTIAL PAIN

by RACHEL KLEIN

We go to Olive Garden all the time because we have officially given up on life. We may only be in our mid-thirties, of neutral good looks, and, as a group, represent a refreshing, but not uncomfortably diverse cross-section of ethnicities, but we are already fully resigned to a life of endless bread sticks that we'll joke look a little like uncircumcised penises, and bowls of mealy pasta drenched in tomato-themed high-fructose corn syrup, because we are dead inside.

Look at us. We look so happy in this commercial, laughing over a joke one of us just made during the voice-over. I will tell you the sad and painful truth: it wasn't a joke. Michael just told us that his dog died. And we laughed. We laughed at Michael's dead dog. Because we are in so much pain that we've come out the other side.

I know what you're thinking: *You look so pleasantly surprised at the way your waitress brings you your multiple shallow bowls of flash-frozen-then-convection-heated-meat-styled entrees. You look like you are enjoying both your meal and your company.* Do not be deceived. We are each living our own personal hell. Not even unlimited refills on salad can revive our withered souls. We are the damned.

Four out of the seven nights of the week you will find us here, trying to drown out our tears with gallon-sized frosted glasses of spiked lemonade. But our tears fall into our glasses, and we drink them up and they are bitter. Bitter and a little bit lemony, from the lemonade. Or perhaps we have begun to cry lemonade tears. It makes no difference to us.

This is the stucco archway of broken dreams. This is the table of the last supper, fed to the innocents who are fattened and led to the slaughter. We would despair if we cared enough to notice the depths to which our lives have sunk. Instead, we plaster on our greasepaint grins, gird our loins, and order the dessert that comes free with our meal. Because, damn it, Olive Garden, you owe us that much.

I'M COMIC SANS, ASSHOLE

by MIKE LACHER

Listen up. I know the shit you've been saying behind my back. You think I'm stupid. You think I'm immature. You think I'm a malformed, pathetic excuse for a font. Well think again, nerdhole, because I'm Comic Sans, and I'm the best thing to happen to typography since Johannes fucking Gutenberg.

You don't like that your coworker used me on that note about stealing her yogurt from the break room fridge? You don't like that I'm all over your sister-in-law's blog? You don't like that I'm on the sign for that new Thai place? You think I'm pedestrian and tacky? Guess the fuck what, Picasso. We don't all have seventy-three weights of stick-up-my-ass Helvetica sitting on our seventeen-inch MacBook Pros. Sorry the entire world can't all be done in stark Eurotrash Swiss type. Sorry some people like to have fun. Sorry I'm standing in the way of your minimalist Bauhaus-esque fascist snoozefest. Maybe sometime you should take off your black turtle-neck, stop compulsively adjusting your Tumblr theme, and lighten the fuck up for once.

People love me. Why? Because I'm fun. I'm the life of the party. I bring levity to any situation. Need to soften the blow of a harsh message about restroom etiquette? SLAM. There I am. Need to spice up the directions to your graduation party? WHAM. There again. Need to convey your fun-loving, approachable nature on your business's website? SMACK. Like daffodils in motherfucking spring.

When people need to kick back, have fun and party, I will be there, unlike your pathetic fonts. While Gotham is at the science fair, I'm banging the prom queen behind the woodshop. While Avenir is practicing the clarinet, I'm shredding "Reign In Blood" on my double-necked Stratocaster. While Univers is refilling his allergy prescriptions, I'm racing my tricked-out, nitrous-laden Honda Civic against Tokyo gangsters who'll kill me if I don't cross the finish line first. I am a sans serif Superman and my only kryptonite is pretentious buzzkills like you.

It doesn't even matter what you think. You know why, jagoff? Cause I'm famous. I am on every major operating system since Microsoft fucking Bob. I'm in your signs. I'm in your browsers. I'm in your instant messengers. I'm not just a font. I am a force of motherfucking nature and I will not rest until every uptight arm-chair typographer cock-hat like you is surrounded by my lovable, comic-book inspired, sans-serif badassery.

Enough of this bullshit. I'm gonna go get hammered with Papyrus.

---

* Read an interview with Mike Lacher about this piece on page 643.

OUR DAUGHTER ISN'T A SELFISH BRAT; YOUR SON JUST HASN'T READ *ATLAS SHRUGGED*

by ERIC HAGUE

I'd like to start by saying that I don't get into belligerent shouting matches at the playground very often. The Tot Lot, by its very nature, can be an extremely volatile place—a veritable powder keg of different and sometimes contradictory parenting styles—and this fact alone is usually enough to keep everyone, parents and tots alike, acting as courteous and deferential as possible. The argument we had earlier today didn't need to happen, and I want you to know, above all else, that I'm deeply sorry that things got so wildly and publicly out of hand.

Now let me explain why your son was wrong.

When little Aiden toddled up to our daughter Johanna and asked to play with her Elmo ball, he was, admittedly, very sweet and polite. I think his exact words were, "Have a ball, peas [sic]?" And I'm sure you were very proud of him for using his manners.

To be sure, I was equally proud when Johanna yelled, "No! Looter!"

right in his looter face, and then only marginally less proud when she sort of shoved him.

The thing is, in this family we take the philosophies of Ayn Rand seriously. We conspicuously reward ourselves for our own hard work, we never give to charity, and we only pay our taxes very, very begrudgingly.

Since the day Johanna was born, we've worked to indoctrinate her into the truth of Objectivism. Every night we read to her from the illustrated, unabridged edition of *Atlas Shrugged*—glossing over all the hardcore sex parts, mind you, but dwelling pretty thoroughly on the stuff about being proud of what you've earned and not letting James Taggart-types bring you down. For a long time we were convinced that our efforts to free her mind were for naught, but recently, as we've started socializing her a little bit, we've been delighted to find that she is completely antipathetic to the concept of sharing. As parents, we couldn't have asked for a better daughter.

That's why when Johanna then began berating your son, accusing him of trying to coerce from her a moral sanction of his theft of the fruit of her labor, in as many words, I kind of egged her on. Even when Aiden started crying.

You see, that Elmo ball was Johanna's reward for consistently using the potty this past week. She wasn't given the ball simply because she'd demonstrated an exceptional need for it—she'd earned it. And from the way Aiden's pants sagged as he tried in vain to run away from our daughter, it was clear that he wasn't anywhere close to deserving that kind of remuneration. By so much as allowing Johanna to share her toy with him, we'd be undermining her appreciation of one of life's most important lessons: you should never feel guilty about your abilities. Including your ability to repeatedly peg a fellow toddler with your Elmo ball as he sobs for mercy.

Look, imagine what would happen if we were to enact some sort of potty training Equalization of Opportunity Act in which we regularized the distribution all of Johanna's and Aiden's potty chart stickers. Suddenly it would seem as if Aiden had earned the right to wear big-boy underpants, and within minutes you'd have a Taggart Tunnel-esque catastrophe on your hands, if you follow me.

Johanna shouldn't be burdened with supplying playthings for every bed-wetting moocher she happens to meet. If you saw Johanna, her knees buckling, her arms trembling but still trying to hold aloft the collective weight of an entire Tot Lot's worth of Elmo balls with the last of her strength, what would you tell her to do?

To shrug. Just like we've instructed her to do if Child Protective Services or some other agent of the People's State of America ever asks her about what we're teaching her.

After all, we've managed to raise a bright, self-reliant girl who achieves her goals by means of incentive and ratiocination and never— or very rarely—through the corrupt syllogism of force. We know, despite what you and a number of other parents we've met have said— as they carried their whimpering little social parasites away—that Johanna's defiant, quasi-bellicose nature only superficially resembles that of an out-of-control toddler, and in truth posits her as more of a latter-day Dagny Taggart than any kind of *enfant terrible*.

Yes, she's blossomed into everything we ever hoped or *post hoc* rationalized she would. In our house we no longer say, "Who is John Galt?" Instead we say, "Who's our little princess?"

HEMINGWAY'S
BLONDE JOKES

by CHRIS RIEBSCHLAGER

Q. Why was the blonde staring at the frozen orange juice container?

A. The container brought to mind the Sunday breakfasts with her mother in the days before she took her life.

- - -

Q. How many blondes does it take to change a light bulb?

A. Margot preferred darkness.

- - -

Q. How can you tell if a blonde has been using your typewriter?

A. The nicotine-stained keys and dried tears.

- - -

Q. Why did the blonde drive into the ditch?

A. She was overtaken with despair. No one was awaiting her arrival.

A McSWEENEY'S INTERNET TENDENCY ORIGIN STORY

SARAH WALKER SHOWS YOU HOW TO SUBMIT TO McSWEENEY'S INTERNET TENDENCY

by SARAH WALKER

H ERE'S SOME ADVICE I GIVE writers before they submit to *McSweeney's*: when you finish a piece, don't send it in immediately. Look at it with fresh eyes only after a night's rest. However, that night MUST be spent in a haunted house. It can be any haunted house of your choosing, but it can't be your own because you have no perspective on how haunted your house is. Also, you must be alone because writing is a solitary practice. Once you make it through the night—if you make it through the night—you'll know what's really important. I'm not talking about your family or your health. If you didn't know those things were important before, I'm sorry to say that you need more than a sleepless, terrifying night in a haunted house to sort out your priorities. No, after spending sunset to sunrise alone in a haunted house, you'll behold your piece with the kind of rarefied clarity that comes after surviving the attempts of an insane Victorian governess to murder you. You'll have a laser-sharp, bloodshot editing eye. You'll delete extraneous sentences and cut jokes with the precision of the poltergeist who cut you to the core both with a shard of stained glass and a comment about your boyfriend jeans before you sent him back to hell screaming, "I don't care if you like them, I like

WELCOME TO PAGE 243

them!" Is "sandwich" still a funny word? No! Cut it! Will the image of a headless child playing the organ appear in the negative whenever you close your eyes? Yes! Who cares! Your thoughts are crystalized into perfect sentences now that you've put the evil alien ghost back into the moon rock that the house's owner stole from a museum... or was it a castle? It doesn't matter! What matters is your clear, concise prose. Your rejection of clichéd comedy words. Your earnest love of sandwiches hoagies. Of course, this is all assuming you haven't been driven mad or possessed. Unless you've become possessed by the spirit of a truly great editor. In which case, lucky! But you can't depend on that. So, be prepared to ward off evil spirits with a mixture of courage, quick thinking and making promises to God you can't keep. In the morning, sane of mind, having seen some really fucked up shit, return to your home, edit your piece and send it in. If you get rejected, which is most likely given everyone gets rejected at least once, don't worry. There are always more ideas and more haunted houses.

III.
ADOLESCENCE
2011–2015

III

AN INTRODUCTION TO THE SECOND HALF OF THIS BOOK

by COLIN NISSAN

H EY EVERYONE, HOPE YOU'RE enjoying the book so far. Lots of funny stuff in here. Lots of yuks. How about that "Guest Columnist Still Getting the Hang of It" piece, huh? Hilarious. Or that list of Hemingway's blonde jokes? Man, that was funny. Almost makes you feel like you could live in this little satire bubble forever, just laughing and laughing as if life's one big joke, you know?

Oh, guess what you guys? Hamsters eat their young. Wait, that doesn't seem very funny, does it? There's a whole side to life that isn't funny at all, like when baby animals think their mom's just licking them but she's actually eating them. LOL, right?

This little section is here to remind you that it's not all fun and games in life *or* in this book. Please take a moment to not enjoy this. Don't worry, you'll be back to your carefree laughter soon enough, but not until you acknowledge the fact that only 8 percent of people who receive CPR survive. Not quite the miracle that movies and TV would have you believe, is it? Sounds more like a death sentence than a miracle. So feel free to pound that sternum all you want, but it's probably in vain.

Speaking of death, 150,000 people die every day in the world. Think about that for a minute, unless you just died, which there's a pretty decent chance you have given those numbers. In which case, maybe you're actually the lucky one who doesn't have to live with statistics like that looming over them. Also, the hamsters.

Fun fact: Scientists recently discovered the loneliest whale in the world. Instead of living amongst a pod as whales typically do, he wanders the Pacific ocean completely alone. Why? Because he was born singing at a frequency that the other whales simply can't hear.

I wonder if *he* would think this book is funny. Truth is, even if he did, we'd never know it because that poor, big dummy can't communicate. We can't hear him. No one can!

Let's hop back on the topic of death for a moment. There are two hundred corpses of failed climbers on Mount Everest that are used as guide points for climbers on their way up. Several of whom will not make it either. ROTFL.

I know what you're thinking, "Jesus, can't I escape the real world for a few minutes and have a little laugh?" Sure you can. But you know who can't escape the real world? The baby sea turtle trying to work his way out of a Doritos bag. And he's not the only one, when you consider the fact that cargo ships and cruise liners dump fourteen billion tons of garbage in the sea every year. That's a lot of Doritos bags. And a lot of baby sea turtle corpses covered in nacho cheese.

Since you guys are such big satire fans, let's take a little satire break: the human brain starts to decline at age twenty-seven. Wait, sorry that's not satire, it's the other thing: a fact.

Let's switch gears to death for a second. If any of you reading this are organ donors, you should be proud that you're doing such a great thing for humanity. Unfortunately, in recent years doctors have begun to suspect that people still feel pain even after dying. They further suspect that removing organs hurts like a motherfucker.

Okay, enough of this doom and gloom. I think you guys have paid your dues, so to speak. Time to get back on the chuckle train. If you're in bed reading this, just settle back in all snug as a bug. Speaking of bugs, and this isn't bad I promise, but during the first ten years of usage, the weight of an average mattress doubles from the accumulation of dust mites and their droppings. LOLZ.

P.S. Droppings are feces.

A TEENAGER TRIES TO MAKE THE BEST OF HOSTING HER MIDDLE-AGES-THEMED PARTY AT THE SAME TIME AS HER OLDER BROTHER'S LACROSSE TEAM'S KEGGER

by JEN SPYRA

Prithee brother-minstrel, quiet your music so that I may address my guests.

Brother-minstrel?

Brother-minstrel?

Dan!

Fair maidens and warriors, welcome. My parents, having gone to Cleve-Land, hath bequest to me their hearth and bid me make merry! Now, I did not know that my elder brother Dan would have a party on the same evening, he's known about my gathering for weeks. No matter. In the land of Acharon, we greet strangers with open arms!

You know what, Dan? In the land of Acharon the cloak and cap that I sport would place me at the very height of fashion, and it is your dungarees that would be the object of fun. But this is not an evening for harsh words. It is one for delicious Cheetos and the season three

Game of Thrones finale. Let us turn now to the magic picture-box where images from near and far dance before our eyes!

Alexa, fair maiden and my own best friend, we are turning now to the magic picture box, not to Dan's game of meade-pong.

Prithee, brethren, bear with me as I search for the remote-wand, which I am quite sure I set upon the coaster when I organized the living room for this eve's festivities.

God's thumbnail. I swear I just spied the thing. Patience, brethren. The spirit Acharon guides my hand.

Dan, you titter. Prithee, reveal the source of your mirth. Prithee.

Mum, eh? No matter. Light will shine on the Mystery of the— okay, very funny.

I notice, Dan, that the remote-wand is wedged between your butt-cheeks. A droll stunt, to be sure, but far beneath your maturity—if not math—level. Hah; I have exposed to the group your struggles with calculus. Isn't it odd, fair maidens, how I am two years younger than Dan, but one grade ahead of him in the mathematic arts? Instead of picking on me, Dan, don't you have a tutor to meet or something? You practically live in Mr. Dambarco's basement. Mr. Dambarco is Dan's calculus tutor, fair maidens.

That blow was harsh, to be sure, but the headlock in which you now imprison me is harsher still!

Far better to lance with words than physical blows, brother! Then again, feats of brawn do not faze you—but ventures of the mind, such as determining the revenue of a charter bus company using a simple parabolic formula, present considerable challenge. I noticed you missed that word problem—and so many of its brothers and sisters—on your latest quiz. No matter, Dan. I also scored a 4/10 on the same quiz— when I was in swaddling cloths! Huzzah!

No, I haven't had a chance to lick Donavan's water feeder this day.

But since my rabbit and I are the closest of friends, I am not ashamed to do so now in front of my gathering, which I've planned for weeks.

I do not gag because of the surprising push you applied to my head as I attempted to debase myself on Donavan's feeder, rather I gag at your gamey odor. There is this new invention that the alchemists of Acharon have gifted to our realm, Dan. It's called deodorant. Have you heard tell of it?

You answer my verbal parry by breaking wind—and a foul, swampy cloud 'tis, brother—but we all know I shall have the last laugh when I tell Mom and Dad that you have not only skipped your study group, but invited a maiden to your room last night and stayed there well beyond sunrise!

Jesus, Dan, P.U.

Alexa, I am certain that you chortle in celebration of my trouncing Dan with that new bit of stratagem, and not because Dan has affixed a blanket around himself as a cape and is miming me having oral sex with Donavan. Methought not.

Well! Now that we've finished that charade, the festivities are finally under way! The time has come, fair maidens and warriors, to fill our goblets with Mountain Dew Code Red, that sweetest of fizzy nectars. In the land of Acharon, Code Red shall not turn our stool into jelly, but until then, it's a delicious sacrifice I trust we are prepared to make. Just as soon as I disinfect this remote-wand.

THE BOY
FROM *JURASSIC*
PARK'S COLLEGE
APPLICATION ESSAY

by JULIA DRAKE

Claws scrabbled at the door, each scratch a shock of fear to my heart. Inside the kitchen, my sister and I hid behind a stainless steel table, slick as the sweat that dripped from my brow. A creak of the door handle. A clicking of prehistoric toenails across the tile floor. I looked at my sister, panic searing through me: the raptors had made it inside.

I never thought I would find myself in such a situation when I went to visit my grandfather on his remote island where he'd created a paradise of living dinosaurs. In fact, my face lit up with childlike joy upon seeing the place, my intellectual curiosity instantly piqued. I got my first taste of fieldwork examining an ailing triceratops with seasoned paleontologists, which instilled in me a passion for hands-on learning. That passion for learning is certainly something I would bring with me to a college classroom; it is also a feeling I have tried to impart to my fellow students in my work as French Peer Tutor.

However, my experience on the park was more than a simple voyage of academic discovery. It was also a complicated and profound transition into adulthood. I overcame copious obstacles such as surviving a Tyrannosaurus rex attack, escaping from a treed car, and being electrocuted by a high-voltage fence. Overcoming these obstacles required great courage and also newfound maturity. Indeed, the adult traits I acquired surviving dinosaurs will make me an enthusiastic and passionate member of a college community, whether I brave a Friday night dance or experiment in a new discipline, such as figure drawing.

My experience there in many ways marked my transition into adulthood. However, perhaps the most important thing I learned was not one of reptilian past but of human present. My grandfather taught me that summer about the ongoing process of learning. Though some critics may read failure in his attempt to safely clone dinosaur embryos, his experience helped me to realize that no matter the age, learning never stops. My grandfather's learning experience with terrible lizards mirrors my personal experience in my position as Senior Class cotreasurer, which required me to learn how to share leadership and how to manage a budget.

In addition, my time at the park marked an intellectual transition into adulthood because it sparked a new interest in history. Though the park itself centered on prehistoric history, I credit my visit there with a lifelong interest in history in general, in particular the French Revolution. My senior capstone project on the Tennis Court Oaths demonstrates my dedication to academics, and I can easily foresee myself continuing this project in a rigorous academic environment. Though the raptors were the guillotine—nay, the *Robespierre*—of my childhood, they helped me realize the importance of intellectual curiosity.

Pliny the Elder once said, "From sad experiences spring new beginnings." Rather than give into sadness and mourn my lost childhood,

I escaped the kitchen, the raptors, and the park. My childhood stayed behind in the jungle, crystallized like amber. Thus I was able to move forward into the world as an adult.

Thanks to my experiences on Isla Nublar, I am comfortable tackling the plethora of challenges that await me on campus, be they academic or physical, modern or prehistoric, quotidian or genetically engineered.

AN HONEST COLLEGE REJECTION LETTER

by MIMI EVANS

Dear Applicant,

The Admissions Committee has carefully considered your application and we regret to inform you that we will not be able to offer you admission in the entering class, or a position on one of our alternate lists. The applicant pool this year was particularly strong, and by that I mean the Admissions Committee once again sent candidates like you multiple enticing pamphlets encouraging you to apply, knowing full well we had no intention of accepting you.

However, you will be pleased to know that you have contributed to our declining admissions rate, which has helped our university appear exclusive. This allows us to attract our real candidates: upper-class kids and certified geniuses who will glean no new information from our courses or faculty, whose parents can incentivize us with a new swimming pool or lacrosse stadium.

As a reminder, we don't aspire to be a socially exclusive learning environment. In fact, we have chosen to actively pursue a more diverse campus and welcome all minorities. But our admissions program is quite unique; we combat past discrimination by discriminating in the present. It is one of the many techniques that our Nobel, Peabody, and Oscar award-winning faculty has helped to develop.

While we consider applicants from all backgrounds who excel both in and out of the classroom, we really want student savants who relentlessly pursue a single instrument, sport, or other activity. Unless you have written a *New York Times* bestseller, won first place in the Intel Science Fair, or cured type 1 diabetes using only solar power and a tampon string, we'll put you at the bottom of the pool.

You may be wondering how a near-perfect SAT and ACT, a dozen perfect AP scores, and your presidency of four clubs did not distinguish you from the pack. Please know that we take many other factors into account as well, including socio-political-monetary context, Asian-ness of name, BMI, and modified-Rorschach (in which one of our assistants holds your application from across the room and we try to discern the outline of your profile).

You should also know that our committee did not fall for your attempts to look "humble" or "well-rounded." Volunteering in developing countries is nice, but truly generous individuals volunteer to improve their local communities, while truly wealthy families buy a third-world country for their child to gentrify. We also realize that your extensive study of how "novel cyclic di-GMP effectors of the YajQ protein family control bacterial virulence" was not influenced by your passion for "volunteering with the elderly," nor was it anything but a résumé inflator. Most importantly, we know that your minimum-wage job did not teach you "patience, teamwork, and leadership." No one learns anything from minimum-wage jobs

AN HONEST COLLEGE REJECTION LETTER

except how much they hate people and that they shouldn't have majored in political science.

The reality is that we are no longer looking for students who are remarkable candidates for college; we are looking for people who have already made a difference, so that we can grow our list of impressive alumni. Your value to our college depends solely on your ability to attract future applicants. Since you are no Emma Watson or James Franco, we urge you to consider your acceptance letters from state universities and equally expensive second-tier schools, and commence nursing an inferiority complex for the rest of your life.

We sincerely hope that you find it in your heart to forgive us for not "seeing" your "full potential." Please remember that we will need your tiger-parent instincts in approximately three decades when you push your own children to the brink of death, and once again help us boost our *US News & World Report* ranking.

Best,
Dean of Admissions

LINES FROM *THE PRINCESS BRIDE* THAT DOUBLE AS COMMENTS ON FRESHMAN COMPOSITION PAPERS

by JENNIFER SIMONSON

"You keep using that word. I do not think it means what you think it means."

"At a time like this, that's all you can think to say?"

"Nonsense. You're only saying that because no one ever has."

"I don't think I'm quite familiar with that phrase."

"I would not say such things if I were you!"

"I do not suppose you could speed things up?"

"Skip to the end!"

"That is the sound of ultimate suffering."

"Inconceivable!"

LITERARY GENRE TRANSLATIONS

by CIROCCO DUNLAP

ORIGINAL TEXT

"I ate a sandwich and looked out the window."

- - -

SCI-FI

"I placed the allotted nutrition capsules on my tongue bed and looked to the Nahin VI-8373 space pod-hole."

FANTASY

"My dragon, Ralfarus, and I, Genflowfla'ii, choked down the hardened cheese curd and two-part-moons-old bread as we peered out of the meeting cavern."

NINETEENTH-CENTURY BRITISH ROMANCE

"Being but a governess with no prospects but a fierce wit and a quick temper which is out of mode, I nibbled a soda biscuit and looked off into the glade, awaiting my dear friend, Mr. Wadswortherton—whom I surely could not come to love."

YOUNG ADULT

"I gagged on rancid human food and instead drank the gushing blood of a rat as my night-kind are wont to do with our pointed tooth-bones. I gazed longingly out of my coffin into the human world where my true lovemate lived (how mortal!) and breathed (MORTALER YET!). The Lofty Council would never allow our soul union."

CHOOSE YOUR OWN ADVENTURE

"You eat a sandwich. You are then compelled to do something so you:

- LOOK OUT THE WINDOW AND REFLECT (Turn to page 65).

- WALK OUTSIDE INTO A DARK CAVE WITH PIRANHA SAND SNAKES (Turn to page 27).

- DRINK FROM A BOTTLE MARKED POISON AND TAKE A NAP (Turn to page 27).

EROTICA

"I nakedly slurped sauerkraut off my engorged bratwurst and looked through the peephole for the endowed plumber."

DRAMA

RICH: Thanks for the sandwich, Dad. Don't think it makes up for all the boozing and you walking out on me and Mom and Baby Boon and Old Lady Glipper and all the beatings with the belt and the stick and the rusty rake and the vacuum cleaner and the Swiffer and the hourglass and the brass pocket watch. *{Rich looks out the broken window.}*

BEAT

"i me you we he she ate a yum yum grubemups smorgasbording it's like breathing take a man out of fish you can fish we all are fish where's that fish the man looks at us like fish through his crystal window and we we we we we weeeeeeee (!) look back"

POETRY

There was nary a doubt,
For my sandwich I'd shout,
If it took its own route
Through the glass I looked out.

RUSSIAN CLASSIC

I, Shanvokovic, steadily finished my becoldened soup made by Gregori-noviczh as if the weight on my conscience weren't pressing deep down into my darkening soul. I looked out the architect's airhole into the bleak grey of the day—grey, indeed, as my morality—as I waited for the sweet nightshade to seep into my bloodstream and for Borsha to find my explanatory farewell tome.

MAGIC REALISM

I ate a sandwich and flew into the air vent.

THE COMMA
FROM WHICH MY
HEART HANGS

by BENJAMIN SAMUEL

1. If nothing else, one ought to know how to treat a comma. Abandonment or abuse of the comma muddles discourse, and this lack of respect is akin to neglect, to a lack of appreciation, to an unreasonable rejection of the very foundation of all worthy human interactions.

2. Even in its more seemingly prosaic applications, appearing to be little more than punctilio, the comma possesses great power. Consider, for the moment, the salutation of a written letter.

    Dear Benjamin,

    That graceful comma is more than ornamentation, more, too, than mere formality. The great missives of history have all begun in such a fashion. But in addition to its magnificent legacy in the history of letter writing, the comma gives us pause to build our anticipation or steel ourselves in preparation. It may tempt us, tickling the foot of that final letter, or it may attempt to hold us back, to warn us before we tumble and fall upon the following line. A comma used thus implies the letter was written with care, with a sensitivity towards its awaiting audience.

3. The comma suffuses language with nuance and delightfully detailed insights, and, by joining together sentences and subjects, it creates unity. For example:

> *I said give me another chance, and she said nothing, refused to look.*

or

> *You're the only one for me, and the only one I'll ever need.*

With the aid of the comma, statements are united, points of view are broadened, and the complexities of reality are more accurately rendered. Here, on the other hand, are examples of less elegant sentences:

> *You're just too difficult to love.*

or

> *I've met someone else.*

These sentences are direct, and yet their meaning is obscured. One must note, of course, the glaring absence of commas, the failure to elaborate, and the disregard for how complicated things might really be. Without commas, one rushes headlong into dangerous declarations and the verisimilitude of reality. Such bare sentences neglect language, neglect the possibilities yet available to us. There is more to say, another story waiting to emerge should one only insert a comma and offer it a chance to explain.

4. Commas, in coordination with a conjunction, are also essential when making comparisons and contradictions. For instance:

    "I'd call you cold-hearted, but you're clearly heartless,"
    Benjamin said.

    or

    "You might call yourself an academic, but you're the only
    one who cares what you think," she said.

5. The comma can also be deployed to separate, organize, and distinguish objects in a list. Consider the list below:

    You left behind your box set of Marlon Brando DVDs,
    ungraded papers, running shoes, and that preposterous Slap
    Chop you bought from the TV.

    Similarly, a comma is needed for the following series of actions:

    She had everything waiting on the kitchen counter (clearly

she hoped to dispatch me quickly), but with a wave of
my arm I knocked it all to the floor, then seized the Slap
Chop, held its spring-assisted blades against my chest,
and claimed I'd Slap Chop my heart to pieces if she hadn't
already left it minced.

6. In written dialogue, commas are part of the mechanics and struc-
    ture of speech.

    "Please," I said.

7. Commas are also necessary for the repetition of words, for when
    insistence and sentiments of great import are required:

    "Please," I said again. "Please, please, please don't do this."

8. It simply cannot be said too often that punctuation, not just the
    noble comma, is crucial to communication and comprehension.
    Truly, a poorly constructed sentence can set worlds crumbling, can
    alter perceptions irreparably. For example, consider how punctu-
    ation affects the following sentences:

    "I love Tom."

    versus

    "I love, Tom."

    In the latter sentence, the speaker does not mistakenly profess
    her love for Tom but simply, innocently declares her capacity to

experience love. The comma, then, is directing her statement to someone named "Tom," someone who might be waiting in the other room, someone who (impossibly) "just doesn't want things to get out of hand."

9. A note on apostrophes: while commas can both provide clarity and allow a sentence to build, to continue, perhaps, indefinitely, the apostrophe is most often used in a frivolous—but not always indolent—manner. Witness the following:

> *"What's so great about Tom?"*

> or

> *"Tom has a proper job with a proper salary, he doesn't waste time 'adjuncting' and claiming to be a scholar, doesn't spend his weekends reading the OED, doesn't judge people for wanting to see a new movie at a regular theater with normal people, and he doesn't correct my grammar in bed—it's dirty-talk you dumb fuck."*

Although the latter example has an arguably excessive use of commas, it does also illustrate the usefulness of an apostrophe in forming contractions—albeit perhaps a bit too much, and one gets the point quite quickly. However, there is another, rather more garish use of the apostrophe: that of possession.

> *"I want to hear you say it," she said. "So there'll be no equiv-ocations, no way that you can call me in the middle of the night claiming something or other about the signified versus*

the signifier. Repeat after me: 'Anne is Tom's girlfriend now.'"

When used in this manner, the apostrophe is clearly stomach-turning. My colleagues might argue that the apostrophe is a perfectly normal, even useful, if not vital punctuation mark. But I say that if language adapts with the times, then it is representative of society, and that if our need for awarding possession is so great as to warrant such a tawdry and sickening punctuation mark, then the apostrophe is indicative of precisely what is wrong with our society: our inability to communicate effectively, to build relationships, to share and support the goals of others—even when those goals mean working temporarily but yet quite hard in a less glamorous position as one pursues a more respectable appointment among his true colleagues.

10. *Dear Benjamin,*

I return you to this salutation. See how that comma hangs there? See how it embraces the end of the name? See how its usage does indeed suggest that care has been taken, thought given? This specific use of the comma, one that accompanies a carefully chosen salutation (in this case "Dear" meaning loved one, one who is close to the heart), should clearly be taken as a sign of glad-tidings, and also as a reason to pause, to take a breath of expectation before proceeding to the following line.

Please stop calling, or coming over.

The foregoing: a flagrantly misused comma that renders the sentence incomprehensible.

Stop evoking destiny, astrology and true love.

Here the absence of the endangered Oxford comma muddles meaning. It is unclear whether the speaker understands that these are separate ideals and concepts, not an elaboration or definition of destiny, suggesting perhaps that she is unaware of her own true destiny.

It's over, I'm through.

The egregious misuses of grammar here suggest the writer is either completely divorced from the reality language represents, or that the sentence is incomplete. It is certainly within the realm of possibility that the sentence above is missing a clause, and the visible, errant comma is a vestige of a now absent sentiment. In other words, perhaps the sentence originally looked something like this:

It's over, this tasteless behavior of mine as well as the cruel game I've been playing in which I pretend to no longer love you, I'm through.

There is hope in a comma.

I mean it, Benjamin. Don't contact me again.

Two utterly pathetic sentences, not one proper clause between them, nothing dependent, just me. Sentences that deploy commas correctly could be endless, like love, boundless, bringing one closer to an idea, or a person, so close and for so long that one could somehow begin to understand the infinite, could stretch on into perpetuity, onwards towards forever, which is itself a word that has lost meaning when so many, many, many times it is uttered alongside other now meaningless words like "love," as in, "I'll love you forever, and ever, and ever."

11. Just as commas accompany a salutation, they also follow valedictions at the end of a letter. Note the commas that attend the traditional and heartfelt valedictions that follow: "love," "yours," "faithfully," "forgive me." Note, too, the aberrant and brute concision of:

—Anne

RAYMOND CARVER'S OKCUPID PROFILE, EDITED BY GORDON LISH

by JIMMY CHEN

MY SELF-SUMMARY

I am a writer and poet, ~~one, bear with me here, of the "major" writers of the late twentieth century,~~ though just typing that felt desperate. ~~I received a B.A. in English at Humboldt State University, then went on to attend the esteemed Iowa Writers' Workshop, thus launching my career.~~ I also like to drink.

WHAT I'M DOING WITH MY LIFE

Working on some short stories but ~~honestly~~ not that into it, which may be why I'm ~~entertaining the prospect of~~ dating again.

I'M REALLY GOOD AT

~~I hate to kick a dead horse here, but~~ I'm really good at writing. I also make ~~a pretty neat~~ beef stew, since I ~~tend to~~ take six-hour naps. It just gets done. ~~My first collection of short stories *Will You Please Be Quiet, Please?* was shortlisted for the National Book Award and sort of revitalized the short fiction form. John Updike selected on of my stories for inclusion in *The Best American Short Stories of the Century*; Robert Altman made a sprawling film out of my stories; writing professors all across the country solemnly mention me as a kind of blue-collar American Camus; so, I'm not saying~~ I'm really good at writing, ~~just noting some examples of how others seem to feel this way.~~

THE FIRST THING PEOPLE USUALLY NOTICE ABOUT ME

I look the way a depressed person looks, if one were not trying to look that way.

FAVORITE BOOKS, MOVIES, SHOWS, MUSIC, AND FOOD

~~*The Trial*; *The Sun Also Rises*; *For Whom the Bell Tolls*; *The Stranger*;~~ *Dear Mr. Capote*; *Kramer vs. Kramer*; *Terms of Endearment*; *Taxi Driver*; *Annie Hall*; ~~*Love Connection*; *Empty Nest*; *Mr. Belvedere*; *My Two Dads*;~~ Miles Davis; Charles Mingus; Bill Evans; pasta ~~all kinds.~~

THE SIX THINGS I COULD NEVER DO WITHOUT

Hendrick's gin; tonic; lime; ice cubes; a tumbler; my typewriter.

I SPEND A LOT OF TIME THINKING ABOUT

~~The triangular yet cyclical relationship between the author, the character of a story, and the reader; how empathy may just be narcissism projected onto others; how nostalgia is desperate memory; the hair-thin line between cliché and truth; showing vs. telling; my kidneys, liver, and spleen; realism, location, and class; linguistic economy; how to say something by not saying it; codependence, alcoholism, and intimacy; rent; whether or not something is a run-on sentence and does it matter.~~

ON A TYPICAL FRIDAY NIGHT I AM

I enjoy turning off all the lights in the house a few hours after dusk, walking over to the window, a drink in hand, and just looking out ~~at the vessels of leafless branches bruised into purple gloom, as if beaten by day.~~ I see a man walking his dog, ~~the diagonal leash sloped downward towards its neck like some slanted guillotine; I see this and think what is wrong with me? As you can tell, I need to be dating again. The bottom of my glass portrays multiple ever receding foci, all working in collusion together as the room fucking spins. The once-frozen lobster ravioli is now paste in my boiling pot, as~~ I've forgotten about dinner.

THE MOST PRIVATE THING I AM WILLING TO ADMIT

I've been cruel to others for material.

I'M LOOKING FOR

~~Just something, or rather someone, to get me away from this writing desk. A jovial date; a flash of tits; some female chatter. We could ride~~

a roller coaster, have way too many corn dogs, and I would hope to die of a heart attack. Anything.

YOU SHOULD MESSAGE ME IF

~~You should message me if you'd like to~~ take a chance on a morbidly depressed yet emotionally available writer near the end of his ~~note-worthy, and in some circles, brilliant~~ career ~~who just wants to tap into this supposed carnal hedonism of art and literature, which I will admit is a heavy-handed euphemism for copulation, which despite all subtleties herein I must now betray and just say will you please be quick~~, please?

A POST-GENDER-NORMATIVE MAN TRIES TO PICK UP A WOMAN AT A BAR

by JESSE EISENBERG

Hey, how's it going? Mind if I sidle up? I saw you over here sitting alone and I thought, that's fine. A woman should be able to self-sustain. In fact, a lot of women are choosing to stay alone, what with advances in salary equitability and maternity extensions, and I think it's an important and compelling trend.

I noticed that you were about to finish your drink and I was wondering if I could possibly watch you purchase another one. And, at the risk of being forward, if you could possibly purchase one for me.

What do you do? And before you answer, I'm not looking for a necessarily work-related response. I don't think we have to be defined by our industrial pursuits, especially when they're antiquated and hetero-normative. I curse my mother, who is an otherwise lovely human person, for not buying me an Easy-Bake Oven when I was younger. I grew up idolizing male thugs like Neil Armstrong and

Jimmy Carter. And, yes, I work at ESPN, but I spend more time being spiritual and overcoming adversity, for example, than I do working for some faceless corporation. And if I were to find a mate, be it you or someone else here tonight, I would be more than happy to tell the proverbial "man" that I quit so I can raise our offspring with gender-neutral hobbies, while my biologically female partner continues to pursue her interests, be they industrial, recreational or yes, even sexual with another mate.

So…

Crazy news about the first female African head of state and Liberia's sitting president, Ellen Johnson-Sirleaf, huh? Announcing her candidacy for 2011 so soon! Wow. What do you think of her chances? I think she's a shoo-in, but I'm admittedly a bit concerned about Prince Johnson making some last minute strides, especially amongst the Gio people in the Nimba region. I'm thinking of launching a letter-writing campaign on behalf of EJ-S or at least cold calling potential Nimba voters over Skype.

Oh, how gauche of me! I've just been chattering away incessantly like some kind of boy or girl who talks a lot. I haven't even properly introduced myself. Although, one often gets the uneasy sense that patriarchy dictates a learned and ultimately damaging order of events with men taking an unearned lead. My name is Terri, with a heart over the *i*, instead of a dot. I have a heart, is what that says, and I'm not afraid to wear it on my sleeve.

So what do you think? Would you like to take me up on my offer for you to buy me that drink?

If you would like to respond, that would be wonderful. Of course, if you would like to continue to sit here silently, staring at me with that powerful gaze, which both breaks gender constructs and also scares me a bit, that would be fine as well.

What's that? I should go fuck myself? I agree! Men should be more self-generative! Thank you for your astute assertion. Why should women exclusively have to bear the burden of childbirth, when men are biologically doomed to fear commitment? It's counter-intuitive and socially degrading.

Ahh, that beer is refreshing! Thank you for throwing it in my face on this warm summer evening.

Okay, okay! I'm leaving!

Thank you for your blunt rejection of me. It takes a lot of courage, which you no doubt have in equal measure to any other human. Now, if you'll excuse, I'm going to the bathroom where I'll cry silently in a stall, questioning my body and texting my mom, but for now, I thank you for your time, which was equal to mine.

IN WHICH I FIX MY GIRLFRIEND'S GRANDPARENTS' WI-FI AND AM HAILED AS A CONQUERING HERO

by MIKE LACHER

Lo, in the twilight days of the second year of the second decade of the third millennium did a great darkness descend over the wireless internet connectivity of the people of 276 Ferndale Street in the North-Central lands of Iowa. For many years, the gentlefolk of these lands basked in a wireless network overflowing with speed and ample internet, flowing like a river into their Compaq Presario. Many happy days did the people spend checking Hotmail and reading USAToday.com.

But then one gray morning did Internet Explorer 6 no longer load The Google. Refresh was clicked, again and again, but still did Internet Explorer 6 not load The Google. Perhaps The Google was broken, the people thought, but then The Yahoo too did not load. Nor did Hotmail. Nor USAToday.com. The land was thrown into panic. Internet Explorer 6 was minimized then maximized. The

Compaq Presario was unplugged then plugged back in. The old mouse was brought out and plugged in beside the new mouse. Still, The Google did not load.

Some in the kingdom thought the cause of the darkness must be the Router. Little was known of the Router, legend told it had been installed behind the recliner long ago by a shadowy organization known as Comcast. Others in the kingdom believed it was brought by a distant cousin many feasts ago. Concluding the trouble must lie deep within the microchips, the people of 276 Ferndale Street did despair and resign themselves to defeat.

But with the dawn of the feast of Christmas did a beacon of hope manifest itself upon the inky horizon. Riding in upon a teal Ford Focus came a great warrior, a suitor of the gentlefolks' granddaughter. Word had spread through the kingdom that this warrior worked with computers and perhaps even knew the true nature of the Router.

The people did beseech the warrior to aid them. They were a simple people, capable only of rewarding him with gratitude and a larger-than-normal serving of Jell-O salad. The warrior considered the possible battles before him. While others may have shirked the duties, forcing the good people of Ferndale Street to prostrate themselves before the tyrants of Comcast, Linksys, and Geek Squad, the warrior could not chill his heart to these depths. He accepted the quest and strode bravely across the beige shag carpet of the living room.

Deep, deep behind the recliner did the warrior crawl, over great mountains of *National Geographic* magazines and deep chasms of *TV Guide*s. At last, he reached a gnarled thicket of cords, a terrifying knot of gray and white and black and blue threatening to ensnare all who ventured further. The warrior charged ahead. Weaker men would have lost their minds in the madness: telephone cords plugged into Ethernet jacks, AC adapters plugged into phone jacks, a lone VGA cable wrapped in a firm knot around an Ethernet cord. But the warrior bested the thicket, ripping away the vestigial cords and swiftly untangling the deadly trap.

And at last the warrior arrived at the Router. It was a dusty black box with an array of shimmering green lights, blinking on and off, as if to taunt him to come any further. The warrior swiftly maneuvered to the rear of the router and verified what he had feared, what he had heard whispered in his ear from spirits beyond: all the cords were securely in place.

The warrior closed his eyes, summoning the power of his ancestors, long departed but watchful still. And then with the echoing beep of his digital watch, he moved with deadly speed, wrapping his battle-hardened hands around the power cord at the back of the Router.

Gripping it tightly, he pulled with all his force, dislodging the cord from the Router. The heavens roared. The earth wailed. The green lights turned off. Silently the warrior counted. One. Two. Three. And just as swiftly, the warrior plugged the cord back into the router. Great crashes of blood-red lightning boomed overhead. Murders of crows blackened the skies. The Power light came on solid green. The seas rolled. The WLAN light blinked on. The forests ignited. A dark fog rolled over the land and suddenly all was silent. The warrior stared at the internet light, waiting, waiting. And then, as the world around him seemed all but dead, the internet light began to blink.

The warrior darted out back over the mountains of *National Geographic* magazines and made haste to the Compaq Presario. He woke up Windows XP from sleep mode and deftly defeated twelve notifications to update Norton AntiVirus. With a resounding click he opened Internet Explorer 6 and gazed deep into its depths, past The Yahoo toolbar, the MSN toolbar, the Ask.com toolbar, and The AOL toolbar. And then did he see, at long last, that The Google did load.

And so the good people of the kingdom were delighted and did heap laurels and Jell-O salad at the warrior's feet, for now again they could have their Hotmail as the wireless internet did flow freely to their Compaq Presario. The warrior ate his Jell-O salad, thanked the gentlefolk, and then went to the basement because the TiVo was doing something weird with the VCR.

I WANT TO MAKE LOVE TO YOU LIKE IN THE MOVIES

by JOSH GONDELMAN

Girl, I'm tired of playing around. I'm ready for that real-deal romance. Flowers and butterflies and fireworks. Baby, I want to make love to you like in the movies.

That's right, girl. I want to serve you that good-ass Billy Crystal dick. That sweet, tender lovin' that'll make you feel like Meg Ryan from 1989 or 1995, depending on which era of Meg Ryan you relate to more. I want to tear that *up* after a long and dramatic courtship where I slowly gain your trust, but lose it at the worst possible moment by revealing our relationship was part of a bet or that I have destroyed your small independent business. Then I'll earn your confidence back with a grand, breathtaking gesture that was foreshadowed months earlier. I want to knock boots with you the way you do after holding a boom box outside someone's window in the rain.

I want to take you home to my apartment. Though my living space is unfeasibly large and furnished well beyond my means with Crate & Barrel accouterments, you'll find it unacceptably messy because *men, right?* Once we get inside, I'm going to tear your clothes off. But, I'll leave the bra on. Women always talk about how they hate wearing bras. How they squeeze and shape and constrict them. But in the movies they always wear them during sex, which seems silly, because lots of great sex things can happen once you remove your bra. I'll take my shirt off, revealing a body which is either *way* too good considering what I do for work, or one that's comically dumpy. I'll leave my pants on. That's how it works in the movies. Girls keep their bras on. Guys leave their pants on. My dick ain't afraid of no zippers.

I want to go at it under the sheets no matter how hot it is. Our feet will extend past the end of the bed, even though you get no leverage that way. We will not notice any unexpected moles or embarrassing tattoos. Everything that happens will be sexy. There won't be any gross sounds or sights. Just like in the movies, our sex will be tasteless and odorless. I will not kiss your neck and get a mouthful of perfume and then you're like what's wrong and I'll be like nothing and you'll get all distant and I'll be like sorry it's the taste of your perfume, and you'll be sad because you only wore it because I said I liked it one time and then all of a sudden you're not in the mood and I think about sneaking off to the bathroom to furtively masturbate but I don't and I just hold you limply until you fall asleep then I check Twitter for like an hour. That doesn't happen.

I'll lay out rose petals across the bed, and they won't get in our butts, though it seems some of them logically would. I'll rub an ice cube all over you, and you won't burst out giggling, causing me to grow self-conscious and lose my erection. I'll drip wax on you, which will be erotic and not at all like the other times you've burnt yourself on something hot, which have not been erotic at all. We'll eat dessert off of each other's nude bodies like that's not the grossest thing two people could do to their sheets and skin. "Can't we just have those strawberries later? I'm going to get all sticky," is something you won't say, in this paradise of physical pleasure.

Then, when we can bear to wait no longer, I will fuck your brains out, which I can only say once because to utter that word again would jeopardize our PG-13 rating. We will make love in every way imaginable, assuming you only know two or three ways and don't expect oral sex. One moment, you're on top of me, gyrating, still wearing that bra. The next, I'm churning rhythmically from above you, my weight perfectly distributed. An instant later, still under a comforter for some reason, I have assumed the "big spoon" position, magically generating torque for each thrust.

We will reorient our bodies effortlessly through jump cuts and other filmic transitions. Your legs will not cramp. My chest hair will not become a sweaty carpet. After less than a minute of athletic, montage sex, you will have a loud, performative orgasm. Or I will have an orgasm before you and feel humiliated and promise to do better next time. Cut to that point, where I'm able to give it another go right away without sacrificing any amount of boner integrity. At the end of our lovemaking we will smoke in bed, like no one I know ever does in New York because of security deposits and lung cancer.

The sex will change the dynamic of our previous relationship drastically and irreversibly. It may bring us together forever. It may drive us tragically apart. That is what sex does. I have seen the movies.

If you suspect you've become pregnant, you will consider keeping the baby, even though you're not religious and we live in a relatively pro-choice state and you had no intention of becoming a mother and I am for sure not ready to be a father. This anxiety will become the crux of our future dealings. You'll decide to keep the baby. We'll stay together, even though we've only been on three dates. One night, while I'm out with friends, contractions will begin, earlier than expected. An ambulance will rush you to the hospital. By the time I arrive, you will have miscarried, just like in the movie *Up*. Though we never discuss it, that night will permeate our relationship forever.

We remain married for sixty years. Childless. You'll die in your sleep at age eighty-eight. I'll pass away the following week, from grief.

That's how I want to make love to you.

I REGRET TO INFORM YOU THAT MY WEDDING TO CAPTAIN VON TRAPP HAS BEEN CANCELED

by MELINDA TAUB

Dear friends, family, and Austrian nobility,

Captain Von Trapp and I are very sorry to inform you that we no longer plan to wed. We offer our deepest apologies to those of you who have already made plans to travel to Salzburg this summer.

Those of you on the Captain's side of the guest list are probably aware of the reason for the change of plans. I'm sure by now you have received that charming "Save the date!" card in the shape of a mountain goat from the Captain and his new fiancée, Maria.

I must confess to being rather blindsided by the end of our relationship. It seems Captain Von Trapp and I misunderstood each other. I assumed he was looking for a wife of taste and sophistication, who was a dead ringer for Tippi Hedren; instead he wanted to marry a curtain-wearing religious fanatic who shouts every word she says.

But I don't want you to be angry at him. We are all adults here. "But

Baroness," so many of my friends have said, "you must be devastated. You yourself are fabulously wealthy, so you cannot have wanted the Captain for his money—you must have truly loved him." It's true. But so, I am sure, does his new fiancée, his children's nanny. Her wardrobe is made of curtains. She's definitely not a gold digger or anything.

I'm sorry. That was crude of me. She seems like a lovely person, and she and the children have a great deal in common.

A great, great, great deal.

Since I will no longer be a part of their lives, I do hope you will all keep an eye on the Captain's children. I am not terribly maternal but I was very fond of them in my own way and I must admit I am worried what will become of them now that I have gone. I had planned to send them to boarding school, since their education at the moment seems to consist mostly of marching around Salzburg singing scales. I think it would have been particularly helpful for the eldest daughter, who seems intent on losing her virginity to the mailman.

Please, friends, don't worry about me. While I was a bit startled to be thrown aside for someone who flunked out of nun school, I assure you that I will be fine, and my main pursuits in life shall continue to be martinis, bon mots, and looking fabulous. You'll also be glad to know I have retained custody of the Captain's hard-drinking gay friend, Max. Anyone who gets tired of sing-a-longs should feel free to look us up.

Again, my deepest apologies for this disruption to your plans. I am currently sorting through the wedding gifts we've already received and I will send them back as soon as possible. The Captain would help, but he is busy learning to play a song about cuckoo clocks on his guitar.

Sincerely,
Baroness Elsa Schraeder

TOTO'S "AFRICA," BY ERNEST HEMINGWAY

BY ANTHONY SAMS

At the airport the young man heard far-off drums echoing in the night. He imagined the young woman in the plane sitting still, hearing whispers of a quiet conversation near the rear of the fuselage. He glanced down at his father's wristwatch—12:30. The flight was on time.

The plane's wings were moonlit and reflected the stars. The moonlight had guided him there, toward this salvation. He had stopped an older man along the way, hoping to find some long forgotten words, or perhaps an ancient melody, for such an occasion. The old man had said nothing at first, and instead stared cryptically into the sodden earth. Then he raised his head and turned slowly.

"Hurry, boy. It's waiting there for you," the old man had said.

The plane was almost gliding. The young man looked at the wristwatch again. His head spun from whiskey and soda. She was a damned nice woman. It would take a lot to drag him away from her. It was unlikely that a hundred men or more could ever do such a thing. The air, now thick and moist, seemed to carry rain again. He blessed the rains of Africa. They were the only thing left to bless in this forsaken place, he thought—at least until she set foot on the continent. They were going to take some time to do the things they never had.

He stood on the tarmac and watched as the plane came in for its landing. He heard the sound of wild dogs crying out into the night. The man thought the dogs sounded desperate, perhaps having grown restless and longing for some company. He knew the feeling. The crying of the dogs reminded him that he would need to do what he knew was right now that she was here. Of this he was as certain as Kilimanjaro rising like Olympus above the Serengeti. He had traveled and sought to cure what was deep inside him, what frightened him of himself.

The plane landed and stopped. He hurried. She would be waiting there for him.

---

* Read an interview with Anthony Sams about this piece on page 644.

WHAT YOUR FAVORITE CLASSIC ROCK BAND SAYS ABOUT YOU

by JOHN PECK

The Doors: You have been bitten by an animal while trying to get it stoned.

The Who: You own a Goldwing with a baby-changing station.

Ted Nugent: Your hair has at some point been caught in a ceiling fan, boat propeller, or lathe.

The Rolling Stones: You own three cars and no stereo.

Canned Heat: You own three stereos and no car.

The Beatles: You can do exactly 1.5 pull-ups.

Badfinger: You are a Beatle.

Deep Purple: Some part of a law named after a young girl applies to you.

Led Zeppelin: The first three things you smoked were banana peels, catnip, and poppies, in that order.

Jimi Hendrix: You are under twenty or over sixty-five.

The Kinks: You have bad teeth and are good in bed.

The Guess Who: You have good teeth and are bad in bed.

Black Sabbath: Your greatest joy is painting in unventilated rooms.

David Bowie: There is still, somewhere, a *Dig Dug* or *Zaxxon* machine with your high score on it.

Mott the Hoople: You are David Bowie.

The Moody Blues: You are a former volunteer at the Liberace museum, a serial killer, or both.

The Grateful Dead: Your stories about the seventies make your daughter's roommates at Tufts very uncomfortable.

T-Rex: No matter how much you clean, there will always be trace amounts of glitter on your stove and blender.

The Eagles: You can only reach orgasm while listening to talk radio.

Pink Floyd: Your garage is full of failed versions of your stereo/barbecue hybrid.

Thin Lizzy: You are often forced to change or cancel your plans due to NO LOITERING signs.

ZZ Top: Your favorite Hank Williams is Hank Williams, Jr.

Chicago: You are incapable of talking about Chicago without mentioning their horn section.

Quicksilver Messenger Service: You become sullen when people don't stick around while you fix their vacuum cleaners.

Crosby, Stills & Nash: You own an oversized hat.

Crosby, Stills, Nash & Young: You own three or more oversized hats.

Jefferson Airplane: You make your living buying and selling oversized hats.

AC/DC: You only remove your socks to shower, and then only reluctantly.

Aerosmith: You know a store that still sells puffy Reeboks.

Van Halen: You have a Peeing Calvin bumper sticker on your Jeep.

Sammy Hagar: You have a Peeing Calvin bumper sticker on your Subaru Brat.

Bachman-Turner Overdrive: You have an actual urine stain on your Subaru Brat.

Uriah Heep: You are the cause of the urine stain.

Santana: You have had an hours-long conversation with someone before realizing it was just a pile of clothes.

Rainbow: You have worn sweatpants to a funeral.

Foreigner: You have a severely wrinkled Jane Fonda poster under your bed.

Styx: You have a severely wrinkled Foreigner poster under your bed.

Allman Brothers Band: You do not own a bong, but can quickly make one from a piece of fruit or an abandoned toilet.

Bad Company: You have sustained several alcohol-related injuries involving sheetrock.

Cream: You know a guy who knows a guy who worked on *Star Wars*.

Journey: You own those running shoes that are shaped like feet.

Lynyrd Skynyrd: You somehow have both long hair and a sunburned scalp.

Yes: Your ideal partner would be into both tantric sex and fat guys.

Creedence Clearwater Revival: You are frequently missing part of an eyebrow.

Rush: You carry a small flashlight everywhere, and use it at least three times a day.

Blue Cheer: You have a subset of friends whose sole purpose is to hold your hair while you vomit.

Boston: Your best friend really likes Blue Cheer.

Steely Dan: You have snorted cocaine off a copy of *Remembrance of Things Past*.

Fleetwood Mac: You have snorted cocaine off a copy of *The Hobbit*.

Blue Oyster Cult: You have snorted cocaine off a copy of *Type 2 Diabetes for Dummies*.

Mountain: You have snorted cocaine off a Blue Oyster Cult record.

Nazareth: You have snorted cocaine off a member of Mountain.

Hawkwind: You sell cocaine to Nazareth fans.

Molly Hatchet: You sell baking soda to Hawkwind fans and tell them it's cocaine.

Jethro Tull: You have a favorite rune.

GLENGARRY BOB ROSS

by ZACK WORTMAN

Okay, I'm just gonna use that same old brush, its working so well. Gonna tap that corner into a little bit of yellow ochre. Just tap the corner, I want very little paint.

What am I painting? Fuck you, that's what I'm painting. You know why, mister? You drive to the store to get your paint supplies in a Hyundai, I drive an $80,000 BMW. That's what I'm painting.

Painting is a man's game. You can't play the game, you can't paint, go home and tell your wife your troubles. Because only one thing counts in life: painting pretty trees. You know me, I always gotta put in a big, happy tree. You hear me, you fucking cocksuckers?

A-B-P. Always be painting. ALWAYS BE PAINTING. G-P-M-B. G, Get a clean paintbrush. P, Put some paint on that brush, M, Make some cute little clouds above some footy hills. B, Be sure to thoroughly clean your paint station afterwards. G, P, M, B!

You see this painting? This painting costs more than your car. You see pal, that's why I'm who I am, and you're nothing. You're a nice guy? I don't give a shit. Good at sketching? Then turn your TV off and go sketch. This is *The Joy of Painting*, not *Needledicks That Love Sketching*.

You want to watch my show? Paint. Paint right now and do not stop until I have told you do so.

People tell me that my demeanor is "off-putting" and "alienating," that I'm "abusive" and "scare away viewers." You think this is abuse? You think this is abuse, you cocksuckers?

You can't take this, how are you gonna take the art critics? They're wolves, vicious. "Bob Ross lacks technical sophistication." "Bob Ross is basically just a landscape painter, and a mediocre one at that." And that's what they say about *me*. Bob *fucking* Ross.

I can go out there with the materials you got. An easel from Michael's. Some boutique paint from Etsy. I can go with that and make $15,000 tonight. In two hours. Can you? Can YOU? Go and do likewise. G-P-M-B.

Get mad, you sons of bitches. Get mad. You know what it takes to paint cozy log cabins that speak the softest parts of the human soul? It takes BRASS BALLS.

I like drinking a nice cup of hot coffee while I paint. You want coffee? Too bad. Coffee is for painters, not nothings like you. Put that coffee down, you think I'm fucking with you? I'm just kidding, you can have a cup too. It'll be our little secret.

I'M SORRY I BIT YOU DURING MY JOB INTERVIEW

by TOM O'DONNELL

Dear Robert,

Thank you for taking the time to interview me for the junior analyst position at Rawles and Hilt. It was great to meet with you and learn more about the company. Please don't hesitate to call or email if you have any more questions for me.

Also, I just wanted to say I'm sorry I bit you during the interview.

Obviously, there is no excuse for biting anyone. But I feel the need to explain what I was thinking at the time in the hope that it might mitigate my disappointing conduct.

The interview was going fine until you threw me a curveball. "Could you talk about your previous work experience?" you asked. I panicked. It's clear to me now that I should have just answered honestly ("No, I can't.") But instead I shrieked and bit you hard on the collarbone. The instant after I'd done it, I knew I'd messed up. It's a testament to your professionalism that you were even willing to continue our interview after such a regrettable lack of judgment on my part.

The second time I bit you, I think I was just hungry. Full disclosure: I hadn't had any breakfast that morning (Okay. Full, full disclosure: I'd had a small breakfast.) When your fingers passed near my mouth, they actually did that cartoon desert-island thing where they seemed to morph into sausages. I think I was still hungry for sausages after the sausages I had eaten right before the interview, so I bit you again. If I'd only stopped and taken a moment to assess the situation, I would have remembered: sausages don't grow out of human hands. But unfortunately, I didn't. The sad irony is that my briefcase was full of leftover sausages from breakfast. That's why my résumé was so greasy.

The third time I bit you, it was supposed to be a joke. In retrospect, I'm not sure it came off that way. I was trying to break the tension created by me biting you and you being all weird about it. It was meant to be playful, like, "Ha ha. I'm biting you again, because I guess I'm 'The Biting Guy' now." But after sinking my teeth into the tender flesh of your calf muscle and holding on for thirty seconds, it started to seem like you weren't getting it. It's obvious to me now that I was misinterpreting your screams of pain as screams of pained laughter.

The fourth time I bit you was honestly your fault. If someone who has already bitten you several times is standing on your desk, completely naked and snarling, don't make any sudden movements! That's practically a recipe for getting bitten. If this situation ever arises again, play dead. Lie on the ground in a fetal position. Curl your face toward your knees and make sure to protect your vulnerable neck area. This will tend to reduce the level of injury sustained in the event of an attack. Once I've realized you are not a threat, I will generally show no further interest.

Frankly I think this all goes back to my childhood, when I would constantly bite people for no reason. I also did this as a teenager and an adult.

Regardless, I am extremely sorry for biting you. I hope you can look past this (not to mention my lack of experience with Excel macros) when making a final hiring decision. After all, who hasn't freaked out and bitten someone during a job interview at some point in their life?

Sincerely,
Mike Edling

P.S. Please apologize to everyone I bit on my way out of your office.

WENDY MOLYNEUX'S EXCERPTS FROM POPULAR McSWEENEY'S INTERNET TENDENCY LISTS THROUGHOUT HISTORY: 1774

LIST

IF EVERYONE ATTENDING THE FIRST CONTINENTAL CONGRESS WAS MADE OF HAM

by TIMOTHEE SANDWICH

7. Ham-uel Adams

8. Benjhamin Hammison

9. George Washing-ham

I JUST FOUND OUT ABC FAMILY IS GOING TO PASS ON MY PITCH

by DAN KENNEDY

It's called *Crashed Cars* and it's about a family of vagrant addicts who live in a junkyard; they shoplift food and drugs; they commit arson to achieve arousal sexually. The only way the male lead can—I don't know how to say this delicately in our meeting here; "make love," I guess will have to suffice—the only way he can make love is if someone holds a loaded gun to his head and keeps telling him they're going to kill him any second. This isn't an abusive thing, this is what he asks lovers to do for him, or asks someone watching him and a lover to do for him. Actually, I should back up a minute and clarify that they're not, obviously, a biological family. They're a family in the road-worn petty thief sense of the word; so, basically, a tight-knit covey of small time degenerates; that's all I mean by family. Like the way Charles Manson and those people were a family. Jesus, I've said the word "family" five times or something; it sounds like I'm really tailoring my pitch to you. It's just that when I started talking about them lighting stuff on fire and holding loaded guns to each other's heads in order to become aroused it occurred to me that I should clarify what I meant by "family." Okay, so moving on... They sleep in a junkyard, like I was saying. They sleep in the cars waiting to be smashed and stacked, so if they were to oversleep, they would be smashed alive on the backseat of whatever junkyard car they dozed off in dreaming of a better life. Those are your stakes, at the beginning of the pilot episode, and those stakes continue through the whole series; we establish this as daily stakes in this life they're living. So, real simple, if one of the shoplifting sexual deviants sleeps on the blood-encrusted back seat of a crashed Monte Carlo that's waiting to get flattened and stacked into the scrap heap, that's where they're crushed to death. So, even though they're a filthy family of miscreant junkies with sex problems, they wake up early and on time, every day, period. Very punctual people, and you wouldn't think it to look at them. Then the unthinkable happens to the female lead in the very first episode: she oversleeps; she is smashed alive. Yep, third act of the pilot, after we've written every trick in the book to get viewers to fall in love with her and after we've clearly invested the whole episode in setting her up as the series' protagonist, she's crushed like a filthy bug in the back of a shitty old limo, sleeping on a rum-stained velour back seat that smells like two decades of middle management cologne and menthol cigarettes; killed, dead, just flattened. So the viewer assumes that the male lead must, in fact, be our protagonist that's going to lead us through the series. Well, we cut to our male lead in a broken down studio apartment having sex with another junkie while a third party, a girl, holds a loaded gun to his head as he makes love. She repeatedly screams that she's going to kill him and suddenly—BLAM! Holy Christ above, the gun was loaded, he's dead. She's shocked, she's covered in blood, how the hell did this go wrong, this was just a sexy game, why the hell was the gun loaded? She's high of course, and wracked with guilt, and she turns the gun on herself—BLAM! Dead. All of this makes the junkie on the bed—the woman our male lead was having intimate relations and intercourse with, and now the only person in the threesome left alive—unexpectedly have an orgasm. Fade to black. End of story. Then we dissolve up on a new scene—a button on the end of the third act of our pilot. We're outside a strip mall massage parlor next to an interstate where both our female lead, our male lead, and the girl we saw turn the gun on herself are talking with the rest of the secondary characters about shaking the massage parlor down; they're jabbering on like a gaggle of filthy gypsies, yammering about working some short con on the johns inside the place. They're smoking, making plans to grift some cash, talking about getting back to the junk yard and into their sleeping cars before the pit bulls are let out to prowl the yard. And you're saying: "Wait, huh? What? I thought those three characters were dead." Okay, get ready for a kick to the head here: these the characters die in every single episode of every single season. Yep, this is the afterlife, folks; this is purgatory; and if you think life is a bitch, just wait till you get to the afterlife. That might be your tagline for the poster, by the way; it just kind of came to me, but that is, in fact, the central message of my show. Anyway, yeah, they're road ghosts. Wait, you know what, new title: *Road Ghosts*. Or it could even be: *ABC Family Presents Road Ghosts*. So, yeah, they're all dead and have been from the second we met them. Back in their earthly days, two of them were young lovers who overdosed in a motel in Michigan. One of them was an upper-middle-class accidental suburban suicide mixing dry saunas with masturbation, wine, and Valium. And one of them had a heart attack in a fast food place, leaving behind a mortal trail of beneficiary relatives, who are all winners now in our litigious nation's lottery of lawsuits against the cash-rich corporations that are killing us all for profit. That's why he does so much heroin in the afterlife—because he can see how wealthy he accidentally made his middle class relatives by dying.

[Long pause. Silence, and then some mumbo jumbo about family comedies and calling me if they're interested in seeing a pilot script.]

THIS IS A GENERIC BRAND VIDEO

by KENDRA EASH

We think first
of vague words that are synonyms for progress
and pair them with footage of a high-speed train.

Science
is doing lots of stuff
that may or may not have anything to do with us.

See how this guy in a lab coat holds up a beaker?
That means we do research.
Here's a picture of DNA.

There are a shitload of people in the world.
Especially in India.

See how we're part of the global economy?
Look at these farmers in China.

But we also do business in the USA,
or want you to think we do.
Check out this wind energy thing in Indiana,
and this blue collar guy with dirt on his face.
Phew.

Also, we care about the environment, loosely.
Here's some powerful, rushing water
and people planting trees.
Our policies could be related to these panoramic views of Costa Rica.

In today's high speed environment,
stop-motion footage of a city at night
with cars turning quickly
makes you think about doing things efficiently
and time passing.

Lest you think we're a faceless entity,
look at all these attractive people.
Here's some of them talking and laughing
and close-ups of hands passing canned goods to each other
in a setting that evokes community service.

Equality,
Innovation,
Honesty

and advancement
are all words we chose from a list.

Our profits
are awe-inspiring.
Like this guy who's looking up and pointing
at a skyscraper or a kite
while smiling and explaining something to his child.

Using a specific ratio
of Asian people to black people to women to white men,
we want to make sure we represent your needs and interests
or at least a version of your skin color
in our ads.

Did we put a baby in here?
What about an ethnic old man whose wrinkled smile represents
the happiness and wisdom of the poor?
Yep.

JAMIE AND JEFF'S
BIRTH PLAN

by PAUL WILLIAM DAVIES

Dear Hospital Staff:

Thank you and congratulations for being on shift for the birth of our child. The following sets forth our wishes for our stay. If a medical emergency requires you to deviate from this plan, please refer to "Jamie and Jeff's Emergency Birth Plan." (Tab J) Please note: Jamie is RH-Negative and BPA-free.

PHILOSOPHY

While we do not have a traditional "philosophy" of "childbirth," we have been heavily influenced by orthodox Whole-Foodism and the "(d) well baby/good design" movement. We believe strongly in the power of the female body and a long-term night nurse. We are opposed to torture/gluten. In the event you are ever unsure how to proceed today, please ask yourself, "What Would Gwyneth Do?"

ENVIRONMENT

We would like mood lighting, like on Virgin America.

The following people, who were with us at conception, will again be in the room with us today: Jeff's mom; Jeff's sister; Jeff's sister's friend, Melanie (plus 2); Jeff Koons.

Please provide Wi-Fi so we can check what you say against Wikipedia and our favorite mom blogs.

Music is very important to us, as music was playing in the Mongolian yurt when we first made love.

In lieu of a traditional hospital gown, Jamie would prefer to be dressed like Zooey Deschanel in *500 Days of Summer*.

Please avoid any use of the words "pulsate," "soiled," or "octo" in the delivery room.

PREP

Jamie would prefer no enema or shaving of pubic hair. If shaving is necessary, she would prefer something in the shape of a vuvuzela. Jeff's pubic hair should NOT be shaved.

Jeff would like an I.V.

LABOR

Please generally avoid procedures that are totally unnecessary or excruciatingly painful.

Jamie would like Jeff to do the pushing whenever possible.

We have chosen a Doctor ("Mr. Cooper") because he shares our desire for a natural, low-intervention birth. Mr. Cooper will deliver the baby via Skype from his home in Taos.

If Jamie starts to sob uncontrollably during labor, please turn off *The Notebook*. In the event the crying continues, please administer the following drugs to Jeff (per Mr. Cooper): Darvocet, Diamorphine, Vicodin, medical marijuana.

If induction is necessary, Jamie would like to try the following before Pitocin is administered: walking, stretching, flipping over, Rolfing, online browsing, nipple stimulation, and/or sexual intercourse.

Nipple stimulation should be done by the resident Jamie met on the tour who looks like Benjamin Bratt.

DELIVERY

We strongly prefer a girl.

If you have not already done so, please now take a few minutes and read *Early Admission: How to Deliver an Ivy League Baby!*

Jeff will remain in the squatting position throughout delivery.

When the crown of the head appears, please turn down the music as Jeff will be reading aloud from *Be Here Now* by Ram Dass.

Please, no texting while suctioning.

Jamie would like a mirror so that she can see the horrible expression on her face if it's a boy.

IMPORTANT: If the baby appears to be black, please immediately escort Jeff out of the room and bring in Jeremy Rayburn from the fifth floor waiting area.

In the event of a Cesarean, please practice Western medicine.

POST-BIRTH

We are interested in the following preschools: St. James, the Schoolhouse at Cedar Point, or Kidsplace. Willow Glen is ONLY a backup.

Jamie would like Jeff circumcised.

Please do not cut the cord until we are through the toddler years.

We would like the baby certified organic by Oregon Tilth.

Please don't put the baby on a scale, as we don't want her to have the same body image issues as her fat mom.

We would like to donate the placenta to the people of the Gulf Coast.

We ask that the baby be bathed in our presence, in the delivery room, in San Pellegrino.

Per Mr. Cooper, do not feed the baby mussels.

Per Gisele Bündchen, do not give the baby a bottle (i.e. chemicals) for at least six months.

If the baby must be taken from the room because of a medical emergency, we would like Jeff to accompany the child. (In this scenario, Benjamin Bratt would stay with Jamie. Please maintain mood lighting and insert the CD in Jamie's handbag labeled, WHEN JEFF LEAVES.)

We will not be vaccinating our baby. Please vaccinate all other babies on this floor.

Namaste,
Jeff and Jamie

HELLO STRANGER ON THE STREET, COULD YOU PLEASE TELL ME HOW TO TAKE CARE OF MY BABY?

by WENDY MOLYNEUX

Oh, hello, person I have never met before! I am so glad you ran up to me on this street where I am walking with my baby. You did not scare me at all with your very loud voice and the way you grabbed my arm! In fact, I am super relieved because I have a series of questions about my baby that I hope you can answer, and I am going to ask them because I know you would never ever offer me unsolicited advice.

First of all, should he be sleeping, ever? If so, should it be at night? Should I keep him in a bassinet or crib or should I let him just sleep in the yard, or the toaster? And when he sleeps, should I just let him sleep as long as he wants, or should I wake him up every fifteen minutes or so for a "baby party" where I give him hard candies and play loud music? Being a new parent is confusing, and there aren't any books or internets about it, that's why I have to rely on kind strangers like you.

Yes, he IS crying, isn't he? You are right. He's probably hungry. Should I feed him? And if so, where do I put the food? His eyeball? His butt? What kinds of cuts of meat do babies like? Should I not give him hot peppers? How much salt is too much, and when can I expect him to use a knife? If he spits up, should I have him put to sleep? There are just so many things I need to know, and that is why I rely on total strangers like you who happen to be experts on child care.

Oh, that rash on his face? Well, the doctor told me that it was just baby acne that would go away in a few weeks and that it's incredibly common. But I really appreciate you pointing it out! I hadn't looked at his face yet! Probably because I couldn't tell which part of the baby was the face. Is his elbow his face? Is his onesie his face? Thank you!

Oh nice lady, you are probably right! I should definitely cover his face always so he doesn't get sun on it. If he is exposed to the sun for even one moment, even as I am simply walking from the mechanic to a coffee shop where I have to unexpectedly stop to feed him because my car broke down, he will probably immediately get sun disease or burst into flames.

I am so glad you stopped me! I can't wait to hear more about your grandchildren. What cuts of meat do they like? Were they ever babies, or did they start out as cats or dogs? And what did you start out as? A regular human being who was generally respectful to others or a nosy monster who is about to get kicked in the neck by a woman with a Baby Bjorn on her chest? What? No! Don't walk away! Please! We were just getting started! I have so many more questions! Am I still pregnant after the baby came out? Can they play with tigers? Aaaaaaaaaaaaaaaaagh! When is it okay for him to go upside down in his car seat!?!

* Read an interview with Wendy Molyneux about this piece on page 646.

25 WORDS YOUR KINDERGARTNER MUST KNOW BEFORE FIRST GRADE

by DAVID TATE

1. your

2. parents

3. are

4. taking

5. this

6. way

7. too

8. seriously

9. their

10. aggressive

11. and

12. goal-focused

13. parenting

14. style

15. will

16. isolate

17. and

18. minimize

19. their

20. ability

21. to

22. parent

23. you

24. effectively

25. puppy

BOAT PARTS OR NAMES OF UNVACCINATED CHILDREN?

by GRANT PARDEE

1. Hopper

2. Tiller

3. Dashiell

4. Stanchion

5. Anais

6. Tallulah

7. Rudder

8. Mason

9. Traveler

10. Flora

11. Portlight

12. Magnus

- - -

Boat Parts: 2, 4, 7, 11
Names of Unvaccinated Children: 1, 3, 5, 6, 8, 10, 12
Both: 9

CLICKBAIT HEADLINES OR TEXTS FROM MY MOM?

by BROTI GUPTA

1. You Are Going to Think Twice About the Next Time You Use That Word in Public

2. You Probably Didn't Hear About This Woman's Death in the Media. This Group Is Making Sure You Will

3. You Probably Didn't Hear About This Woman's Death in the Media. Aunt Meredith Is Making Sure You Will

4. You Will Not Believe What Dad Did Today

5. With This One Simple Trick, I Figured Out Facebook

6. These 11 Photos are Accidental Two-Second Videos of My Chin

7. She's Not Saying You Have to Stop Eating It, but Eating a Little
    Less Lets Three Great Things Happen

- - -

Clickbait: 2.

Mom's texts: 1, 3 (after Aunt Meredith clicked on a clickbait link),
4, 5, 6, 7

Both: 7 (but different "great things.")

SOMETHING IS WRONG WITH MY IPAD: I STILL HATE MY LIFE

by SAM WEINER

I hope you Apple Geniuses are up to snuff because I'm pretty sure my iPad's busted. No matter how much I use it to check email, surf the web, or tag photos on Facebook, I'm still gnawed at by a horrifying emptiness that no amount of fiddling with your magical gadget can fill.

Is it too much to ask that the mere act of owning your products fills me with utter, unbroken contentment? I think not.

Now, don't treat me like some tech newbie. I've done all the stuff the Apple support page says—I restarted the iPad, I upgraded to the latest version of iOS, I even sleep next to the iPad in hopes that it will turn into a beautiful, understanding woman—but for some reason I can't pass by a mirror without gagging then giving myself the finger. The iPad, like my spirit, is completely broken.

For instance, it didn't even come with a headphone jack. Headphone Jack, I assume, is an outrageous skateboard guy who will recommend music to me and be my new best friend. Oh, it's just this music hole? Then, yeah, it did come with one of those.

Well, something is definitely wrong with the iPad's Shared Photo Streams. It lets me browse my friends' photos, but in every picture, they appear to be smiling—I *know* that's not possible in a world that is literally a bottomless pit of loneliness, metaphorically.

And I don't mean to go off on a rant here, but the only thing smart about this Smart Cover is how well it works! It's not smart at all at reawakening my childhood sense of joy or my ability to deserve an erection!

Side note: you know what's great at getting fingerprints off the Retina Display? Tears. And you know what's great for getting tears off the display? Kisses.

Look, I bought all this Apple gear because it's all supposed to work seamlessly together. And sometimes it does. But when I download an album from iTunes on my iMac then use iCloud to download it to my iPhone then use AirPlay to send it to my Apple TV, no matter what song I select, the only thing I can hear is myself softly whispering *You are garbage*, inside my own head. I restart my Airport Extreme thinking that'll do the trick but all I get is even scarier whispering.

Alright, alright, I see that look in your eyes. I'm willing to leave this Apple Store on only one condition: You let me stay here as long as I want and don't make me leave.

The second condition is that you find the voice of Siri and make her marry me. She doesn't have to call me "Sex Hotshot" like I programmed the Siri on my phone to do, but she can. And she has to.

Also, are nightmares covered by AppleCare? Because my sleep mode is NOT working right.

A DAY IN THE LIFE OF A TARGET-MARKET FEMALE

by KATIE BRINKWORTH

At 6 a.m. on the dot, the twenty-five- to forty-five-year-old target-market female wakes up and stretches with delight, excited to greet the day.

For breakfast, the target-market female debates whether to eat the yogurt brand that encourages her to be herself, or the one that helps her poop. Today, like most days, the target-market female chooses regularity over self-worth.

After drinking a cup of the orange juice brand that makes her look the thinnest, the target-market female lotions up every inch of her body and gets dressed for the day. She then takes a short, breezy walk to a local café, where she patiently awaits signs of male appreciation for her noticeably soft skin.

While she waits, the target-market female daydreams about fiber, smaller pores, and easy-but-creative recipes she can make with precooked sausage. When she realizes the time, the target-market female rushes home to begin the most rewarding part of her day: doing the laundry.

At home, while waiting for the end of the spin cycle, the target-market female fantasizes that a male model has materialized in her kitchen and is making her a salad. He works slowly—first carefully washing the organic produce, then cutting the vegetables with his own chiseled facial features.

When he's finished, he feeds the target-market female bites of the kale-based salad while sensually describing how it will help reduce her belly bloat. Afterward, he does yoga on her while they both indulge in the yogurt brand that makes the target-market female feel sexy and independent.

Hours later, the target-market female wakes up on the floor of her laundry room in a daze. She notices that the spin cycle is complete, and opens the lid of the washing machine. When she sees what the combination of premium bleach and stain-fighting detergent has accomplished, her knees weaken beneath her and her bowels release for the very first time in her life.

In her giddy, almost orgasmic state she decides to forgo her internet-enabled, whisper-quiet dryer, opting instead to "carpe diem!" and dry the brilliant whites outside on a clothesline. With the help of a talking stuffed bear (which her anxiety medication's animated-blob mascot assures her will disappear within four to six weeks), the target-market female hangs her symbols of domestic bliss proudly in the warm, gentle breeze.

Later on, the target-market female meets up with her racially ambiguous friend for an afternoon coffee and daily discussion of their respective yeast infections. The target-market female feels comfortable discussing such personal topics because the rich aroma of her coffee has whisked her away to the calm, soothing mental state that her rage therapist has conditioned her to visit whenever she feels envious of her friend's perfectly toned biceps or sleeveless-ready underarm skin.

After coffee, the target-market female returns home, making it back just in time to catch a falling piece of dust before it touches the floor. While re-cleaning her kitchen for the seventh time, the target-market female hallucinates that she and the mop are engaged in a quasi-sexual relationship that's been broken up by the Swiffer. She tries playing hard to get with the mop, only to discover that it has begun a fling with the basket of pinecones she uses as holiday decor.

Unsure whether the jealousy is real or fiber-induced, the target-market female builds a fire with the pinecones and every other romantically threatening knickknack, producing a very real and uncontrollable inferno. By the time the fire trucks arrive, the whole house is ablaze.

When she realizes her loss, the target-market female begins to cry like women always do.

Fortunately, in the end, the target-market female is oddly comforted by the fact that she can wipe up all the tears, spilled gasoline, and broken dreams with one illogically absorbent, quilted paper towel.

NATE SILVER OFFERS UP A STATISTICAL ANALYSIS OF YOUR FAILING RELATIONSHIP

by JORY JOHN

While data shows that overall happiness in your relationship fell eight more points, there is still a 31 percent chance of makeup sex this Friday, depending on average energy levels after work and how proactive you're feeling (see chart). However, if you just order $18 of Chinese takeout like you did last weekend, projections show a 16.8 percent drop in possible intercourse and a whopping 74.2 percent upswing in Netflix-streaming, with both of you falling asleep long before the movie is over.

In an exit poll from Monday evening, exactly one half of the duo in attendance said they had an unfavorable opinion of the chosen restau-rant—Arby's—wondering if it was some sort of retribution, or if this is sadly what it's come to.

Between the hours of 6 and 7 p.m. tonight, there was a 77.1 per-cent increase in annoyance and a 54 percent rise in revulsion based on the way you slurped your capellini, drank 65 percent too much wine, and prattled on about your ex-girlfriend Sarah for some reason, even though she has a new boyfriend with a sailboat, and you've supposedly moved on, too. The logic here is that you are 44 percent over Sarah after three years, but there is only a 3.6 percent chance of her taking you back, which is reduced by nearly half of a percentage point every time she steps foot on that boat.

In a very local poll released just this week, 50 percent of those in your current relationship said it bothers them when you leave your shoes in the middle of the carpet and added that, if you could clean a dirty dish or two—putting in a minimal effort of just five minutes—stress would be reduced by 39 percent, along with a telling 54 percent decrease in shouting matches and escalating threats to leave forever.

You've lost nearly a hundred hairs on your head every day since March, 2011, when you met, which is almost 36,500 hairs in the last year and nearly 73,000 hairs in the last two years. This is, ultimately, why you'll be 84 percent bald by the time you're forty-five.

In a survey conducted with your partner's biological parents between Tuesday and Wednesday, you are currently ranked seventh most popular on the list of known boyfriends, after Andrew R., Bryan, Kevin, Seth, Shawn and Kyle, but before Andrew Y. who refused to apply labels to relationships and wanted to "keep things loose."

Of the seven ex-boyfriends listed above, two of them (Andrew R. and Seth) have sent a combined two emails to your girlfriend this month, totaling about 2,200 words, both of which have gone 100 percent unmentioned.

The aforementioned emails were placed in a folder marked "SAVE," which actually contains twenty-six messages you've never seen, twenty-three of which would immediately increase your base paranoia by 87 percent.

There are upwards of 12,000 couples within ten square miles of your house who had more measurable fun than you did in the last eight weeks, as evidenced by this graph (right). The red line is indicative of genuine laughter, the purple line represents long, meaningful stares, the blue line shows a water sport or plane ride, and the orange line depicts sunsets or sunrises enjoyed without irony or arguments.

Your current net approval rating is at 42 percent, revealing a divided house. If you look to your approval rating at this same time last year, it stood at 59 percent while, two years ago, it was at an all-time high of 81 percent, excepting that flu-week when you wore the same sweatpants for six straight days. Your incessant, fever-stricken whining lowered your then-approval to 54 percent (although sympathy conversely rose 13.6 percent in that same timeframe). However, it's important to note that there *is* no rebound this time, according to polls with a margin of +/- 1. Across the board, you're less popular now than ever before.

According to a survey conducted last month, your partnership ranks as the second most doomed on your block, behind the couple who stand on their lawn and shriek at each other. Yours is statistically guaranteed to end three years sooner than that really attractive woman's, the one who recently moved in across the street and is home a mere 32 percent of the week. Of the sixteen occasions you've peered through your blinds and noticed her walking to her car, she is on the phone with her boyfriend 53 percent of the time and there's a 91.5 percent chance that it's serious.

The trend line shows that the odds of remaining in this current relationship hover steadily at 1 in 52, the very same chances of drawing the queen of hearts out of a deck of well-shuffled playing cards.

My procedures are not skewed toward your relationship failing, as I have a macro perspective on commitment and monogamy. By using quantitative polls and demographics—and after talking to numerous individuals who knew dozens of unhappy couples—I've accurately predicted exactly fifty out of fifty breakups this year. There is no reason to doubt my system. Valuations show that yours will meet a comparable end and that I will be right for the fifty-first consecutive time.

My breakup forecast shows you losing thirty-five of the albums you bought together at garage sales, leaving you with only fifteen, including Sting's fourth solo record, *Ten Summoner's Tales*, which neither of you really wanted. The album *does* contain the song "If I Ever Lose My Faith in You," which seems prescient in hindsight and which made it to #17 on the Billboard charts in 1993. There is a 97 percent chance you'll listen to the song at least twenty times.

Additionally, there is a 62.8 percent likelihood that your girlfriend will be dating somebody new within three months of your split. If this happens, there is an 84 percent chance that it's that new friend from the gym you keep hearing about (see photo).

Ultimately, please don't give me too much credit for this accumulated data. Although 0.0 percent of your mutual friends were willing to say anything, 93.9 percent of them saw this coming from the start.

NIHILISTIC PASSWORD SECURITY QUESTIONS

by SOHEIL REZAYAZDI

What is the name of your least favorite child?

In what year did you abandon your dreams?

What is the maiden name of your father's mistress?

At what age did your childhood pet run away?

What was the name of your favorite unpaid internship?

In what city did you first experience ennui?

What is your ex-wife's newest last name?

What sports team do you fetishize to avoid meaningful discussion with others?

What is the name of your favorite canceled TV show?

What was the middle name of your first rebound?

On what street did you lose your childlike sense of wonder?

When did you stop trying?

CORPORATE TIME EQUIVALENTS

by MARCO KAYE

"Just a sec" = 5 minutes

"Just a minute" = 10 minutes

"Pick your brain" = 17 minutes or, in rare cases, 90 seconds

"Quick chat" = 48 minutes

"No more than five minutes" = 1 hour

"End of day" = 2 hours after the delivery guy brings dinner

"Quick meeting" = 3 hours

"Deep dive" = the time it takes to eat half a bag of baby carrots

"Exploratory" = only the intern knows for sure

"Brainstorming session" = the entire afternoon, but everyone involved gets to sneak out early

"Could use a hand" = 1 week

"Could really use a hand" = 1 week + the weekend

"Onboarding" = 3 weeks that felt like 3 three years

"Stint" = 2-3 weeks

"Gig" = 3-4 weeks

"Boondoggle" = 1 month of hotel food and daydreaming at strange buildings

"Pitch in" = 1 month here and there

"Help out" = 1 month + 2 harrowing weeks

"Assist on" = 3 months + 1 month plotting an escape

"Build-out" = why those tech people make shitloads of money

"Ramping up" = must happen before the end of the fiscal quarter

"Gearing up" = really should happen before the end of the quarter, but don't hold your breath

"Strategize" = don't ask, don't tell

"Cool little project" = 6 endless months

"Wonderful opportunity" = 8 months

"Interesting opportunity" = 2 years

"Immediate need" = still hasn't been resolved

"Got my start at" = too long or too short to fully explain

"Job" = holy shit, has it really been X years?

"Current job" = 1 more year and then I'm out

"Career" = 15 years trying + 5 years coasting + 15 years wondering if all that trying was worth it + 5 years just sitting there, collecting a paycheck, fondly reminiscing about the coasting

"Let's revisit this later" = never shall we speak of this again

"Loop back" = 50/50 chance we shall speak of this again

"ASAP" = unquantifiable

LESSER-KNOWN TROLLEY PROBLEM VARIATIONS

by KYLE YORK

THE TIME TRAVELER

There's an out-of-control trolley speeding towards a worker. You have the ability to pull a lever and change the trolley's path so it hits a different worker. The different worker is actually the first worker ten minutes from now.

THE CANCER CAPER

There's an out-of-control trolley speeding towards four workers. Three of them are cannibalistic serial killers. One of them is a brilliant cancer researcher. You have the ability to pull a lever and change the trolley's path so it hits just one person. She is a brilliant cannibalistic serial killing cancer researcher who only kills lesser cancer researchers. 14 percent of these researchers are Nazi-sympathizers, and 25 percent don't use turning signals when they drive. Speaking of which, in this world, Hitler is still alive, but he's dying of cancer.

THE SUICIDE NOTE

There's an out-of-control trolley speeding towards a worker. You have the ability to pull a lever and change the trolley's path so it hits a different worker. The first worker has an intended suicide note in his back pocket but it's in the handwriting of the second worker. The second worker wears a T-shirt that says PLEASE HIT ME WITH A TROLLEY, but the shirt is borrowed from the first worker.

THE ETHICS TEACHER

There's an out-of-control trolley speeding towards four workers. You are on your way to teach an ethics class and this accident will make you extremely late. You have the ability to pull a lever and change the trolley's path so it hits just one person. This will make you slightly less late to your class.

THE LATTE

There's an out-of-control trolley speeding towards five workers. You're in a nearby café sipping on a latte, and don't notice. The workers die.

THE DICKS

There's an out-of-control trolley speeding towards two workers. They're massive dicks. You have the ability to pull a lever and change the trolley's path so it hits just one person. He's an even bigger dick.

THE BUSINESS ETHICS VERSION

There's an out-of-control trolley speeding towards three workers. You have the ability to pull a lever and change the trolley's path so it hits a teenager instead. At a minimum, the three workers' families will receive a $20,000 insurance payoff each, and the families will no doubt sue the company, which in this scenario you represent. The trolley driver seemed to die instantly from a freak aneurysm, so your company might not be faulted for negligence under the FELA and might come out okay. The teenager's parents, on the other hand, make a total of $175,000 a year, and can afford a pretty decent lawyer.

THE REAL STINKER

There's an out-of-control trolley speeding towards four workers. You have the ability to pull a lever and change the trolley's path so it hits just one worker instead. But get this: that one worker? It's your fucking mom. Bet you weren't expecting that shit, were you?

THE SURREALIST VERSION

There's an out-of-control trolley speeding towards four workers. You have the ability to pull off your head and turn it into a Chinese lantern. Your head floats into the sky until it takes the place of the sun. You look down upon the planet. It is as small as the eye of a moth. The moth flies away.

THE META-ETHICAL PROBLEM

There's an out-of-control trolley speeding towards Immanuel Kant. You have the ability to pull a lever and change the trolley's path so it hits Jeremy Bentham instead. Jeremy Bentham clutches the only existing copy of Kant's *Groundwork of the Metaphysic of Morals*. Kant holds the only existing copy of *Bentham's The Principles of Morals and Legislation*. Both of them are shouting at you that they have recently started to reconsider their ethical stances.

LOOK, WE CAN EITHER STUDY FOR OUR LAW SCHOOL FINALS, OR WE CAN BRING ABOUT THE VIOLENT DISSOLUTION OF THE AMERICAN LEGAL SYSTEM

by ERIC HAGUE

It's been a long semester. At this point we've read hundreds of pages of judicial opinions and sat through countless hours of lectures on legal theory and case law, and now we're down to the wire. Exams are less than a week away, and the way I look at it, we've only got two options: we can either buckle down and hit the books harder than we ever have in our entire lives, or else we can attempt to bring about the violent downfall of the institution of rule of law in the United States of America.

And between you, me, and this three-hundred-page Crim. Law outline I got from a 2L, that second one just sounds more viable.

Sure we can study. We can go over our notes and take a couple practice tests and pray we get good enough grades to land a sweet summer firm job. But let's be realistic. How hard is it going to be to understand the complex web of choice-of-law analysis implicated by *Erie Railroad*

Co. v. Tompkins? Now how hard is it going to be to instigate a bloody nihilistic revolution the primary result of which will be the complete collapse of the federal and state judiciaries and the instantaneous and complete invalidation of four centuries of American law and jurisprudence? You're shaking your head.

Let me ask you this: Have you even tried to wrap your mind around the English common law system of easements and servitudes? It's perverse. It's the kind of perverse that makes you want close your copy of the Restatement, put the caps back onto your rainbow highlighters, and then proceed to organize a paramilitary overthrow of one of the most democratic and legally equitable societies ever established in the history of humankind.

Seriously—just think about how stressed out you are right now. Now think about how unstressed you'll be when you're roasting marshmallows over a bonfire whose flames are fed by the nullified volumes of the *United States Reports.*

Now, I figure if we can seize control of the broadcast media first, we can more readily disseminate instructions to comrades and partisan fighters near—hold on. Why are you looking at me like that?

Sure I may be "starting to really freak you out"—but is what I'm saying even half as freaky as the explanation of Coasian theory in our Property casebook? Where's your sense of adventure and militant, vaguely anarchist anti-patriotism?

You know, H.L. Mencken once said, "Every normal man must be tempted at times to spit on his hands, hoist the black flag, and begin to slit throats." Note that he did not say, "Every normal man must go ahead and follow through with law school and not dismantle the American polity through armed revolt simply because if he fails his Torts final he'll probably never be able to get a six-figure associateship and have any hope of paying off his Grad PLUS loans."

And what would the founding fathers have done, huh? What would James Madison do if he was staring down a four-hour, closed book Constitutional Law final? I mean besides, you know, not writing the Constitution. I like to think he would have just broken down and started destroying stuff rather than confront the reality of his own intellectual inadequacy and poor post-graduate educational decisions.

So who's with me? Who among you will tear off the manacles of history and cloak yourself in the mantle of noble insurrection against the tyranny of law and the final examination thereof?

Fine. I'll leave.

But know this—when the streets of Washington are thick with the perfume of cordite and the strains of the Internationale; when the Smithsonian's tablet of Hammurabi's Code has been ground into a fine dust whose motes will be contemptuously scattered across the plains, forests, and mountains that separate the Atlantic and Pacific; when the citizens of the new America gaze upon the cracked-egg dome of the defunct capitol building and contemplate the metaphorical spoiled yolk of the sort-of-hard-to-understand laws its legislature previously produced—when these inevitabilities come to pass, you shall be held accountable for your cowardice and collusion with the law school-industrial complex. Know that when the revolution comes, you—all of you!—will be the first against the wall.

Also, please give me back my outlines and rainbow highlighters.

A McSWEENEY'S INTERNET TENDENCY ORIGIN STORY

WHAT I IMAGINE HAPPENS TO MY McSWEENEY'S INTERNET TENDENCY SUBMISSIONS

by JESSE EISENBERG

FROM: ME

TO: TENDENCY EDITOR

Hey there. I just finished a little humor essay—think it's pretty funny. It's called "Pigs in a Blanket." But happy to change the title if you hate it ;-)

FROM: TENDENCY EDITOR

TO: ME

Thanks Jesse! Looking forward to reading it! Will get back to you soon!

FROM: TENDENCY EDITOR

TO: McSWEENEY'S CEO

Hey Boss, just read Jesse Eisenberg's humor submission, "Pigs in a Blanket." Funniest thing I've read in a long time. Should we put it online next week?

WELCOME TO PAGE 357

FROM: MCSWEENEY'S CEO
TO: TENDENCY EDITOR

My goodness. I just put down "Pigs." In my twenty years writing great books and publishing *McSweeney's* award-winning writing in quarterlies, magazines, and online, I have never read something so piercing, so delicately wounding yet, at the same time, meditative. That Kevin character slayed me! He feels classic yet contemporary; nostalgic yet prescient. Before we get back to Eisenberg, let me send to a few people. We don't want to unleash this prematurely.

FROM: TENDENCY EDITOR
TO: MCSWEENEY'S CEO

Shouldn't someone get back to Jesse? At least let him know how much we liked it?

FROM: MCSWEENEY'S CEO
TO: TENDENCY EDITOR

Hold off on getting back to Eisenberg. He's not worried about us. I'm sure he's working on some killer new humor piece right now, not sitting around waiting for us to get back to him.

On a side note, I slipped "Pigs" to my mother last night. We're back on speaking terms. (!)

FROM: ME
TO: TENDENCY EDITOR

Hey there! Checking in to see if you read my last submission "Pigs in a Blanket"? It's been a few weeks. If not, no prob—I'm sure you're swamped! As always, happy to make any changes to it. It doesn't have to be about pigs. Could be funnier with dogs.

BTW—If you'd prefer to read a hard copy, I'm more than happy to swing by your office. Always so nice to see you and I know you love my cupcakes ;-)

FROM: MCSWEENEY'S LEGAL DEPARTMENT
TO: MCSWEENEY'S CEO

Dear CEO, You were smart to send "Pigs in a Blanket" to our department. We ran it through every algorithm and it does appear to be an original text.

However, we had a team of historical literary experts take a look and they all red-flagged it. Our Shakespeare scholar thought this might be the text of an undiscovered folio (esp. the part where Kevin throws a tea party with Uncle Jerry).

Our Egyptologist ran it through his Rosetta Stone and said it aligns with theories on early methods of embalming.

Obviously, we love the piece and publishing it online would be a massive boon for the website, with Nobel buzz and exploding sales. We just cannot, in good legal faith, advise publishing something with such potentially historic tentacles.

FROM: HEAD OF PARAMOUNT PICTURES
TO: MCSWEENEY'S CEO

So there I am in KwaZulu-Natal, South Africa, poaching tusks when my assistant flies in to hand deliver this tear-stained, astounding piece of humor-writing, "IN A BLANKET," to adapt for a major film.

Frankly, I got into this business forty years ago because of stories like this—stories that reach into your chest and pull out the throbbing organ we call our heart. Stories that read like the most private diary entry and the loudest call to action. The moment when Kevin falls off the unicycle? I felt like I was falling. When Kevin prank calls the pizza parlor? I felt like he was prank calling me.

The sad truth is, the world wants to see fighting robots and flying men in tights. A film adaptation of "IN A BLANKET" would show audiences what we've been withholding and cripple our already struggling industry.

In short: if we make "IN A BLANKET," no one would ever watch a movie again.

FROM: MCSWEENEY'S FOREIGN CORRESPONDENT
TO: MCSWEENEY'S CEO

Hey Boss, Sorry it took me a week to get back to you. I've been embedded in the Middle East and it's been absolute chaos; just when you think the threat of ISIS has been quashed, the thud of a mortar jars you back into the hellish reality of this forgotten place.

Anyway! I LOVED "Pigs in a Blanket"! It's a brilliant metaphor for the Balkanization of the Middle East by shortsighted Western powers. It's the harshest criticism of Sykes-Picot I've ever read.

In light of this, I would not publish this story. There's already so much trouble in the world, do we really need "Pigs in a Blanket" holding a mirror up to our worst flaws? Yes, it's brilliant. Yes, it's a masterwork. But it'll set a fire that I don't think the world is ready to extinguish.

FROM: THOMAS PYNCHON
TO: MCSWEENEY'S CEO

I have just read "Pigs in a Blanket." As you might imagine, I have spent my entire literary career chasing the dragon that is this earth-shattering work. How fitting, then, that the deft hand that created "Kevin" and "Farmer Stu" is the same hand that plunges the dagger of envy into my heart.

All of my books combined do not come close to the literary achievement of a single sentence from "Pigs in a Blanket." When Peter the Parrot squawks, "Balloons are for popping!" I realized that I am in the wrong profession. I think I may pursue a career as a bike messenger once the sting of my inferiority wears off.

Please do not print this. It will destroy my legacy.

FROM: MCSWEENEY'S CEO
TO: TENDENCY EDITOR

Heard back from some of my contacts about "Pigs." Don't think we should publish. Can you inform the writer?

FROM: TENDENCY EDITOR
TO: ME

Hey Jesse! Sorry for the delay! Unfortunately, "Pigs in a Blanket" is not for us but thanks for submitting! If the offer for cupcakes is still on the table, though, stop by the office anytime

;-)

AMERICA: A REVIEW

by MEGAN AMRAM

How to begin this review? Few countries that debuted in the 1700s have been as controversial or long running (it's into its 237th season now) as *America*. It may not have the staying power of perennial favorites such as *China* or the credibility of indie darlings such as *Finland*, but *America* has proven that it can at least make some cultural impact. It's not the best, but hey, they can't all be *Louie*.

America was originally a spinoff of the long-running *England*. Airing from the 1776 to 1777 season through today, *America* focuses on a small ensemble of white people using things in the ground to become rich or kill brown people. A sprawling dramedy, it combines all of the loose plot points of a Tyler Perry sitcom with all the fun of being white.

It has widely focused on the themes of war, freedom, sitting, Fenway Park, maps, the one true Christian god, rugs, pregnancy tits, *Vice* magazine, butter-faces, coal, butterdicks, "Where's the Beef?," Chicago,

Larry Flynt, colonialism, Terri Schiavo, NBC single-camera sitcoms, toddlers, suicide pacts, Atari, penny-farthing bicycles, SpaghettiO's (Cool Ranch flavor), tiny dolls, the TLC show *Sister Wives*, H1N1, television, and genocide. It has some unique perspective every once in awhile, but honestly, *America* can be super derivative. Most of the stories have already been on *The Simpsons*.

A lot of episodes in *America* don't really hold up. Slavery? Parachute pants? White slavery? It just feels really overdone now. Among the most memorable episodes are "The Civil War," "Texas," "World War" (a two-parter), and "Black President."

Some of the storylines are also a bit of a stretch. Are they really expecting us to believe that they killed all the Indians and that all those Indians did to deserve it was invent diabetes?! And *come on*—that stuff in the 9/11 episode could not have happened without someone working on the inside. That makes no sense. "9/11" jumped the shark. Hard.

It's been on so long that no one wants to comment on the OBVI-OUS PLOT HOLES. Such awful continuity. Like, how could it be explained that in season 170, George H.W. Bush fathered a mentally disabled son, but then in season 225, that son became president?! Really terrible continuity. I would like to point out that I do appreciate a recent callback to earlier plots. Around seasons 174 to 184, some of the anti-feminist and sexist storylines were put on the backburner, but it's nice that we've seen a resurgence in this last season.

America has time and time again proved itself as a launching ground for young starlets. It's fun seeing people before they became huge stars, like John Ritter, Stella McCartney, Theodore "Ted" Kaczynski, and Ted "Ted" Bundy. But the ensemble works best when we see the regulars yearn for a raise or promotion, struggle with Mary Tyler Moore's foibles and be there for Mary Tyler Moore when the going gets rough. I stole this from a review for *The Mary Tyler Moore Show*, but I think it completely and entirely makes sense to literally lift from that review and drop it into this context as well.

As someone with more quirky and alt tastes, I can't say that *America* is my favorite thing to watch. I'm more into *Breaking Bad*. Have you seen season four?! Season four of *Breaking Bad* is flawless. Season four of *America* is VERY very uneven. It had no main black characters. *Girls*, much?! I love *The Wire*!

I just hope to God (the American/right one) that they don't pull some deus ex machina shit at the end of this series. Like, there's nuclear war with North Korea, or they've been dead the whole time or something.

Anyway, it may have veered off wildly from the pilot, but *America* is definitely worth a look. It's an interesting experiment in the world of primetime sovereign nations. What the characters lack in consistency, they make up for in body weight, lingering racism, and inconsistency. But it makes for a quick and easy viewing, and can often surprise you with heartfelt turns. It's like eating Cool Ranch SpaghettiO's on a warm summer's eve. And hey, sometimes things get really good right before they're cancelled.

MY RATING: 50 stars (out of 100).

THE FOUR HORSEMEN OF GENTRIFICATION

by ZAIN KHALID

Then I saw when the Landlord broke one of the rent-controlled seals. I heard one of the four living creatures saying as with a voice of thunder, "Gentrify." I looked, and behold, a green horse, and he who sat on it had a mason jar; and a fedora was his crown, and he went out pickling and to pickle.
—*Millennials 6:1, New Standard Greenpoint Bible (NSGB)*

BRINE

Greenpoint biblical scholars from the early twenty-first century were the first to interpret this horseman as not only the emergence of artisanal pickle shops, but of all unnecessary goods. It is said that after Brine visits your village, products will be made out of coconut oil for no reason whatsoever. The horse's green color represents the thousands of dollars that will soon be wasted on items like serrano pepper dishwashing liquid.

- - -

When He broke the second seal, another, a horse with tortoise shell glasses went out; and to the rider it was granted to take peace from the newly acronym-ed neighborhood, and that men would drolly insult one another; and a great Twitter account was given to him.

—Millennials 6:2, NSGB

SNARK

Snark is thought to make his first appearance at a house party with a DJ who is "the truth," where people say *Vice* showed up, even though *Vice* probably did not show up. Chalkboards will materialize outside of local stores as if from thin air, and they will have written on them a quote from Bill Murray or a reference to the chalkboard itself in an attempt to be what the experts call "meta." Residents will be mocked for their inability to taste notes of stone fruit in single-origin Ugandan espresso.

- - -

The third seal was broken by Him, and verily there was a horse the color of poached egg; he who sat on it had a food and cocktail menu in his hands. And I heard something like a voice in the center of the four living creatures saying, "A quart of mimosas for Denise, and three Bellinis for Kyle; but do not separate the hollandaise."

—Millennials 6:3, NSGB

BRUNCH

There are those who believe Brunch to be the most destructive of the horsemen. Once he takes hold, an underage girl will line the streets with vomit because she heard once that tomato juice cancels out vodka. Brunch is often followed by the demon Tapas who ensures appetites are never more than whet. Wine will be served out of thimbles and all will despair.

- - -

When the Landlord broke the fourth and final seal, a ravenous horse emerged; and he who sat on it had the name Whole Foods; and Urban Outfitters was with him. Authority was given to them over the remaining area, to kill with overpriced chicken breast and with Vampire Weekend vinyls and with alpine-style cheeses and by the small dogs of the purse.

—Millennials 6:4, NSGB

WHOLE FOODS

As Whole Foods arrives, hope departs. Ethnic restaurants will be replaced with half an aisle dedicated to "international ingredients." Greek will be the only variety of yogurt and the quality of kale will be as high as the rent for an alcove studio. Lana Del Rey will be elected to the city's council. There will be a great migration of former residents to more affordable housing. As they are loading their U-Hauls, one of them, a man without a ukulele, will look to the heavens and ask "Why?" He will hear the voice whisper a single word: "Kombucha."

A GUIDE TO
AMBIGUOUS GRAMMAR

by VIJITH ASSAR

Depending on whom you ask, the use of the active voice over the passive is arguably the most fundamental writer's maxim, thought to lend weight, truth, and power to declarative statements. This absolutist view is flawed, however, because language is an art of nuance. From time to time, writers may well find illustrative value in the lightest of phrases, sentences so weightless and feathery that they scarcely even seem to exist at all. These can convey details well beyond the crude thrust of the hulking active voice, and when used strictly as ornamentation, they needn't actually convey anything at all.

As a thought experiment, let's examine in extremely close detail a set of iterative changes that can be made to a single simple grammatical structure, turning it from a statement taken at face value into one loaded with unrealized implication. This makes for rich writing which rewards—or even demands—close scrutiny.

The quick brown fox jumps over the lazy dog.

The most fundamental feature of the passive voice is the conversion of the object into the subject by way of a stative verb. This often requires complete structural inversion of the sentence, since the two clauses are changing position, but it allows the roles of the nouns to shift, bringing the secondary participant to the foreground.

The quick brown fox jumps over the lazy dog.

The lazy dog *is jumped* over *by* the quick brown fox.

It's also helpful to switch to past tense; this very slight change often lessens the impact of the statement. If the action being described happened at some point in the distant past, it is no longer an immediate concern, so other parts of the sentence can be more easily emphasized instead.

The lazy dog is jumped over by the quick brown fox.

The lazy dog *was* jumped over by the quick brown fox.

Remove definite articles whenever possible, replacing them with indefinites. This diffuses the verb: in this form, the notion that *any* actor may have performed the action is a logical conclusion. The exact referents can still be intuited upon closer reading.

The lazy dog was jumped over by the quick brown fox.

A lazy dog was jumped over by *a* quick brown fox.

The verb is still concrete, but it shouldn't be. In fact, the verb can be removed completely: convert it into a present participle adjective, and then use that participle as a modifier for a broad, general-purpose noun. In this example we'll use "incident" to at least acknowledge that the events took place along a common timeline, but even that much is still an unnecessary concession to specificity—we could just as easily substitute "thing," which is so broad that unpacking it will command the reader's complete attention.

In addition, there is still a distinction between the subject and object which can be further erased. Both subject and object were "involved" in the proceedings, simply because both are present in the sentence. That new verb can apply to both nouns, making them equal and indistinguishable partners.

A lazy dog was <u>jumped over by</u> a quick brown fox.

A lazy dog was *involved in a jumping incident with* a quick brown fox.

The adjective can be made vaguer still simply by implying that it is a class of modifier, rather than the specific modifier itself. That is, an apple can itself be fairly called apple-related, and a banana is itself also truly banana-related, so this adjective modifier can likewise be fairly described as adjective-modifier-related—a grammatical identity theorem, if you will.

A lazy dog was involved in a <u>jumping incident</u> with a quick brown fox.

A lazy dog was involved in a jumping-*related* incident with a quick brown fox.

Further in pursuit of turning the two operators into equal partners, we are now in a position to alter the broader structure of the sentence to present them alongside one another. This removes the last vestiges of the initial phrasing, in which an object was being operated upon by the subject. Both nouns are now equally implicated based on their position in the sentence.

> A lazy dog <u>was</u> involved in a jumping-related incident with a <u>quick brown fox.</u>

> A lazy dog *and* a quick brown fox *were both* involved in a jumping-related incident.

The word "both" is now redundant here, so it can be removed in the interest of concision. The participation of both parties in the action is logically implied simply by their presence, so it does not need to be explicitly stated to the reader.

> A lazy dog and a quick brown fox <u>were both</u> involved in a jumping-related incident.

> A lazy dog and a quick brown fox *were* involved in a jumping-related incident.

It's time for another major structural leap. We have carefully converted both subject and object into equal participants, but they are still both acting—both are now subjects. But what if neither of them was taking action? We can divert the reader's attention to a completely separate entity and recast the entire scenario around it, moving both nouns into passive slots. Both actors are now being acted upon as objects instead of acting as subjects, and the reader's attention is now drawn to a specific quality which had previously been a disposable attribute of one of the nouns.

> A lazy dog and a *quick* brown fox *were* involved in a jumping-related incident.
>
> *Speed was* involved in a jumping-related incident *with* a lazy dog and a brown fox.

Having already turned one attribute into the new active subject of the overall sentence, let's similarly recast the other attribute, such that the noun is now just a passive recipient of its descriptive qualities.

> Speed was involved in a jumping-related incident with a lazy dog and a brown fox.

> Speed was involved in a jumping-related incident with a lazy dog *while* a fox *was* brown.

We have finally fully arrived at the ultimate in passive voice: the past exonerative tense, so named because culpability is impossible when actions no longer exist. For the most extensive erasure of direct communicative value, the original object can now even be removed entirely.

> Speed was involved in a jumping-related incident while a fox was brown.

When **a police officer shot a black man** on August 9, 2015, the St. Louis police department sent the following description to the media:

"**The St. Louis County Police Department was involved in an officer-involved shooting after officers came under heavy gunfire.**"

---

* Read an interview with Vijith Assar about this piece on page 647

PRODUCT REVIEW: THE INVISIBLE BACKPACK OF WHITE PRIVILEGE FROM L.L. BEAN

by JOYCE MILLER

(Thank you, Peggy McIntosh.)

The Invisible Backpack of White Privilege is pretty decent, I guess. I've had one as long as I can remember. My parents said it just showed up in the mail when I was born, and L.L. Bean's policy is to replace the backpack for free if it ever breaks, so I don't have anything to compare it to. It's $8 extra to get your initials monogrammed, which I personally think should be free of charge. The backpack comes in different colors, more recently Irish, Italian, and Buffalo Plaid.

The Invisible Backpack of White Privilege is great for carrying questionable things like weed, Ponzi schemes, and sex crimes. I have lived in dense urban areas my whole life, and the cops never once search my Invisible Backpack. Then again, that's probably just because, like people always tell me, I have a really trustworthy vibe as a person.

My roommate Sam has a *visible* backpack from the North Face, which he says cost him so much that he and his family are still paying for it, whatever that means. Personally, I prefer function over trend. Sam had the nerve to suggest that if I were to trade my backpack for his backpack, I'd see what he means. I told him if he's really that dissatisfied with his own backpack, he should just return it to the store and buy one like mine instead of criticizing me all the time, because from what I can see, my backpack's only advantage is that it comes with a more positive attitude and frugal spending habit than all the other backpacks. He got really quiet and things between us have grown uncomfortable.

The backpack also includes one or more upwardly mobile forefathers who had special opportunities to garner and accumulate family wealth during times of legalized overt discrimination against people without Invisible Backpacks. According to the L.L. Bean catalogue, my great-grandfather was "a poor country boy who put himself through Harvard in the 1800s and worked incredibly hard to build a fortune on nothing but his own merits." I guess that's one of the backpack's cooler features, but it's not like it changes the fact that I have to do the work of picking up and putting on and walking around with a backpack on my back, just like anybody else.

The Invisible Backpack of White Privilege is by no means immune to hardship. As an inner-city youth, my artist mom and small business-owner dad struggled financially with no margin for luxury. Having one of the shabbiest Invisible Backpacks at private school and college gave me a complex, and I perpetually felt like "a poor boy in a rich boy's school," to quote F. Scott Fitzgerald.

In fact, the Invisible Backpack contains the complete works of F. Scott Fitzgerald, along with the Western canon, largely written by people with my same Backpack. In rough weather, it's handy to have a rich literary tradition to provide a validation of selfhood verging

PRODUCT REVIEW: THE INVISIBLE BACKPACK OF WHITE PRIVILEGE FROM L.L. BEAN

on the grandiose. Combined with a detachable Gore-Tex underdog mentality that serves to justify the backpack's pathological egotism, it often makes me consider writing a novel of my own. Should I choose to do so, the Invisible Backpack of White Privilege comes with the instructions and encouragement to create a writing career/funny video/ indie band/online satirical essay based on various unpleasant situations experienced while wearing the backpack.

The Invisible Backpack of White privilege can occasionally get pretty heavy. Its one design flaw is a hidden zipper compartment on the bottom containing anonymous multitudes slaughtered in the name of Western Civilization, yet I have no idea who these people are or where they come from. I inquired about it with an L.L. Bean customer service representative, who seemed to know nothing about the product. Thankfully, the manager was very familiar with the demands of my backpack, and explained to me that without this secret pocket, the backpack could not exist. It is a burden I complain about often, but could never imagine actually taking off.

A nice little detail about the Invisible Backpack is its built-in cosmetic mirror. The mirror enforces the basic conformity of my facial structure to an arbitrarily Caucasian globalized standard of looks. When I gaze into this mirror, it fills the void of human longing with the subconscious Pavlovian reassurance: *I am a valued citizen, I can have love.* Regardless of weight, age, injury, disability, a thoughtful nature, and other characteristics alienated by modern society, I can strain my features to approximate an internalized construct of what advertising defines as the default human face. I can garner instant trust and acceptance despite countless unexamined character deficiencies. Deficiencies such as always wearing a backpack, even in the shower.

All in all, the Invisible Backpack of White Privilege is a satisfactory product. To be completely honest, I kind of have trouble connecting with people who don't own one. I'm giving 2½ out of 5 stars because I have really high standards. I'd give 3 stars except there's no mesh water bottle holder on the side (wtf). I am a big fan of L.L. Bean and just ordered the Heteronormative Long Johns as a Christmas gift for my daughter.

FAKE
MASSACHUSETTS
TOWNS

by MICHAEL ANDOR BRODEUR

Lameham

Methol

Shamesbury

Blight Falls

West Lameham

Mansocket

Whitefolk

Leominsterlingburghamshireton

Scroughton

Unstable (/unst'-a-bull/)

Hamham

Braintree

THIS WAS NOT SUPPOSED TO BE A HAUNTED HAYRIDE

by DJANGO GOLD

Attention, passengers! I need you all to listen to me right now! Put down your souvenir Smallwood Farms cider mugs and pay attention. There can't be any uncertainty surrounding what I'm about to say to you: This is *not* a haunted hayride, and the horrific events of the last fifteen minutes were *not* planned or scripted in any way.

Truly, none of the madness that you have witnessed today was intended as part of our Fall Fun Time Hayride. Not the strands of animal entrails decorating this remote stretch of forest, not the sinister laughter echoing around us, and, most crucially, not the berserk individuals who have been raiding our hayride wagon. Actually, it would in fact appear that these maniacs wish us very real harm.

This isn't a joke. We are all in terrible danger.

Yes, I understand that Spooky Acres, Fright Forest, and various other attractions in the area operate haunted hayrides during the

Halloween season, but please take my word that this is not one of them. Our hayride is a family-friendly excursion consisting of hot apple cider, group sing-alongs, and some of the most beautiful autumn foliage upstate New York has to offer. It does not involve a swarm of deranged men flitting through the trees around us and shouting horrible threats while gleefully mutilating themselves with broken bottles.

Those men are not Smallwood Farms employees.

I wish you had listened. But when I first aired my concerns after seeing that the wooden bridge leading back to Smallwood Headquarters had mysteriously collapsed, leaving us to follow the direction offered by that crudely fashioned detour sign, it was clear from your "knowing" chuckles that you believed this to be part of a rehearsed performance. Similarly, you cheerfully ogled the increasingly appalling warning signs: the occult symbols carved into the surrounding tree trunks, that gruesome altar, the large piece of plywood with GO HOME FEDS scrawled on it in glaring red letters. The evidence strongly indicated that we had wandered into some sort of depraved backwoods murder haven—cause for alarm, not something for you to eagerly Instagram.

That pile of human heads was almost certainly real.

Still, you couldn't stop "oohing" and "aahing," even when the first wave of gibbering lunatics mounted our wagon and set upon our driver, slicing his throat from ear to ear as he begged for mercy. Let me assure you right now that none of that was special effects. There are no special effects. This is a cart being pulled by a tractor, and Patrick is dead, god damn you, his body dragged off into the woods for some kind of unimaginable desecration while you all applauded like fools.

And not to belabor the point, but I would think that the frantic nature of my own confrontation with that machete-wielding behemoth as he and I desperately wrestled for control of his blade would have suggested the profoundly dire nature of this hayride, particularly that part in the fight where I upended our tureen of scalding hot apple cider onto his deformed face while screaming, "Die, you son of a bitch! Die!" Rest assured that I did not mean any of that in a fun or "spooky" way.

Nonetheless, casting blame is not a luxury we have at our disposal at the moment. This wild pack of hillbilly psychotics knows that we're on the run—yes, they've got a taste for it now. And once they regroup and take another pass at us, we'll have two options: fight them off, or join them in the dark heart of the woods as unwilling participants in some Satanic rite that the civilized mind cannot comprehend. That is the choice as it stands before you on this grim Smallwood Farms afternoon.

Oh, I can hear them now. Scrambling through the woods, moaning and slavering like something out of a fever dream. They'll be here soon, and when they arrive, I say beat them back with your fists, with your souvenir mugs, tear the planks from our besieged caravan and bludgeon these savages back into the darkest corridors of Hell. Do this, and you may yet return to a world in which the monsters are imagined and true evil but a gray shadow skulking in the woods. Kill them! Kill them. Can you freaks hear me out there? I hope that you can. Happy Halloween, you diseased maniacs!

SNOPES INVESTIGATES THE ANDERSON FAMILY'S HOLIDAY LETTER

by ALLEN REIN

To our dearest friends and family,

FALSE. While this letter was indeed sent to dear friends and family, it has been confirmed that the recipient list also included immediate neighbors, members of the PTO board, and Beth from work.

We hope this little note finds you well, and that you're enjoying the holiday season. We've already had our share of snow here in upstate New York, and we've spent much of the last month digging out Tom's beloved BMW!

MOSTLY TRUE. It did snow a ton in upstate New York, and Tom's car therefore required frequent digging out. However, the use of "beloved" is undoubtedly a sarcastic jab from Rachel, who is not known to be particularly fond of the BMW, having been heard on multiple occasions to refer to it as, "Tom's dick."

It's been a wonderful year for all four of us.

FALSE.

Connor finished eighth grade with flying colors. He continues to follow in his father's footsteps, fervently pursuing basketball and excelling in his science class, especially in the areas of chemistry and physics.

TRUE. Connor, like his father before him, is playing basketball because of intense paternal pressure. Connor shares his dad's hatred for the sport and has already secretly vowed to make his future son play as well. Also true is Connor's love for science. He experiments with Boone's Farm Strawberry Hill (chemistry) on a regular basis from the roof (physics).

Chloe wrapped up tenth grade with a beautiful presentation on the Women's Suffrage Movement. She spent much of her summer at an outdoors camp and has hit the ground running this school year. She has even found a new love for art! Who knows what she'll come up with next?

FALSE. Except for the part about Chloe finishing tenth grade, this paragraph appears to be entirely fabricated. One could argue that Chloe has, in fact, found a new love for art, but one would have to be talking about her ankle tattoo of a spider on fire. Interestingly, Chloe did go to an outdoors camp three summers prior to this holiday letter. We believe this to be a copy-and-paste error of either the computer or cerebral variety.

Tom had his busiest year yet at the law firm. His client base has been expanding, and he's found himself traveling all over the country to handle various contracts negotiations. He was even out of town for the big snowfall, which left quite a bit of shoveling for Rachel. She sure expanded her vocabulary that day!

TRUE. Tom was on the road constantly throughout the year, because work is more important to him than key life moments, like Connor's first basketball game, the fight over Chloe's tattoo, and, yes, that incredible snowstorm. Rachel is still out-of-her-mind pissed.

Just kidding! Ha ha!

FALSE.

Rachel has had a marvelous year of self-discovery. She knew it would be hard to shift gears to consultant work, but it's been such a joy to work with everyone at the agency. She continues to blog and attend her hilariously insightful improv class. Look out for a live performance after the holidays (rim shot)!

TRUE and **FALSE.** Rachel hates her new job, and she hates her coworker Beth with the heat of a thousand suns. She also hates her blog, which seemed like a perfectly good idea at the outset, but how much is there to say, really, about scrapbooking and wine? Her love for improv, however, cannot be overstated. She spends all day thinking about class and her teacher Seth, who has taught her so much about her own creative mind. Improv is about acceptance. In improv, one always responds with, "Yes, and…" One never negates. Improv isn't about being funny; it's about being attentive and open. "Listen with your ears, your mind, and your heart," Seth once said as he took off his outdoor knit cap and replaced it with his indoor knit cap. Seth says the most beautiful things, and Rachel silently responds to every single one with, "Yes, and…"

In closing, friends, we wish for you what we wish for ourselves: to have a safe and happy holiday and a peaceful start to the New Year.

UNCONFIRMED.

—The Andersons

TRUE.

IT TAKES 42
TO TANGO

by MATT INGEBRETSON

The tango is a partner dance that originated in the late 1800s on the border of Argentina and Uruguay. Tango is characterized by long elegant steps, syncopated rhythmic footwork, and traditionally requires forty-two people.

Two partners, who we will refer to as #1 and #2, begin the dance by making eye contact from opposite sides of the room, approaching each other, embracing, and moving across the dance floor in time with the music. #1 leads, #2 follows.

A third person (#3) enters the dance by tapping #1 on the shoulder and asking permission to "cut in," thereby displacing him in the dance.

Person number four (#4) enters holding her seventh drink of the night. She accidentally spills it all over #2's dress, forcing #2 to angrily excuse herself to the restroom. #4 makes eyes at #3 and they begin to dance.

Person number five (#5) is in a serious committed relationship with #3, and had no idea #3 started dancing with #2 and subsequently #4 while she was having a cigarette on the patio. She enters the dance by asking #4 just what in the hell she thinks she's doing dancing with #3. #4 responds by vomiting and stumbling off the dance floor.

Person number six (#6) enters the dance when #5 pulls him away from his partner (#7), and begins aggressively grinding on him, attempting to incite jealousy in #3 as retribution for dancing with #2 and #4. #3 reciprocates by aggressively grinding on #7.

Number eight (#8) is #7's father. He is owner of the dance club and head of a crime family. He has been watching from the balcony with numbers nine (#9), ten (#10), and eleven (#11), who are members of said crime family. #8 motions for #'s 9 to 11 to protect the dignity of his daughter (#7) by taking #3 out into the back alley and teaching him what happens when you disrespect #8's daughter (#7).

Numbers twelve (#12), thirteen (#13), and fourteen (#14), members of a rival crime family headed by number fifteen (#15), enter the dance when they see #'s 9 to 11 to grab their brother, #3, and begin dragging him off the dance floor. They pull out handguns and begin shouting threats at #'s 9 to 11, who drop #3 and also pull out handguns.

Numbers sixteen through thirty-nine (#'s16 to 39) enter the dance as they attempt to dodge stray bullets from guns being fired by #'s 9 to 11 and #'s 12 to 14. #19 is hit squarely in his left thigh and falls to the ground, writhing in pain. #22 and #27 are critically wounded and die within minutes.

The dance continues as #'s 9 to 11 and #'s 12 to 14 barricade themselves behind tables and continue firing on one another. #13 shoots #9 in the forehead. He dies instantly.

Numbers forty and forty-one (#40 and #41) enter the dance when they arrive on the scene in record time in their police cruiser, guns drawn. They open fire on #'s 10 to14, while crime lord #15 slinks out the back door unnoticed.

The dance comes to a climax just as #40 and #41, believing they have squashed the threat to public safety by killing #'s 10 to 14, holster their guns and turn their backs on the scene, giving #3 an opportunity to pry a gun out of his dead brother's (#14's) hand, and shoot them both in the back.

Number forty-two (#42), a stunning brunette wearing high heels and a knock-out red dress that could cause a man's heart to rocket into his throat, enters the dance through the front door of the club, looks at #3 and coyly asks, "Am I late?"

The dance concludes as #3, despite being devastated by the death of his brothers, is charmed by the gall of #42, drops his gun, walks across the dance floor, and, in a moment of pure disregard for the tragedy that life has thrust upon him, embraces her. The two begin moving across the dance floor in time with the music. #3 leads, and #42 follows.

I WILL NOT WRITE UNLESS I AM SWADDLED IN FURS

by JOHN BABBOTT

I will not write unless I'm swaddled in furs and am roosted to perfection upon the couch. Perhaps I could write upon the divan, but never a table. And there must be furs.

I will not write unless I am oriented perpendicularly to a large window. I'm not picky, but it must be quite large, and there must be sheets of cold rain pouring down outside. If the rain stops, so do I. I will not write without a bracing rain.

I must have fuzzy slippers. They must be slightly worn on the inside, because if the fuzz is too fluffy, my feet become claustrophobic, and my writing naturally follows suit. They must not be too worn, though, or else it feels as if I'm merely wearing warm shoes with no socks, which makes me feel ill-prepared. They must be just fuzzy enough.

The beverage is of utmost importance. It must be hot, to contrast the rain, and must be either a coffee of reputable origin or a tea that no one has ever heard of, as the writing that follows (if the conditions are correct) will likewise be uniquely energizing and unexpected.

I should mention that while I require cold, pouring rain, I also require, at some point, the sun to emerge unexpectedly. The sunbeams will illuminate the rising motes of steam from my beverage. The rising steam will resemble, and thus stoke, my Original Creative Fire, and this shall signal the crystallizing moment of artistic creation that sets my writing apart from the work of others. Then, it should begin pouring rain again.

My implements, whichever I choose for the occasion, must be of appropriate heft. I am sorry, I cannot reveal their specifics, as their characteristics are clues that indicate my identity as an artist, which is a secret I must guard at all costs. They are all slightly different, and even I don't fully understand my criteria for choosing one over the other on any particular late morning. Nonetheless, each and every implement must catch the page deliciously and leave elegant trails of ink, their subtle praxes reminding me with each flourish that something mysterious is happening.

There must be a cat. It must purr, constantly. The cat may knead and stretch, but it must not move from its parenthetical orientation next to my left thigh unless absolutely necessary.

The window must be on my left.

It must be early morning, but not dark. I must be well-rested, clean, warm, shaved, manicured, and pleasantly hungry. I must be well-hydrated, but not so much so that I have to use the bathroom, as it takes some time to extricate myself from the furs without disturbing the cat. Just before the kettle heralds my writing's approach, I should be finishing a satisfying, soothing bowel movement. I'm not picky, but it should be well-integrated, smoothly long and tapered at one end. Any other kind would ruin the metaphor.

There should be a moon, and it should be waxing full. I do not need to see the moon—it will be raining, I realize. It's enough just to know that it's there.

A friend once told me that Ansel Adams would trek for days and then wait days longer in a location before he took one single, iconic photograph. I don't know if that's true about Ansel Adams, but if I were a photographer, I'd work in exactly the same way.

As the correct conditions for writing are difficult to cultivate and come by, I've only written three times over the course of my career. Colleagues implore me to be more flexible, pointing out that I would write more if I relaxed my requirements. I always listen, but then dismiss them with a wave. The three pieces I have produced have changed the landscape of contemporary art. Their sequence was conceived at the correct moment, under the correct conditions. They will be posthumously released.

Anyway, I trust the accommodations here will meet all my needs. I've heard splendid things about this Motel 6. I will now retire to my room. Ring me when the fur delivery arrives.

KAFKA'S JOKE BOOK

by JOHN MCNAMEE

Why did the chicken cross the road?

It had been crossing so long it could not remember. As it stopped in the middle to look back, a car sped by, spinning it around. Disoriented, the chicken realized it could no longer tell which way it was going. It stands there still.

- - -

"Knock knock."

"Who's there?"

"Knock knock."

"Who's there?" Alois asked again, more insistently.

"Knock knock."

And so it went for years. It wasn't until his deathbed Alois realized he was on the outside of the door.

- - -

"Why is a raven like a writing desk?"

"I don't know," Gregor told the faceless interrogator for the fiftieth time.

"We can't help you if you won't work with us. Perhaps another day in the machine will convince you to cooperate."

- - -

What's the difference between a lawyer and a catfish?

Nothing after Albert's inexplicable transformation. Every breath was agony.

- - -

[*To heckler*] Hey, I don't come down to where you work and expose the bureaucratic machine in which you're embedded as the dehumanizing monolith it is.

- - -

A horse walks into a bar. The bartender asks, "Why the long face?"

"I was born into servitude, and when I die, my feet will be turned into glue," replied the horse.

The bartender realized he would not be getting a tip.

- - -

[*Holding a rubber chicken*] Behold this mockery of food.

- - -

Yo momma's so fat, that she hasn't left the flat in three years. Her only solace is the figurine of the ballet dancer that she stares at day in day out. One day, you slip on a banana peel, destroying it.

- - -

If the system has no place for you, and you're forced to live on its fringes teetering between poverty and anarchy... you may be a redneck.

- - -

[*Wearing arrow through head*] This arrow does not bring the release I so desperately crave.

- - -

Take my wife, please. I can no longer support her and don't wish to since we lost the child.

- - -

What's black and white and red all over?

The prisoners in the penal colony. The sun was especially brutal that day, and the warden had taken their roofs as punishment for an unnamed crime.

- - -

A first sign of the beginning of understanding is the wish to die. Am I right, ladies?

FEMINIST
HUMBLEBRAGS

by LINDSEY FINN

"My doctor says I'm underweight, but I don't care what a man thinks about my body."

"I was promoted to partner at the firm. It comes with a 30 percent raise that still isn't as much as my male counterparts make, thanks to the wage gap."

"My father wants to walk me down the aisle at my seaside wedding. I told him that I don't adhere to patriarchy, even on a yacht."

"The objectification of women has got to stop. I can't even go for a jog without guys commenting on my ass."

"Four guys at the bar last night offered to buy me a drink. Thanks, but I'm an independent woman and I can buy my own."

"After the mariachi band finished playing at sunset, Robert got down on one knee, told me I was the 'most perfect person' he'd ever known, and asked me to make him the 'luckiest man alive' by marrying him. I said, 'I hope you don't expect me to change my last name.'"

* Read an interview with Lindsey Finn about this piece on page 648.

1915's SLUTTIEST HALLOWEEN COSTUMES

by BROOKE PRESTON

Lady Bare-Ankles

Blushing in Public

Chatty in Church

Brazenly Bobbed

Begging for It in the Bread Line

Jaunty Joyride Jezebel

Suffragette Strumpet

Munitions Factory Minx

Lonely Clerk, Loose Corset

Steamy Sweatshop Seamstress

Petticoats Galore

White-Hot War Widow

Sexy World War I Field Nurse (comes with unsterile tourniquet garters)

Slacks

REASONS YOU WERE NOT PROMOTED THAT ARE TOTALLY UNRELATED TO GENDER

by HOMA MOJTABAI

You don't smile enough. People don't like you.

You smile too much. People don't take you seriously.

You're abrasive, for example, that time when you asked for a raise. It was awkward and you made the men on the senior leadership team uncomfortable.

You don't speak up. We'd really like to see you take on more of a leadership role before we pay you for being a leader.

You're sloppy. Like when you sent that email with a typo. You need to proofread your work.

You're too focused on details. Leaders need to take the 50,000-foot fighter pilot view. No, I never served in the armed forces, what's your point?

You're not seasoned. Oh, wait, you're thirty-five? Well, you look young. Maybe if you were more mature, like if you were married or had kids (why don't you have kids, by the way?), then we could envision you as being a leader in this organization.

Oh, you do have kids? Well, we're concerned about your ability to balance everything and you look really tired all the time and I feel guilty asking you to stay late, so I just ask good old Tom who's a great guy and simple and easy to talk to.

You're argumentative. For example, right now you're upset that you didn't get a promotion and you're asking for concrete examples of what you can do better. I really don't want to get into the nitty-gritty and you should trust my judgment anyways.

You're a pushover. When Tom came up and gave you that totally platonic hug in the shareholders meeting you should have just told him to not touch you instead of telling me you thought it was inappropriate. Leaders handle their own problems.

You're not a team player. If you'd just wait a few years, there will be some great opportunities here for you, we need you in this role right now.

You aren't good at promoting yourself. I mean, toot your own horn a little!

I'm not sexist and this organization is not sexist and I have to say you're developing a little bit of a reputation as a troublemaker. Five years ago we promoted a woman who happens to be black—I mean, African-American... or maybe just African, I can't remember—and that proves that we are tolerant and committed to diversity.

---

* Read an interview with Homa Mojtabai about this piece on page 650.

A McSWEENEY'S INTERNET
TENDENCY ORIGIN STORY

THE EXTREMELY TRUE
STORY OF THE FOUNDING OF
McSWEENEY'S INTERNET TENDENCY

by KASHANA CAULEY

M CSWEENEY'S INTERNET TENDENCY WAS founded on a cloudy, 76-degree day in July 1863, typically referred to as the "Battle of Gettysburg." Everyone was in Pennsylvania. Union soldiers threw scrapple at Confederate soldiers while the Confederates slung Virginia boiled peanuts back, since they had a lot of extra ones, just like slaves.

After two days of food-fighting, an enterprising Union soldier said to another Union soldier, "We're never going to win this battle without conceptual humor." The two of them, covered in peanut shells, snuck off to the back of the battlefield to write the first issue of the Tendency with a quill that they kept dipping into ink while peanuts flew all around them.

Due to the soldiers' tightly-packed schedule, the first issue of the Tendency only had one article titled, "It's Decorative Musket Season Again, Motherfuckers." The founding editors slung copies of the publication at the other side using fishing nets, hence the name Internet Tendency.

The Confederate soldiers were so distracted from laughing at the inaugural issue that they put down their peanuts and missed the part of the battle where the Union soldiers grabbed their actual guns. "These aren't decorative muskets, motherfuckers!" the advancing Union Army yelled. They scored a decisive victory in just thirty seconds, and changed the course of both our country and conceptual humor forever.

WELCOME TO PAGE 411

IV.
EMERGING ADULTHOOD:
2016–2019

IV

PLEASE DON'T
GET MURDERED AT
SCHOOL TODAY

by KIMBERLY HARRINGTON

Do you have everything? Homework? Lunch? Field trip money?

I love you.

I remember that one of the Sandy Hook parents said that they took comfort in the fact that they had seen their child off to school that morning—you know that morning—and said, "I love you." So before their first-grader was gunned down in her classroom, she knew that she was loved. I bet they all did though.

But just in case, I love you.

We've talked about all kinds of scary things, like I've told you never to get into a car with anyone you don't know and don't ever believe that an adult needs your help finding a puppy or a kitten. Also: no one will ever give you a free iPad or Legos from their car, that's just not how the world works.

But for some reason, amidst all the talk of stranger danger and pedophiles, cancer and dying, and me sheepishly asking your friends' parents if they have a gun in the house, we haven't really talked about one of the scariest things of all. Those lockdown drills you're always having at school? No one's being straight with you about those. They're to prepare you in case someone decides to come into your school and murder you, your friends, your principal, the secretaries, and teachers before killing himself (it's pretty much always a him). Sorry about that.

I love you.

I know that may sound scary, but what you need to remember is that this country was founded on freedom. And that includes the freedom of all people (sane, crazy, whatever) to have unchallenged access to guns that are capable of executing at least twenty first graders or twelve moviegoers or nine of the faithful at a church service or even a baby asleep in her car seat. This is very, very important in terms of staying true to the principles and spirit upon which this country was founded. Just ask the internet.

I love you.

Also: I think the real victims here are the politicians, how can they be expected to do what's morally right when they lost their way, not to mention their souls, so very long ago? These politicians—most of whom have children, grandchildren, maybe even great-grandchildren of their own—have no qualms about walking past grief-stricken parents who clutch photos of their murdered children to their chests and telling them in so many words, "You don't have to go home but you can't cry here."

They have to know, deep down, that what they're doing is wrong and the world certainly knows that what they're doing is wrong but they put their suits on like it's any other job or maybe they're convinced that they're righteous people doing God's work. But they are no more doing God's work than the ones who have pulled the trigger over and over again.

And again.

And yet again.

Ad infinitum.

I love you.

I'm sorry, I wish I had better news. But let's keep our sympathies where they belong—with the powerful and the armed. With those who feel threatened in the face of the most toothless efforts to hold back the bloodshed and those who believe scary monster stories about their guns being taken away. Let's face it, it would be easier to take away the ocean or the stars. Did you know that there are more guns than people in this country? That means everyone in your class already has a gun with their name on it, so to speak. Maybe mention that at share time.

I love you.

You could also tell your class that sometimes when I hear a lot of ambulances and fire trucks go by, sirens filling the air with panic, I pay close attention to whether they're heading in the direction of your school. And if they are, I check Twitter and our town hashtag and the fire department account to see if anyone's mentioned your school. When I get the all-clear I think, "Someone else's tragedy today, suckers!"

And sometimes I wonder, what if one or both of you gets murdered at school? How will I ever forgive myself for sending you there? You know, to school. But do you want to know what makes me feel better? The fact that you could be massacred pretty much anywhere these days! Such a relief, right? So off you go!

I love you.

Yes I know, I know, you're going to be late. Just to wrap up, our country has chosen to shift all of the weight regarding your safety away from our lawmakers and gun manufacturers and instead put it squarely on the shoulders of your principal and teachers. These people who kneel down on the first day of school so they're just as tall as you. These people who shake your hand and say, "Good morning!" and help you rehearse for the spring concert and take you on field trips to see different rock formations—they are now in charge of keeping you from getting murdered. Which really is the least they can do for all that money they make.

I love you.

Oh hey, quick reminder, tell your teacher that I'll be picking you up at two o'clock for your dentist appointment.

And please don't get murdered at school today.

I love you.

I WENT TO A TRUMP RALLY. WHAT I FOUND THERE WAS A BUNCH OF OTHER JOURNALISTS ALREADY WRITING THIS ARTICLE

by DAN HOPPER

"Go home! We don't want you here!"

The sneer comes from a scruffy individual in his early twenties sporting a short-sleeved blue flannel shirt and a press lanyard from a site called *WonkCrush.ed*.

"We don't need another person writing this article."

His immediate disdain for me strikes a familiar chord here at the press tent outside the Pensacola Bay Center. The Trump rally is jam-packed with jaded writers from all corners of the internet— PolitiWord, MindLeashUntruthed, The Honeydew, VERY BEST TEACHER SHARES, the Paypal Blog—each hoping to wring some traffic out of yet another "inside Trump rallies" article.

Desperation is a common theme here. For many writers, paid opportunities simply don't exist anymore, and on some level, their collective, swelling frustration is understandable.

"I already have a thumbnail picked out," one writer declares, showing me a screenshot on his phone of Trump mid-speech with his eyes slightly closed, possibly while saying something goofy. "Just need some racist quotes and this baby's GTG." The image is a bit blurry and will end up costing him clicks, but I know better than to rile these people.

"Trump just has such huge balls," yells another man to my right, filming an on-location character bit with his sketch group. He's clad in a SHILLARY SHNEVER T-shirt showing a crude pic of Hillary in an old timey jailbird outfit holding a serial number that says EMAILS and chained to a metal ball that says BENGHAZI with a cap that also says EMAILS. The entire event is full of similarly boorish, vulgar T-shirts—a far cry from those excellent T-shirts you see all the time.

At this point I realize I should probably throw in a tactile detail. I look around perceptively and notice a hot dog cart with a yellow and blue umbrella. It says either SCHILLMAN'S or SKILLMAN'S or something, but the details don't matter to these people; rally goers line up, undeterred by such vagaries and motivated probably by the bad parts of religion, eager to scarf down their ready-made hot dogs and bottles of lukewarm water.

"I'm working the 'we don't trust journalists' angle," another attendee offers unprovoked, showing me her outline so far. "But if I snag some f-words I might lead with that." The vulgarity of the crowd is indeed striking; they're likely sick of the constant condescension they receive from every writer but me.

More yelling and more chants erupt in pockets throughout the growing crowd. I initially came here to write a story about people yelling at Trump rallies, but this? This was not at all what I expected.

"Sorry, I don't have you on the list?"

I'm snapped out of my ruminations. These thunderous words from the organizer at the press tent flawlessly underscore an evening of burgeoning divisiveness. I explain to her that I haven't called ahead for credentials, but that I just plan on quietly standing with the press corps, jotting down ridiculous things I see and maybe firing off some incredulous low-quality pics on Twitter. I even show her my awesome shareable article title with swear words in it (our site can do that), but she remains predictably unconcerned.

I've been deported from the Trump rally. The irony is so thick, I'll probably make it the Facebook share description.

"Lock her up!"

"She's a Satan Woman!"

"Emails? SHE-FAILS!"

These are three things people are conceivably shouting inside the arena, I imagine, as I stride poetically away from the now-filtering-in crowd.

On my way out, I stop for a hot dog. I bite into the mustardy flesh, hungry for instant gratification but knowing, deep down, that there's nothing of substance to this meal. I finish the last bite, stride past the rows of metal crowd control barriers, and head off towards a third taut metaphor.

THE VAST
LEFT-WING
CONSPIRACY

by TEDDY WAYNE

Hillary Clinton enters a bunker where many people are waiting.

CLINTON: Good to see you all for our secret weekly meeting. What are you watching?

MEDIA MEMBER: One of the many existing videos of Muslims in New Jersey celebrating 9/11 that we are keeping under wraps.

CLINTON: (*smiles and shakes her head fondly*) Ah, memories. How's our war chest?

FEMALE STAFFER: It's flush for dishonest attack ads on Donald Trump, thanks to money from the international bankers.

CLINTON: Send them some bagels and lox. And the global warming initiative?

FEMALE STAFFER: Our Chinese friends tell us the hoax is working perfectly. No one suspects that the planet is actually getting colder and that we need more factories to keep it warm.

Clinton coughs for several minutes then opens an unmarked bottle of pills and swallows several.

CLINTON: Sorry about my sickly health. Now I temporarily have more stamina because of these Mexican drugs.

MEDIA MEMBER: Secretary Clinton, we are having trouble coming up with new ways to rig the election because we are not intelligent. We have already ordered the journalists at all the failing biased news outlets to slander Mr. Trump with lies, but it's not working—he is too charismatic and honorable, and everyone knows he is the best at making deals.

FEMALE STAFFER: For that is all that matters, in the presidency and in life: deals.

CLINTON: I was afraid of this, just as I am afraid of many things. Since he is superior to me in every way, we must concoct a story that Mr. Trump sexually assaulted a woman.

FEMALE STAFFER: But... but... that would imply that there exists a woman somewhere who did not desire Mr. Trump's seductive advances.

CLINTON: I see your point; he is so sexually magnetic that such an outcome defies logic. Forgive me—my health problems cause me to think irrationally, on top of the fact that I'm a postmenopausal woman.

FEMALE STAFFER: Surely there are outtakes of Mr. Trump speaking on camera in a manner that might upset the East Coast liberal elite he invites to his weddings to be nice.

MEDIA MEMBER: We have found nothing from scouring the many guest appearances he has made on TV shows to boost their low ratings out of the kindness of his heart.

FEMALE STAFFER: How about this clip of him talking to Billy Bush in 2005?

MEDIA MEMBER: Which part?

FEMALE STAFFER: When he discusses the ways women always willingly allow him to partake in gentlemanly foreplay.

MEDIA MEMBER: Oh, I didn't know what you were referring to, because there is nothing inappropriate about what he said. It is simply a truthful, colorfully narrated account of how alluring women find him.

FEMALE STAFFER: (*dreamily*) Yes. And nobody respects us more than he does.

CLINTON: I know and you know that it's simply locker-room banter, which is a phrase I just learned because in school I studied like a loser all the time instead of playing sports. But the American people are gullible and overly sensitive in this politically correct climate that the president and I invented, along with ISIS. We will say that this is vulgar, and they will believe us and be offended on their cyber blogs.

MEDIA MEMBER: What about also bribing some beautiful Hollywood actresses and Czech supermodels to falsely corroborate the claims in the video?

FEMALE STAFFER: We tried, but they all said no because they have either already had the best consensual sex of their lives with Mr. Trump or they really want to and are afraid of ruining their chances, in the unlikely event he and Melania ever divorce just before her prenuptial bonus kicks in.

CLINTON: Of course—I would do the same. Despite the obvious implausibility, we will just have to get desperate, unattractive women. Bill knows plenty.

She faints. No one wants to help her. Eventually she recovers.

CLINTON: Gosh, I really am weak and unlovable—no wonder I'm doing so badly in the latest accurate Breitbart News Network anonymous polls.

She fans herself with Barack Obama's birth certificate from Kenya and mops her brow with uncounted Emmy votes for The Apprentice.

SHORT EXISTENTIALIST PLAYS STARRING YOU AND YOUR COWORKERS

by MICHAEL JUNGMAN

HOT

COWORKER: It's hot in here right?

YOU: Yeah, it's pretty hot.

[*Beat*]

COWORKER: Are you hot?

YOU: Yeah.

[*Beat*]

COWORKER: It's hot in here. Right?

YOU: Yes.

[The conversation repeats until the sun burns out and everything on the planet freezes to death and it finally stops being hot.]

THE WEATHER OUTSIDE

[Your COWORKER *stands in front of his cubicle dripping wet. He shakes out his dripping wet umbrella.* YOU *enter dripping wet.* YOU *put your soaked coat on the coat rack and shake out your dripping wet umbrella.]*

COWORKER: Is it still raining out?

[YOU *can only speak to what you experienced outside several seconds after your coworker entered the building, but several seconds before* YOU *yourself reached your cubicle.* YOU *do not know if it is in fact still raining out.* YOU *say nothing and are forever plagued by the unknowable nature of the immediate present.]*

BLACKLIST

COWORKER: Did you see *Blacklist* last night?

YOU: Oh, I don't watch that show.

[Your COWORKER *asks you this every Friday morning and* YOU *are unsure if he is forgetful or if* YOU *are locked in a* Blacklist-*watching struggle he is determined to win. Either way,* YOU *will fight on, for it is the only thing to do.]*

GOSSIP

[*Your* COWORKER *leans over your cubicle wall.*]

COWORKER: Did you hear?

[*Your* COWORKER *begins inaudibly whispering.* YOU *rise from your chair, your ear extended.*]

YOU: What?

[YOU *bring your ear to your* COWORKER's *trembling lips but hear nothing.*]

LUNCH

COWORKER: Where'd you get that sandwich?

YOU: From the deli around the corner.

COWORKER: The one on 9th?

YOU: No, 8th.

COWORKER: Sal's?

YOU: No, that's on 9th. This is from Reggie's.

COWORKER: Where is Reggie's?

YOU: Around the corner on 8th.

COWORKER: Do they make good sandwiches there?

YOU: They are OK.

COWORKER: Sal's has really good sandwiches.

YOU: ...

[YOU *stare at your sandwich.* YOU *lied about it being OK.* YOU *taste nothing when you absentmindedly feed yourself at your desk.*]

COLD

COWORKER: "It's cold in here right?"

YOU: "Yeah, it's pretty cold."

COWORKER: "Are you cold?"

YOU: "Yeah."

[*Beat.*]

COWORKER: "It's cold in here. Right?"

YOU: "Yes."

[*The conversation repeats until the sun explodes and everything on the planet experiences excruciating heat death and it finally stops being cold.*]

ALTERNATIVES TO RESTING BITCH FACE

by SUSAN HARLAN

Thanks for Behaving So Predictably Badly Face

Stop Looking at the Clock While I'm Talking Face

This Is All a Bunch of Bureaucratic Nonsense Face

You Haven't Told Me Anything That I Didn't Already Know Face

I Would Prefer Not to Face

A Smidge of Self-Awareness Would Not Go Amiss Face

The Situations Are Really Not Analogous Face

Please Tip a Bottle of Bourbon Down My Throat Immediately Face

Your Tone Raises Some Real Questions Face

I'm Just Now Registering That Horrible Thing You Did Face

That Is Not What I Meant At All Face

All the Things You Just Said About Your Baby Are Really Very Interesting Face

This Email Is Surely a Joke Face

Your Facebook Page Makes Me Not Like You Face

You're Clearly Struggling with My Failure to Conform to Your Stupid Expectations Face

That Is Only Going to Make Things So Much Worse Face

Please Stop Touching My Knee Face

That Compliment Strikes Me as Sort of a Dig Face

Thanks So Much for Your Unsolicited Advice Face

What Would the Point of That Really Be? Face

I Can't Believe I Have to Fill Out Another Effing Form Face

Yes This Is What I'm Wearing Face

I'm Trying Not to Judge You But I Am Face

No I Don't Really Think That's How All of Humanity Is Face

Sorry Your Authority Is Such a Burden for You Face

You're So Right That It's Amazing That I'm Pretty and Not Married Face

Way to Tip Fifteen Percent on Your Bill Before Taxes Face

The Best Lack All Conviction Face

You Are Still Talking About Yourself Face

This Is an Astonishing Waste of Time Face

For the Love of God Please No More Platitudes Face

You Really Know Nothing on This Subject Face

I Don't Really Know Where You're Going with This Face

Please Do Keep Checking Your Phone Face

Tell Me Again About How as a Man You're Terrible at Administrative Labor Face

This Other Email Is Surely a Joke Too Face

Would It Have Been Worthwhile? Face

Will You Be Talking for Much Longer? Face

Your Unquestioned Assumptions Are Astonishing Face

I Don't Have the Energy to Give You the Approval You Need Face

Tell Me Again About That Thing I Didn't Care About the First Time Face

Please Stop Touching My Shoulder Face

I Would Do Well to Question Your Motives Face

You Would Do Well to Question Your Motives Face

Way to Not Say Thank You Face

My Dog Is Not My Baby Face

There Are Far Too Many Steps in This Process Face

I Need a Cheeseburger and Possibly Two Face

What You Just Said Makes No Sense to Me Face

You Are Correct That You Do Not Need to Wait in This Line Face

This Smile Must Look Fake Because It Totally Is Face

Please Don't Make Me Talk to the Trader Joe's Checkout Person Face

This Too Is All a Bunch of Bureaucratic Nonsense Face

You Are Definitely Mistaken There Face

Your Premise Could Not Possibly Be More Flawed Face

Don't Stand So Close to Me Face

The Vacation You Just Told Me About Is My Worst Nightmare Face

I Won't Be Responding to That Email Face

Yes I Really Do Just Want to Sit Here and Read My Book Unmolested Face

This Form Is Designed to Drive Me to Distraction Face

Don't Feel Obligated to Be on Time Face

Way to Not Say Please Face

I Can't Believe That People Are Still Allowed to Say Things Like That Face

No Jane Austen Is Not Just for Women You Idiot Face

Your Smugness Reveals More Insecurities Than I Care to Count Face

You Make So Much More Money Than I Do and You Do Nothing Face

You Would Die if You Knew What I'm Thinking Face

The Worst Are Full of Passionate Intensity Face

What You're Talking About Is So Not What You're Talking About Face

It Is Impossible to Say Just What I Mean Face

Did You Just Sort of Correct Me Face

I'm So Glad That Is Just Your Opinion Face

I'll Be Going Now Face

OBITUARIES FOR TEENAGE GIRLS IF THEY ACTUALLY DIED WHEN THEY SAY THEY'RE DYING

by KAREN CHEE

Huang, Jamie, age 14, died suddenly upon seeing a tiny Labrador puppy walk successfully through a set of revolving doors.

Phillips, Ema Arlene, age 15, passed away when she saw Taylor Swift exiting the neighborhood gym. She died three times before realizing that the woman was not in fact Taylor Swift, whereupon she died once more.

Thomas, Morgan, age 15, tasted the perfect mango mousse cake just before succumbing to death. During her life, she was a "mousse lover." She loved mousse. She was tragically killed by the perfect mousse.

Hruby, Sierra, age 13, heard that Emma said Dan told Rebecca that Maggie was hosting a party that Henri would also attend, but it was actually Rebecca who told Dan that Molly was throwing a get-together and Emma was wrong, but it was so confusing that she just gave up and died.

Brenner, Lianna, age 15, lived a healthy life until she made the fatal decision of watching a video of a puppy splashing in a puddle. She clung to religion until the very end, crying out to God via the YouTube comment section, typing "omg omg" in interest of time, but it was too late. She was dying, dying, omg, and then proclaimed dead.

Lee, Rachel, age 14, suffered from an asthma attack at the local dog park. When she cried out in fear of death, her friends responded, "I know, the puppies are so cute!" and "I didn't think my joke was that funny." Genuinely unable to breathe, Rachel... actually passed away. Her memorial service will be next Saturday afternoon at St. Paul's Cathedral. All are welcome.

IF WOMEN WROTE MEN THE WAY MEN WRITE WOMEN

by MEG ELISON

There is a particular look about a teenage boy that lets you know what kind of man he'll be. A certain fullness of lips, a frank sensuality in his gaze. We all know what the word for that is, but it's not polite to use it until he's proven he's that kind of boy.

- - -

Hugin was chosen, among all the boys of the village, to compete in the Races. He had grown up, the child of a simple, lovely baker, and his wife, the wolf-hunter. Hugin wore his hair in simple golden waves and had the longest legs anyone had ever seen, coated in fine, silky down. When the yearly selection began, other boys watched Hugin. They knew he would be the one, and they pouted.

What they did not know was that Hugin was torn; torn between tall and silent Joina and her younger sister, Kika the Maker of Knives.

As the old men pulled him on stage to crown him as the Racer, he could see Joina's eyes upon him. He could sense Kika's longing for him as her lips formed his name.

Which one of them would choose him? Who would he belong to? The question would have to wait. He was a Racer now, and nothing else mattered. Not even love.

- - -

Brett pulled his tank top up over his head and stared at himself in the full-length mirror. He pushed down his jeans, then his boxers, and imagined the moment when Jennifer saw him nude for the first time. His feet were average-sized, and there was hair on his toes that he should probably take care of before tonight. He liked his legs just fine, but his thighs were wide and embarrassingly muscular. He tried standing at an angle, a twist at his waist. Some improvement. In that position, it was easier to see his ass and notice that it was not as pert as it had been at twenty-two. He clenched both cheeks, hoping that tightened its look. He sucked in his tummy and pulled his pecs up high, trying to present them like pastries in a bakery window. Would she like him? Were the goods good enough? He pouted his lips and ran his hands over his thighs, masking their expanse. *Maybe.*

- - -

Prof. Redgrave looked down to find Stephen gazing up adoringly at her. She blinked down at him, unimpressed.

"But what is Nabikova trying to tell us with this transgressive tale? Is it really just elevated pornography? Or is there a deeper meaning to this titillating tale of a middle-aged woman seducing her teenage stepson?"

Stephen's look didn't waver. Redgrave knew there wasn't a single original thought in the little tart's head. She had seen the way he lounged, long in his desk, inviting the girls in class to look at him and then crying foul when they prefaced their arguments with a harmless little "sweetheart." She had graded his papers, marking them down for their puerile assertions and childish leaps of logic. She and her grad student, Gertrude, had privately giggled over his pathetic striving.

"That one is not 201 material," Gertrude clucked. "Fail him out already. It's sad watching him struggle like this."

But of course, it had to be the Nabikova where he showed a little glimmer of hope. What other book would serve?

"Professor," Stephen began, one well-tanned arm in the air. "What if it's not really about the boy? What if, like she says, he's a safely solipsized something else? What if the plaything isn't the jailbait kid, but the English language itself?"

And just like that, Redgrave knew who her next TA would be. She drank him in, the combination of nubility and fragile academic curiosity and knew he'd fall for her wise advisor act. Kid had mommy issues written all over him.

This semester was looking up.

- - -

"But I don't get it!" Shea was panting, trying to catch up to Michael as he fled. "The monster ate everyone else. How did you escape?"

Michael reached the boat first, flinging himself in. He waited for Shea to follow him and take the oars, guiding them smoothly away from the shore.

"It's because I was different from the other boys," he said, pushing his hair behind his ear and looking away.

"What do you mean, different?" Shea's muscles rippled and flexed as she rowed them to safety, and Michael could not tear his eyes away.

"Different. Pure, the monster said. Because I'm... I've never..." He looked away again, and the moonlight caught on his throat, outlined his clavicle.

"You're a virgin," Shea said, realization dawning. "What a waste." Michael blushed.

"If we get out of this alive," she said. "I'm going to fix that."

- - -

"You're so good-looking," said Chester. Antoine was patting his hair into shape in the mirror, fretting again. Antoine knew that his friend meant well, but his opinion just didn't mean anything. Was Chester going to give him a class ring? Was he going to hang that all-important varsity dance team jacket over his shoulders when he was shivering? Would Chester wrap his arms around him, hold his hand, kiss him so deeply that his toes curled? Antoine looked at his best friend in the mirror, seeing him in an entirely new way. It wasn't the same as Barbara, he knew. It would never be as overpowering, or as fulfilling. But maybe...

Barbara found them twenty minutes later, wrapped around each other. Antoine looked up in horror.

"I'm so sorry! It didn't mean anything!"

Barbara smirked, crossing her arms and taking in the scene. "Now, this is interesting. Don't freak out, babe. It's not like it's really cheating, after all."

The two boys looked at each other, flushed and excited.

"Maybe…" Chester bit his lip. "Maybe you'd like to join us?"

She smiled again and began to undo her belt. "That's just what I had in mind."

- - -

Andrew didn't mind that he never came when they had sex. Bianca would climb on top of him and ride his pubis, grinding her clit until she spasmed and fell on top of him, exhausted and mumbling about love. He liked the way it got him excited and sometimes, later, he would take care of himself. He really just wanted to feel the power of her body on top of his, to know that he was exciting to her. Besides, what are orgasms when compared to true love?

---

* Read an interview with Meg Elison about this piece on page 651.

WENDY MOLYNEUX'S EXCERPTS FROM POPULAR McSWEENEY'S INTERNET TENDENCY LISTS THROUGHOUT HISTORY: 1860

LIST

LINES FROM WALT WHITMAN'S REVIEWS OF MOVIES STARRING THE ROCK

by ELDREDGE SWIFTMAN

4. Simplicity is the glory of *Jumanji*.

5. Let your soul stand cool and composed before a million universes, but do not bother standing in line for *Skyscraper*.

6. Do I contradict myself? Very well then, I contradict myself. I contain *Moana*-tudes.

7. And there is no trade or employment but the young man following it may become a hero, especially when that young man is Dwayne Johnson, and he is driving that road as the enigmatic Luke Hobbs in this triumphant return of the *Fast and the Furious* franchise.

8. Every moment of light and dark is a miracle, but *The Tooth Fairy* sucked.

FAMOUS AUTHORS REPLY TO YOUR UNSOLICITED DICK PIC

by JAMIE CRICKS

JANE AUSTEN

It is a truth universally acknowledged, that a single woman in possession of a smart phone may not be in want of your dick pic.

However little known the feelings or views of such a woman may be on her first opening a text, this misconception is so well fixed in the minds of the men online, that she is considered as the rightful viewer of their penises.

My dear sir! Have you not heard that women may not enjoy your images? It is true, for my friend has just been here, and we talked all about it. Do not you want to know what we thought of it?

Well, my dear, you must know, we agree that your penis is obviously one of a young man of large fortune in the southern region; but that you don't care at all for the maintenance of your private area, and we were much disgusted with it and did not enjoy viewing it; and sincerely request that you send me no more, and remember that no woman of sensibility wishes to wake up to your cock before their own cock crows with its morning's call.

VIRGINIA WOOLF

There it was before me—your dick pic. Your dick pic: I thought but I did not finish my thought. I took a look at the image, for I had a constant sense of it there, something turgid, something imposing, which I shared neither with my friends nor my Twitter followers. A sort of interaction went on between us, in which I was on one side, and your dick pic was on another, and I was always trying to zoom in on it, as it was of me; and sometimes we eyed each other (when I was alone); there were, I remember, furtive staring scenes; but for the most part, understandably enough, I must admit that I felt this thing that I called your dick pic was sudden, intrusive, and would be quick to pounce on me if I gave it a chance.

LANGSTON HUGHES

What happens when your dick pic is ignored?
Does it dry up like a raisin in the sun?

CHARLOTTE BRONTE

Most true is it that "beauty is in the eye of the gazer." Your colorless penis, turgid, massive head, broad and hairless balls, deep eye, strong shaft, firm, rounded head—is not disgusting, according to rule; but it is more than disgusting to me; admittedly it is full of power, an image that quite mesmerized me—that took my thoughts from my own volition and tethered them to your penis. I had intended to want you; I had struggled strongly to grow within my soul the seeds of want; but now, at the first erected view of you, they spontaneously die, shriveled and impotent.

MAYA ANGELOU

Out of your sack and follicle's nest
You rise
Up from a shaft that's rooted in groin
You rise
You are average length, thin and unspent,
Welling and swelling, and terribly bent.
Leaving behind images of hope turned fear
You rise
Thrusting me into an evening of beer
You rise
Sending me pictures and hoping I'll save,
You are a crooked mast in need of a shave.
You rise
You rise
You rise.

SYLVIA PLATH

All the disgust and disappointment have purged themselves. I feel surprisingly calm. I hold the dick pic suspended a few feet above my head. I am open to the offending image.

ANNE BRADSTREET

Your dick pic was so irksome in my sight;
Yet being your own, at length photoshop would
Thy shortcomings amend, if so I could.

OSCAR WILDE

There are only two tragedies in life: one is not getting a dick pic, and the other is getting yours.

MARY SHELLEY

I behold the wretch—the miserable monster whom I had help create. He takes up the entire screen; and this dick pic, if dick pic it might be called, is fixed on me. The veins throb, and it lurches forward disturbingly, while a single tear weeps from the tip. Your one hand is stretched out, seemingly to grip him, but I avert my eyes and delete the image. I take refuge in my Candy Crush challenges, where I remain during the rest of the night, dropping candy pieces up and down in the greatest agitation, listening attentively, catching and fearing each text sound as if it were to announce the approach of the demoniacal snake to which I had so unintentionally given life.

ZORA NEALE HURSTON

It seems to me that trying to look at your dick pic is like milking a bear to get cream for your morning coffee. It is a whole lot of trouble, and then not worth much after I do it.

A McSWEENEY'S INTERNET
TENDENCY ORIGIN STORY

KEEPING IT IN THE FAMILY

by RIANE KONC

M CSWEENEY'S WAS ALWAYS A family business, owned by Baron McSweeney's and passed down from Son McSweeney's to Son McSweeney's. My father worked for McSweeney's, and my grandfather, and his grandfather, too. As far back as my family line goes, we've always done good, honest work for McSweeney's.

For my father, working for McSweeney's was supposed to be a nine to five gig. He'd drive to the office, punch in, do some McSweeney's, eat lunch, balance the McSweeney's, and then punch out. But the job was all-consuming, and he often had to bring McSweeney's home with him. "Shh, your father is doing McSweeney's," my mother would whisper as we begged to be hugged. He worked so much, we often found him passed out in his easy chair, just covered in McSweeney's. One time—I'll never forget it—my father hoisted me up on his lap and let me work on McSweeney's with him. He pulled out a sketchpad, handed me a pencil, and we both wrote "McSweeney's" until the sun came up. I had hand cramps for weeks, but from that night on, it was settled: I was a McSweeney's man.

Things were different when my grandfather worked for McSweeney's. To hear him tell it, he was out in the fields before sun-up, tilling the McSweeney's so that new McSweeney's could be planted. It was hard work, he said, but worth the bountiful McSweeney's harvest it produced. My grandfather said that some days, after the harvesting was through, he would run his hands through the barrels of McSweeney's and thank god he was alive. Then he'd ride through town on his bike and shout, "Free McSweeney's! Free McSweeney's for all!" The children would run out of their houses, and he would toss the McSweeney's from his bike. Things were simpler back then.

He learned everything he knew from his father, my great-grandfather. My great-grandfather used to handmake McSweeney's, making every stitch by hand. He would put his own little signature at the bottom of each McSweeney's, so you would know it was an authentic McSweeney's. Of course, that all changed when the machines came into town. All of the sudden, you could make 200 McSweeney's with the flick of a switch. Soon, it seemed like everyone had to have a McSweeney's. Demand shot through the roof. Some people still bought my great-grandfather's homemade McSweeney's, because they recognized the quality, but it was hard for him to keep up with Big McSweeney's.

I could go on and on: about the McSweeney's Revolution or the Suddenly Everyone Had to Have a McSweeney's Merger or the Great McSweeney's Crash of 1972, but that's for another time. Now, I have a more important job to do: helping my son get his first summer McSweeney's job, stocking McSweeney's.

MY HUSBAND HAS BEEN A GARBAGE BAG FULL OF BEES THIS WHOLE TIME

by KATIE BRINKWORTH

Friends, relatives, and neighborhood beekeepers, I'm sure you're all wondering why I've asked you to meet me here and not wear any perfumes or bright colors. Unfortunately, I have some disappointing news. My soul mate, the love of my life, and my husband of ten years isn't who he says he is. The truth is, he's been a garbage bag full of bees this whole time.

Now I know what you're thinking. How could this be(e)? Our love, our life together, and the face I drew on the outside of the garbage bag all seemed so real. But even though it hurts, I have to admit that it's true. My husband has been leading a double life, or approximately fifty thousand different lives if you consider the volume of an average hive.

It's the kind of devastating secret I never could have expected when I married him. This news has me questioning everything now, and I'm sure you have questions too. Like should you still use the name "Frank" when addressing the bag, who will get the house in the divorce, and how exactly was I able to navigate the logistics of a sexual relationship with a plastic bag full of bees for so many years? But I'd prefer to keep the sordid details of "he said/she said" and "garbage bag full of bees made a buzzing noise" to ourselves for now. After all, there are kids involved.

And even though I know now that our relationship was based on a lie, I can't help but remember the good times. I remember the day we met, and the way my heart swelled when we first touched. I also remember the way my lips, mouth, eyelids and throat also swelled. It was a feeling unlike anything I'd ever experienced. Maybe it was because I'd never felt true love before, or maybe it was because I grew up in a city with limited access to nature, but either way I knew then that this relationship was special. In fact, to this day I still get butterflies in my stomach whenever we see each other. Yes, I'll admit it's probably because there's a huge hole in the bag and I've swallowed some of the bees, but that hole isn't nearly as big as the hole in my heart. Which is also full of bees.

I suppose a few of you may have seen this coming, and even voiced your doubts early on in the relationship. Although I ignored them, I wasn't unaware of the concerned whispers behind my back: "Is she sure about this?" and "Has she stopped taking her meds?" and "OH MY GOD BRENDA, YOU KNOW I'M DEATHLY ALLERGIC TO BEES—WHY WOULD YOU BRING THAT HERE???" But no matter how many times I heard it, or how many people went into anaphylactic shock as a result, I just wasn't ready to face the truth. I guess I was blinded by love. And also, as I mentioned earlier, my eyes were completely swollen shut for most of our marriage.

But I guess this is nothing new. After all, this isn't the first guy I've been with who hasn't been completely honest with me. In fact, every guy I've ever dated has turned out to be some kind of liar, cheater, international scam artist, pile of dirty laundry, small wooden puppet who dreams of one day becoming a real boy, the word "MAN" spelled out in a stack of children's blocks, a chalk outline of a dead body at a crime scene, or even a Republican presidential candidate. But for some reason, this betrayal stings more than the others. And it's not just because stinging is a bee's natural defense mechanism, it's more like a metaphorical pain. It's also very itchy.

It's been a tough road, and after all this, I fear I'll never be able to trust again, that I may never find real love. But I just have to remember to stay positive and keep my heart open. After all, love can be unpredictable, and can show up when you least expect it. Sometimes it even falls right into your lap, like a burlap sack full of wet rats flung onto your porch by an irresponsible pest control employee. Speaking of which, I've gotta go. Have a hot date tonight!

HOW TO DE-FERALIZE YOUR CHILDREN FOR BACK-TO-SCHOOL

by SARAH HUTTO

1. Find them. Where are they? Nobody knows for sure. Seems like one might have been enrolled in a facility of some kind and another was left with a family member in a part of the country with reportedly different values. Was there a third one? There definitely was a tiny one somewhere. Jayden. Or Kayden. One of those. Drive by the playground while yelling "Aiden" out of the driver's window and see what turns up.

2. Get them medical treatment. Set broken bones, dress wounds, and provide antibiotics for new strains of disease they are sure to be carrying. After living in the wild for three months they are likely harboring various strains of bacteria and pathogens that should not be reintroduced into the general population.

3. Remove any creatures that have come to know them as a host. Using bolt cutters, remove all small mammals currently using their hair as a habitat. This includes, but is not limited to, bats, badgers, opossum, chinchillas, ferrets, lemmings, and meerkats. Any creatures misappropriated from local zoos should be returned once liberated from your child's pelt. Reptiles should be turned loose into wetlands and bird's nests should be carefully placed high in the branches of native trees.

4. Bathe them. This is best done in an open area out-of-doors where you won't be clogging your septic system with their waste. A firing line with a spray hose works very well, being sure to focus extra attention to ears, armpits, and nether regions, all while avoiding direct contact, preventing further infection. After the preliminary rinse, a Borax scrub will remove lingering soils, followed by a final pressurized rinse.

5. Minimize rough edges. Clip talons, exfoliate callouses, and ebb budding horns with a micro-planing tool. A simple haircut can be persuasive in the illusion of their not having spent most days of the summer at least partially naked urinating on trees while acquiring disturbingly large mosquito bites that you had to look up on WebMD. Lingering animal musk can be temporarily obscured with baby oil and a dab of vanilla extract behind the ears.

6. Transition them from their steady diet of acorns and bugs back to table food. Expect some resistance here, but be persistent. It's important that they be able to eat people food once they begin school so they're not walking around all day snacking on handfuls of gravel from their pockets. If you continue to find them nibbling

on dead leaves and mulch well into autumn, don't lose hope. By the end of the year, all of their natural food sources will be snow covered, forcing them to revert to the traditional macaroni and cheese cuisine until the ground thaws. An occasional small pine-cone can be provided as a treat.

7. Replace footwear. Whatever they've been shod with all summer (if anything) must now be destroyed. Shake out shoes to release hidden pockets of sand and tiny animal bones, as well as lost valuables, like your wedding band and original brain cell count. Usher the shoes from the earth permanently in an elaborate cere-mony of incineration. Spread the ashes over multiple locations of varying distances to be sure the remains won't re-congeal into a radioactive pair of zombie footwear that will find its way back into your home each night without you knowing and track mud into every room.

8. Confiscate all tribal effects and weaponry acquired during ascen-dance to power in local child horde. This includes, but is not limited to: headdresses, crowns, conch shells, chain-link armor, back tattoos, shields, spears, kilts, and tooth necklaces. Turn these in to your local police department, and replace with the (slightly) more socially acceptable rope bracelet from the boardwalk gift shop.

9. Get them some notebooks with cats on them or something.

AN ORAL HISTORY OF QUENTIN TARANTINO AS TOLD TO ME BY MEN I'VE DATED

by ALI ELKIN

CHRIS, 25, *took me to the Upright Citizens Brigade Theater*: Improv is where they make up the show totally on the spot, in case you didn't know. What were we talking about? Probably directors. My favorite director is definitely Quentin Tarantino. You know that shot in *Pulp Fiction* where John Travolta and Samuel L. Jackson are pointing their guns straight to camera? I had that poster in my college dorm room. Very cool and unique, right? Do you know the names of any directors?

- - -

MIKE, 30, *met me at* The Whiskey Ward *(or similar)*: Awesome that you can order a whiskey, by the way. So, Quentin Tarantino dropped out of high school and never even went to college. That's why I like him a little bit better than Paul Thomas Anderson, who had some college before he dropped out. That's actually a great story. Paul Thomas Anderson knew his screenwriting professor was bullshit, but to test her he submitted a David Mamet scene instead his own homework assignment. The professor gave him a C+, so he quit. Sorry, what did you say? Well, yeah, it's plagiarism but that's beside the point. Anyway, back to Quentin Tarantino.

- - -

ALEXANDRE, 29, *left his hat in my apartment*: I do not care much for American cinema, but do you know the films of Quentin Tarantino?

- - -

JASON, 28, *took me to some Naples-style pizza spot*: The first feature Quentin Tarantino wrote and directed was called *My Best Friend's Birthday*, and a lot of it was lost in a fire. It's OK, though, because a lot of that script wound up going into *True Romance*. Here's the thing: Even though he lost that physical copy of the film, Quentin Tarantino is totally against digital! He says he'll stop making movies once it becomes impossible to shoot on film anymore. You just have to admire that kind of integrity and love of the craft. Oh, and not sure if you know this, but in Italy they actually eat pizza with a knife and fork.

- - -

ANDREW, 27, *never took me anywhere (I'm starving)*: What places are delivering right now? So, in the early '90s, right around when *Pulp Fiction* came out, Quentin Tarantino and Mira Sorvino were dating. I always thought *Romy and Michelle's High School Reunion* was a dumb chick flick, but I caught part of it on cable the other day and there was an ad for Red Apple cigarettes in the background of one of the shots! Do you know about Red Apple cigarettes?

- - -

FRANK, 26, *also took me to the Upright Citizens Brigade Theater[1]*: Red Apple is the made-up brand of cigarettes that Quentin Tarantino uses in all his movies. There are all sorts of little Easter eggs like that in his movies, if you're paying attention. Like there's this scene in *Pulp Fiction* where Mia Wallace is talking about a movie she acted in and years later that description turned into *Kill Bill*! This improv team is supposed to be pretty good, by the way. One of them had a small part in *Broad City*. You know that show?

- - -

ALEXANDRE: I have actually been to several of the locations where they shot *Inglourious Basterds*, but what you might not know is that most of them are in Berlin and not in Paris.

- - -

ANDREW: Oh, sorry, I don't have a working card hooked up to my Seamless right now. Mind if we order on yours? Oh, so this is a badass story: At Jamie Foxx's first rehearsal for *Django Unchained*, he was reading the part with, like, too much finesse. So, Quentin Tarantino takes him aside and just rips him a new one, telling him to play the part more honestly. Didn't walk on eggshells or anything just because Jamie Foxx is a star. Jaimie Foxx said Quentin Tarantino was a tyrant but that he'd work with him again in a second. That's the kind of film-maker I'd want to be, you know? When does the delivery window start?

- - -

MIKE: It's totally cool that you got your whiskey on the rocks, but just so you know, you should really taste it neat first, then maybe add a bit of water. Where was I? Oh. So, when Quentin Tarantino was making *The Hateful Eight*, the script leaked. He said after that he was going to write it in the form of a novel instead of a movie, and I have to say that was devastating. It turned out fine, though, because he changed his mind. Then they released it on 70-millimeter and that was just, like, a religious experience for me. I know a lot of people don't care about that sort of thing, but I'm just, like, a purist.

- - -

JASON: Oh, man. Seeing *The Hateful Eight* on 70-mil? I know a lot of people wouldn't care about that sort of thing but I'm just, like, a purist. Anyway, Quentin Tarantino says that he probably won't get married as long as he's working because right now is his time to make movies, and I just think that's the way to go, man. Why muddy things up with kids and a marriage when you're in the prime of your career? That's definitely what I'm going to do. I mean, I guess maybe it's different if a woman wants to make movies, but how often does that happen?

- - -

CHRIS: Quentin Tarantino's movies have a lot of strong, female char-acters. There's the Bride in *Kill Bill*, Shoshanna in *Inglourious Basterds*, the chicks that don't get murdered in *Death Proof*. I find that a lot of movies have female characters. Have you seen a movie?

- - -

ALEXANDRE: I find most American women to be vulgar, but you are very sweet.

- - -

[1]It turns out that students of the Upright Citizens Brigade are required to see improv shows, and the dating apps kept sending me aspiring comedians.

WENDY MOLYNEUX'S EXCERPTS FROM POPULAR McSWEENEY'S INTERNET TENDENCY LISTS THROUGHOUT HISTORY: 1870

LIST

BAD THINGS TO PUT IN YOUR POCKETS IF YOU'RE A COWBOY

by GALLOPIN' JOE SHOEMAJOR

44. Fudge.

THE LIFE-CHANGING MAGIC OF KEEPING ABSOLUTELY EVERYTHING

by JENN SHAPLAND

Have *you* ever sworn off waste, only to find yourself dragging the cans to the curb once more? If you find yourself backsliding, remember the three *R*s you learned in fifth grade: Reduce, Reuse, Recycle. Then, cut out two of those *R*s and focus on the middle one: Reuse. If you adopt this approach—the KeepEverything method—you'll never revert to discarding again.

WHY CAN'T I STOP THROWING THINGS AWAY?

Every time you go to throw something away—an eggshell, a used wrapper, a straw, a dirty paper towel, a broken DVD player, a sock with a hole in the toe—pause, and gently ask yourself *How else can I use this?* Give it time. Let the item speak to you, however quietly. Be patient. Perhaps keep the item—a screw of unknown origin, a ball of lint, a soiled Kleenex—around for a bit. Set it on the counter, stash it in a drawer. Behold the power of *shelving*—leaving things unused until their time, their power reveals itself to you.

Empty bottles, cardboard boxes, bubble wrap. Or, a place for future potions, the walls of cat forts, protection for your shoes. I've heard of people saving all of their chewed gum, which may sound extreme. I'm not here to tell you how to reuse. Remember, this is a personal journey. It's between you and your things. But I am encouraging you to treat all of your things equally. To love every piece of threadbare furniture and old grocery list, every coupon and every unworn, ill-fitting pair of shoes you bought on sale the same. To love them equally, to keep them safe.

HOW DO I MAKE ROOM FOR EVERYTHING?

As your collection grows and your waste decreases, you may find yourself craving space. It might be time to move somewhere vast—New Mexico, Siberia—where you can have a compound, some land, adobe walls to protect your wares, your family. Allow likeminded others to live on the compound with you and your things. Your ex-boyfriend, Jim. The Tibetan religious man you met in AA. *They, too, are a part of your collection.* They should not be thrown out. Perhaps, as time goes on, some of your new tenants have a mind to clean things up, pitch things out—a broken rowing machine, a legless desktop, a cockeyed lamp. Take these, cold from the curb, and *find a home for them.* Your front porch will do, as will piles under tarps, or the giant plastic garbage cans your son brought over when he offered to help you "get organized." Place them alongside the ripped, disintegrating outdoor cushions that birds were nesting in when your tenants pitched them over the wall. The Tibetan can surely find a use for them. He built a prayer wheel from a garbage can and perched it atop the dead tree you've been keeping around. He will use the desktop to secure the walls of his trailer fortress in the driveway. Reuse is the perfect opportunity to exercise your creativity to its fullest potential.

WHAT IF I CAN NO LONGER LEAVE MY HOUSE?

As your collection grows, you might stop leaving the house altogether. But do you need to leave the world you've created? This is why you have so many things: they are your memories, your friends, your outside world. Dead lightbulbs, scratched CDs, moldy succulents. Mold! One of the promises of *keeping everything*, especially if you expand outdoors. Collections breed collections of their own. Moths will flock to you, too. They will live in the floorboards. They will find plenty to eat among the vintage sweaters you bought and never wore. The moths are there to use them. Save cat hair from the vacuum cleaner in jars or bags. After all, Georgia O'Keeffe kept all her chow dogs' fur and had it woven into a shawl. The possibilities are endless.

All great artists are hoarders. When you can't find your copy of *The Life-Changing Magic of Tidying Up*, a book that at least three well-meaning, oblivious friends gave you in 2014, call up a better friend, a minimalist sculptor. She has a copy buried in a stack of thirty dusty books to lend you. Keep this book, along with all the library books you never returned, not to read, but for some other purpose: fashion a doorstop, a shelf, a low wall around yourself.

Andy Warhol wasn't a hoarder; he was a collector. Take a page from his book. Place everything you might have thrown out over the course of a day into a box. Seal the box, sandwich crusts, beer cans, soggy newspapers, *Life-Changing Magic* and all, and place it in a stack in some heretofore underused corner of your property. Call it a time capsule, if anyone asks. An archive. A life.

I HAVE SIGNED
THE GUESTBOOK
OF YOUR CHARMING
COTTAGE BY THE SEA

by DAN KENNEDY

We had a wonderful stay at the cottage. The apple tree was loaded with fresh fruit, so we picked plenty, and even have a few to take home. Our days were spent at the beach, evenings were spent in the sauna looking out at the sea and the full moon. I had a bit of insomnia, so the night descended on me like a sky full of angry ravens and specters full of fury. A black aurora borealis, the ghosts of ex-friends, lovers, and drinking buddies, all screaming down from the inky abyss, a collective earth-bound howl. The voices counted off the years, demanding answers, presenting me with a full accounting of time, dead-end self-involved precocious ambitions, things I thought I wanted and found out differently, and plans that never came to fruition. The moon was an interrogation light, blinding me on the patio of your fairytale cottage. A voice from behind the light demanded I reconcile its ledgers of this life; square up the shortfalls, explain the overages. I ran off of the patio and out to the apple tree between your Fairytale Cottage and Seaside Main House. The fucking apple tree. Where I stood only nine hours ago, picking fruit, making jokes, laughing, smiling. So normal did all of this seem, sweaters were worn, photographs taken with telephones and posted up into an ether of mostly strangers so that they might admire, and like, and approve. I stared at the photos too, convinced I looked good on the surface, calm in the face of time and life doing what they do. Does the cottage, in fact, have a history rich with golden era Hollywood icons staying here while looking to escape the scandal and countless little deaths that came with celebrity and outsized success, even back then? Tonight, having headed down the slippery slope of comparing myself to the curated lives depicted in the guestbook entries of previous travelers, I envy anyone whose life was torn asunder, destroyed, and reordered by fame's sweet venom and hurricane momentum. In the previous entry, just one week before my arrival, I see that Steven proposed to his girlfriend Melissa on the deck overlooking the bay. Congratulations to Steven—only God and the Devil know why I've struggled to accept all of the love that has come my way in this life. I see in an even more recent entry that just two days prior to my arrival, Mike and Stephanie from North Carolina sat at the very table I write at now, serene, having a glass of wine, and recalling their stay. I agree with Mike and Stephanie's estimation that no other place on Earth is quite as magical as your little cottage here, but Mike and Stephanie need to learn that magic, like reality, has a light and dark side. What Mike and Stephanie don't seem to understand that life is a cobra in a terrarium, cornered by invisible walls, confined by boundaries it cannot see. It is beautiful, but also savage by nature, impartial to what it strikes, fucks, eats, in order to carry forth with its biological imperative. I wonder if Mike and Stephanie have ever considered that. Maybe it is incumbent upon other guests to stay awake nights in your delightful cottage, trying to make sure the metaphorical cobra of life is warm. Maybe it's up to an unfortunate few itinerant weirdos to feed the cobra of life, all the while hoping it does not strike at the wrist and paralyze the heart. My girlfriend is calling for me to return to bed now; a kind and comical small whisper of a whistle that she does, a playful pulling me back as the sun comes up now and ends what feels like my funeral, trial, and spectrum of maladies. In closing, we enjoyed riding the bikes to the farmer's market on Saturday for fresh cinnamon buns, sitting in the sun, cooking on the outdoor grill, and sitting by the fire at night... the dark, dark, night, in which so many questions seem to arise.

Dan Kennedy
New York, New York

P.S. While I'm impressed with Stephanie's photo-realistic charcoal sketch of your apple tree, I'd like to point out, on the facing page, my rendering of guitarist Slash from the American rock band Guns N' Roses. I started working on it immediately after checking in nine days ago, and it's meant to represent Slash in the 1991/1992 *Use Your Illusion* period.

IF BOSTONIANS LOVED OTHER LOCAL INSTITUTIONS THE WAY THEY LOVE THEIR LOCAL SPORTS FRANCHISES

by MICHAEL HARE

—Hear that new one from the BSO?

—Shit, yeah, that Brahms? That one knocked me square on my ass. Even more so than the Shostakovich. Pardon me, the *Grammy Award-winning* Shostakovich.

(*They toast.*)

—We should repeat.

—We should but we won't, because the Recording Academy hates Boston. Watch. Watch them give it to the frigging New York Phil, which is a fine orchestra if you like listening to a bunch of soulless prima donnas collect paychecks.

(They nod, drink.)

—Gotta respect Andris Nelsons.

—The kid can conduct his ass off, in the bravura tradition of Seiji Ozawa.

—Friend of mine down in Quincy just named his pit bull "Ozawa."

—Remember '02, when Ozawa did Beethoven's Seventh?

—Course I do.

—Course you do. We all do, because it was an indelible performance. An indelible performance that the *New York Times* called "plodding." Please. Please do me one favor, Mr. Big New York City Critic, please don't talk to me like I don't got two ears and a brain. Because I do, and also a heart, which Seiji touched with that masterful Seventh.

—They act like there's no culture north of the Triborough. Like guys like us don't know a sublimely realized Seventh when we hear one.

—Just don't talk shit about Seiji, all right? You come up here and you try to talk shit about Seiji—I don't care if you got a Pulitzer or a MacArthur or a Pulitzer and a MacArthur and an award from the frigging National Book Critics Circle—I'll lay you the fuck out.

—Figuratively speaking.

—Of course. This city once aspired to be the Athens of America. I'm

IF BOSTONIANS LOVED OTHER LOCAL INSTITUTIONS THE WAY THEY LOVE THEIR LOCAL SPORTS FRANCHISES

not about to disrespect that majestic civic aspiration by acting like a goddamned fucking barbarian.

- - -

—Other day I went over to the Museum of Science.

—How was it?

—Well it was the fucking Museum of Science, so how the fuck do you think it was? It was superlative. It was a testament to our region's proud tradition of rational inquiry.

(*They toast.*)

—Meanwhile, all you hear is, "Silicon Valley this, Silicon Valley that…"

—Because they hate Boston, because they're jealous of Boston. And I'm sorry, but making an app to call a cab isn't science. You know what is science? Life science is science.

(*They nod, drink.*)

—Gotta respect our biotechs.

—I swear to god, I get all these disgusting frigging fantasies about a bunch of these Silicon Valley guys coming up here and talking shit about our biotechs. Being like, "Oh yeah, Boston's got a nice little biotech scene." And I'm like, "Little?" And then I very figuratively lay them all out. I very figuratively beat them back to Cali using the gold Nobel medal awarded to Dr. H. Robert Horvitz.

—Friend of mine out in Walpole just got a Horvitz tattoo.

—Sick.

- - -

—So I'm in the MFA last weekend, where I volunteer as a docent.

—A valuable service to an invaluable institution.

(*They toast.*)

—I'm in Gallery 242, and this kid comes over, says, "Are these the only Rembrandts?"

—And this kid is from where?

—From a state that wants so hard to be part of New England but is actually just part of New York, and it knows it, and so it's got all this twisted anti-Boston resentment.

—Friend of mine up in Lowell deals cards down in Connecticut. Says it's awful.

—What it is is anti-Boston.

(*They nod, drink.*)

—Kid asks for more Rembrandts. That's some true Connecticut bullshit.

—You want to see a hundred Rembrandts? Here. Here's a bus ticket. Enjoy Manhattan. P.S., it sucks. You want to see five Rembrandts, and really see them? Really engage with each canvas? Come to Boston.

—Because there's far, far less to see and do here, and so it's easier to concentrate.

—Exactly.

- - -

—Know where I haven't been in a wicked long time? Plimoth Plantation.

—I'm there two, three times a month. It's a jewel.

(*They toast.*)

—You wonder why it's not constantly crammed with people coming in from all over to experience what life was like in the seventeenth century in a fledgling agricultural settlement on the outskirts of what would one day become Boston.

(*They nod, drink.*)

—Could be the thing about people hating Boston.

—So it's guys in costumes speaking in an archaic vernacular and churning butter under a hot sun or whatever. Not flashy enough for you? Here. Here's a bus ticket. Go numb your brain in Times Square.

—The quiet of the place, its frank modesty, that's part of what makes it so moving. That, and its brave refusal to ignore the darker aspects of our history.

(*They nod, drink.*)

—Ever feel like some people, like non-Bostonians most especially, might be sleepwalking through something major? Like, not the shit we see, but the shit behind the shit?

—Like America's silent epidemic of depression? Its festering addiction to distraction? Like how some people mistake conspicuous consumption for meaningful experience? And how some others mistake hatred for virtue? Like how so many have lost contact with the communities that should help to sustain them and that they should help to sustain?

—Yeah, dude. Basically that. I worry that one day soon we're all going to find ourselves condemned to lives of isolation and sorrow, all trapped inside the same airless, boundless nightmare anti-community.

—Like Fairfield County, Connecticut?

—Exactly.

—If the whole world turns into one big Fairfield, that'll make us two guys from Connecticut.

—Two guys from Connecticut, just begging to get laid out.

THE
ORAL HISTORY
OF THIS
ORAL HISTORY

by KEVIN SECCIA

A FIRSTHAND ACCOUNT OF THIS ORAL HISTORY,
AS TOLD BY THE PERSON WHO WAS THERE.

"You have to remember, at that time, right now, no one was doing anything like that. It was unheard of."

KEVIN SECCIA (WRITER): I remember what I was doing when I first thought of the idea to write an oral history of this oral history. I was procrastinating. That's the truth. I was avoiding actual writing work, and I thought to myself (in the beginning, it was just me—this was before all those other people didn't come aboard), wow, why not? Why not write an oral history of this oral history, the one you're reading right now? I couldn't think of a reason.

K. SECCIA (WRITER): You have to remember, at that time, right now, no one was doing anything like that. It was unheard of. People wrote oral histories about great TV shows and classic films and sometimes they'd do one on the making of a legendary album. Like, music. Also, I'm pretty sure there are sports ones.

KS: Yeah, there are definitely sports ones. But this one isn't about any of those things, it's about this thing you're already reading.

KEVIN SECCIA: Here's the ironic thing—and no one ever talks about this—this oral history is taking time and effort that could've been used in pursuit of a legitimate accomplishment. Something that might've eventually garnered enough interest to justify the making of an actual oral history.

K. SECCIA: Before this piece, if you'd wanted an oral history you needed to have a great idea, execute it perfectly, then attract an audience, and eventually, critical acclaim. And then years later someone would round everyone up for an oral history. But I didn't see it that way, I was like, shit, why don't we just do it now? About this thing you're already reading.

KS: Here's what no one ever realized until now. Those things are always written by like ten people, all weighing in on different aspects of the thing they did. I was like, I'm just one person! I can't do all that. But then I figured out a way. And that's when everything clicked.

KEVIN SECCIA: Hey, it's me again, the same guy from above. What I've done is formatted this thing in such a way that you think this is someone else writing right now, but it isn't. And that was the moment we all realized this could be something special.

K. SECCIA: Just to clarify, this is one guy writing all of this. Look closer, it's all variations on the same name.

KEVIN SECCIA: Also, it's being written but no part of it was ever oral… and I think the moment we realized it could be that way was when we knew we were onto something.

KS: You've gotta understand, people just weren't doing oral histories that way, at all. Until us.

KEVIN SECCIA: He said that? That's hilarious. Yeah, that's true.

K. SECCIA: Wait, is there that much crosstalk in these things? Maybe go easy with that. The first time it's kind of funny but not the second time.

KS: Wow. Oh yeah, you're right.

KEVIN SECCIA: Someone else may have said this already but we knew we needed more than just this initial conceit. The whole meta aspect of the title and then the first few beats would only get us so far…

K. SECCIA: Some of us were concerned early on. We knew that around the fifteenth chunk of dialogue people were bound to start asking themselves, "Is this like, all it's gonna be?"

KS: Or, "Do I even need to keep reading this thing? I mean, we get it."

KEVIN S: And that's the moment when everything changed. Someone, I forget who, maybe it was KS? This feels like a Kevin Seccia thing, honestly. Anyway, someone had the idea to introduce a new, separate story into the narrative, that went beyond just the oral history gimmick. Which is why we've decided to kidnap your dad. You, the person reading this, we have done a home invasion and taken your father hostage.

K. SECCIA: Whoa. Okay, no. That felt really weird. Like it was part of some other piece, in a totally different style.

KS: That was bad. Not the right tone at all.

VIN SECCIA: I think we were all getting a little complacent and things happened but we will not mention the kidnapping thing again. I'm so sorry.

KEVIN SECCIA: I'll tell you my favorite moment of that whole time, when I was writing this oral history of this oral history. Most of it I never think about, because I'm not that guy anymore, you know? The guy who started writing this. You get older, you start to think about something else you'd like to write, or maybe you should just do the writing work someone has already paid you for. So, the best moment, for me, was this line… Because that's when you were like, "Uh, the wheels are starting to come off of this thing, a little bit? How's he gonna end this?"

K. SECCIA: That's when the momentum definitely started to slow down and even the structure of the piece seemed to suffer. It was like, has he even read a lot of these things, or did he read like, two?

KEVIN SECCIA: Here's the real crime. Maybe someone out there really loves these oral histories and they would've done an awesome job with the premise but now this guy got to it first and ruined it for everyone.

That's what I still think about.

K. SECCIA: I've heard that argument, and I get it, I really do. But you gotta understand, we were just a couple of kids messing around, but really it was one guy, and we didn't know what we were doing. We, meaning I, had no idea how it would be received or even if anyone would ever read it. You're telling me one guy can write an oral history, about nothing? No one had ever done that before.

VIN SECCIA: Let's have fun, and try to make ourselves laugh. That's basically all I was thinking about during that whole time, right now.

KEVIN SECCIA: Should someone else have written this piece? Yeah, maybe. But they didn't. And I'm glad, because when all is said and done, it was the best job I've ever had, except for all of the actual jobs. That's the thing you find out later, this meta idea, this experiment or kinda vague premise driven into the ground or whatever you want to call it... we did it, and no one can take that away. And no one had ever done that before.

VIN SECCIA: Oh, and you'll never see your father alive again.

THE RULES OF THIS BOARD GAME ARE LONG, BUT ALSO COMPLICATED

by BRIAN AGLER

I'm so happy you all could make it to board game night! We're going to have a blast. OK, so, what do we want to play? What'd you bring?

Clue? Ok.

Monopoly? Hmm.

Those are all good options, but we could also play this new game that I just picked up. It's called The Secret of the Golden Tomb. It's really fun, and it's super easy to learn.

Sorry, did I say, "super easy?" I meant needlessly complicated.

We start by setting up the board. See that stack of 750 tiles? Each one goes into its own unique space, like a jigsaw puzzle. But it's way worse, because any sense of accomplishment you achieve is drowned out by the fact that this is just the prelude to a multi-hour process.

Oh, also, I'm missing a few of the tiles, so we'll just have to imagine that they're there. It probably won't be a big issue, but then again, it almost certainly will.

To move around the board, all you have to do is roll a die. Well, actually, thirty-two separate dice, rolled one at a time. The goal is for each roll to result in a higher number than the last. If it doesn't, you have to start over. You might be wondering, "Die only have six sides. How can there be thirty-two ascending numbers?" Exactly! It's a challenging game!

You'll notice that the board is divided up into different areas. Specifically, there are four quadrants. Also, there are seventy different sectors. And that's in addition to the ever-shifting and often indeterminate number of cosmo-zones. Once a player controls at least two quadrants, twenty-three sectors, the square root of a negative number of cosmo-zones, and correctly answers a series of trivia questions about the 1973 Cincinnati Reds, we move into the next phase of the game. This is where it gets a little tricky, but you'll catch on.

We'll add up the number of everyone's power cubes and convert them into resource tokens using an algorithm that's roughly based on the complex math undergirding Bitcoin. After this conversion (which could take up to a week, depending on how slow my computer is) the player who was winning may still be winning. Or maybe, the player who was losing will be winning. Or maybe, another player whom we haven't met yet will be winning!

That brings us to Elijah's Cup. Go ahead and grab that chalice out of the box. That's for the prophet Elijah, who may or may not join the game. We'll cover what to do if that happens—but it probably won't happen. He's only appeared like three times, and one of those times, he just wanted to watch us play and eat our snacks.

This next section of the rules is on how to build and maintain your fortresses. It's not really necessary, so we'll just skip it, but rest assured, I will invoke an obscure rule from this section to win later on, and you'll have no idea what I did.

Quick question—is anyone here left-handed? Marjorie, you are? OK, you can't play.

This is an important rule, so pay attention—if you reach the Ranch you become the Sheriff. This part of the rule book explains what happens when you become the Sheriff... but it's written in Greek. I could translate, but you'll grasp the nuances of the game better if you read the rules in the original Greek. While you all are learning Greek, maybe I can go get everyone some *spanakopita*? That's spinach pie. See, you're picking it up already!

Oh, I almost forgot to ask, does anyone want to play with the expansion pack? We don't have to, but it will make the game marginally more fun and infinitely more confusing. You know what, I'll just go grab it.

Now, you're probably asking—why is there a loaded revolver in the box? Honestly, it's never come up... but that's the great thing about this game: it totally could!

And of course, there's the big question: how do you win the game? Have you read Nietzsche's *Thus Spake Zarathustra*? That's basically what you're trying to do.

Oh, one last thing to remember, if you have anything you're confused about, ask now—because once the game starts, we have to burn the rule book. But don't worry, if you have any questions, I'll be sure to explain the answer to you in an extraordinarily patronizing manner. Ready? Let's play.

WELCOME TO OUR STARTUP WHERE EVERYONE IS 23 YEARS OLD BECAUSE WE BELIEVE OLD PEOPLE ARE VISUALLY DISPLEASING AND OUT OF IDEAS

by BOB VULFOV

Hello, and welcome to our startup. We hope you're enjoying your complimentary snifter of vaporized coconut water. Once you're done, please place the glass into one of the blue receptacles around the office, which will send the glass to be washed and dried. Do not place it into one of the red receptacles. The red receptacles take whatever you put inside of them and launch it into space.

If you look to your left, you'll see one of our employees using a state-of-the-art ergonomic sleeping desk. Most startups have standing desks, but we have sleeping desks, dancing desks, and even skateboarding desks. The skateboarding desks are just large skateboards you can use to skate around the office. Be careful while skating, though, because we don't offer any sort of medical insurance, since our benefits budget all goes toward cool desks.

As you can probably tell by looking around, every employee at our startup is twenty-three years old. On the morning of your twenty-fourth birthday, the barcode on your employee ID stops working and you can no longer enter our building. We do this to ensure our company has a ceaseless, youthful energy. We believe old people are displeasing to look at and also, bad at ideas.

We do things a little differently here at our startup. First of all, we have a completely horizontal, non-hierarchical organizational structure. There are no bosses, no subordinates, and no mugs with jokes about people's job titles written on them. Nobody has a job title here. All of our employees put "Thinkologist" as their occupation on their résumés. We show our commitment to a completely flat hierarchy by not giving anyone a salary. No one at our company earns a single dollar because everyone is equally important here.

One of the perks of working here is that our workspace offers a dizzying array of complimentary dining options. Breakfast, lunch, and dinner are free for all employees. Sometimes we wonder why our employees would ever want to eat anywhere else! To that end, we outfit each new employee with a tiny device inside his or her mouth that makes any food purchased or cooked outside of our office taste like sewage. Everyone tends to eat all of their meals at the office because of the sewage mouth device and because there's nothing like getting to know your coworkers over some delicious poke bowls. If you try to eat a single meal elsewhere, you will throw up because the food will taste like wet garbage.

We want everyone who works here to show a lot of company pride, so several times per year, we print and distribute free apparel for all of our employees. Whether it's a hoodie, a T-shirt, or a snapback hat, we want our employees to rep our startup. This summer, just in time for beach season, we're going to be distributing company flip flops! If our employees are ever caught wearing anything other than official branded clothing with our startup's logo on it, they get zapped by a drone.

When our employees have some downtime or want a morale boost, they are encouraged to pop into our rec room for some fun and relaxation. We have: ping-pong tables; massage chairs; pinball machines; work tasks disguised as video games; big screen televisions; a printer that can print actual living safari animals; board games; talking robots that ask you when you're going to get back to work; poker tables; cotton candy machines; cameras that watch you at all times; and a glowing orb that you should never touch. We believe when you work hard, you should also get to play hard! We also believe nobody should touch the glowing orb because its powers cannot be wielded by any mortal.

Care for a nap? Well, you are more than welcome to take a quick, refreshing nap in one of our many nap pods. You will be lulled to sleep by the soothing sound of our twenty-three-year-old founder softly whispering startupy things such as, "Disruption," and "Like Uber, but for horses."

Oh, you have to meet our office dog! His name is Series B and he is a labradoodle. Our office is extremely pet-friendly, so employees are encouraged to bring in their pets. However, this policy comes with the understanding that those pets will be put to work if they're here. We're in all-hands-on-deck mode right now, so no one gets to just sit around. Series B is currently working on a pitch deck for a few of our international investors.

Did we mention we're not like all the other startups? At our startup, employees are encouraged to fail. Failure is good. Failure represents progress toward success. We don't focus on things like profit, or overhead, or returns on investment. Those things are boring and stupid, like old people.

As soon as a company starts caring about a bottom line more than an awesome time, workplace culture dies. Our employees never have to worry about the bottom line. We continuously shred all of our financial documents and refuse to comply with the IRS. We rent our building from the Armenian Mafia and receive all of our electricity from private generators. We are completely off the grid. Any time an auditor comes to our office to solicit financial information, we wipe their memory by making them touch the glowing orb from the rec room. One auditor held on to the orb for too long and now he's trapped in another dimension.

You noted on your application that you'll be turning twenty-four in two months. As much as we're impressed with your background and previous experience, we can only offer you a contract for two months. Once those two months are up, you will become nothing more than an old bag of bones with a rapidly decaying brain. So, can you start this weekend?

PLEASE FORGIVE US AT BLUE APRON FOR THIS WEEK'S MEALS. WE'VE BEEN HAVING A TOUGH TIME LATELY

by LUCY HUBER

This box contains the ingredients and recipes for this week's Blue Apron meals. We know you've come to expect a high standard of quality from Blue Apron and normally we are happy to provide you with the best quality recipes and ingredients possible, but look, stuff has been rough for everyone lately and we're doing our best. Things kind of got away from us this week.

SCRAMBLED EGGS

PREP TIME: 45 seconds

COOK TIME: 1 minute

SERVINGS: 2

This is 4 eggs. We were going to do a whole soufflé thing, but we had a bunch of stressful meetings and then someone turned on CNN in the office kitchen and everyone got kind of depressed. We all kind of wanted to go home early, sit down on the couch with a glass of wine and watch a few *Great British Bake Offs* before going to bed. Honestly, this could also be fried eggs if you wanted.

INGREDIENTS: 4 eggs

KNICKKNACKS: You probably have some kind of cheese somewhere, right? You can throw that in.

PREPARE THE INGREDIENTS: Crack the eggs into a bowl. Use a fork or a whisk, we didn't test it, someone really yelled at Claire in Customer Service over the phone because we forgot the watermelon radish in last week's bibimbap recipe right after she read an article about cuts to Planned Parenthood, and she was feeling pretty down so we all took her out to lunch instead.

Using a nonstick pan if you have one, heat some butter or oil, and then just sort of pour the eggs in there. Swish them around a little bit. You'll know when they're done because they won't be liquid anymore—what else do you want us to say? It's eggs. We were going to research the best technique but we decided to spend the afternoon calling our senators and asking them not to support a ban on Muslims.

PLATE THE DISH: Put the eggs on a plate. A clean one if you have it.

WINE PAIRINGS: Do you have an open bottle of wine in the back of the fridge somewhere? It's probably fine.

ROLLED-UP DELI TURKEY WITH VARIOUS FRIDGE CONDIMENTS

PREP TIME: 30 seconds
COOK TIME: None
SERVINGS: 2

We're sorry, really. This is just a piece of deli turkey. At this point checking Twitter for the latest news is basically a full-time job so we're all pretty burnt out. We all just wanted to catch up on the new *Pod Save America* and just chill for a little while. We took a long walk and Damien from UX pointed out this really beautiful tree outside the office that had just begun to blossom and then wondered out loud if all the trees in our neighborhood will die if Trump does away with the Clean Power Plan. The turkey is organic and nitrate free.

INGREDIENTS: Four pieces of deli turkey.

KNICKKNACKS: You have condiments, right? Mustard? Mayo? An old jar of olives that you've been saving because you're pretty sure olives don't go bad but not 100 percent sure? Use those.

PREPARE THE INGREDIENTS: Simply roll up the turkey and stare into the fridge while you try to decide what condiment you're going to squirt on it, contemplate what will happen if you and your loved ones lose their health coverage. It's fine if you just put ketchup on it. No one will see you. You are all alone.

PLATE THE DISH: If you haven't already eaten this while you were standing in front of the fridge, go ahead and eat it sitting down while watching the new season of *Orange Is the New Black*. Don't turn on the news, just stop and give it a break for like thirty minutes.

WINE PAIRING: 3 to 4 Miller High Lifes

SOME CEREAL

PREP TIME: 20 seconds

COOK TIME: None

SERVINGS: 2

Sometimes we think we've got this whole cooking thing down and then sometimes we're like, why do we even bother we're the worst at this and everything is just a total mess. We're all going to our parents' house for the weekend to just catch up on some sleep. We were going to think of something better than cereal but then Sarah from Finance mentioned that she read somewhere there are roughly 32,000 gun deaths per year in the United States and yet the government isn't doing anything to make it harder to obtain firearms, and we just didn't feel up to it.

INGREDIENTS: Cheerios. Maybe. You might also have gotten Honey Bunches of Oats. We ran out of Cheerios.

KNICKKNACKS: Just eat it dry, OK?

PREPARE THE INGREDIENTS: Open cereal bag.

PLATE THE DISH: Pour the cereal into a bowl or mug or reach in there and pick out pieces of it while you scan through Twitter, compose a tweet with a joke about Paul Ryan's vacant, emotionless expression and then delete it because honestly, what's the point? Go to bed at 9 p.m. Wake up at 12 a.m. in a cold sweat, remember Trump pulled out of the Paris Climate Agreement and the polar ice caps may melt, leaving much of the United States underwater. Eat a few more handfuls. Just shove the shit directly into your mouth.

WINE PAIRING: A shot, oh fuck it, two shots, it's Thursday. Chase it with half a capful of NyQuil. Go crazy while you still can.

REFLECTIONS FROM A McSWEENEY'S INTERNET TENDENCY WRITER

by LUCY HUBER

I WAS WORKING AT 826MICHIGAN as their Field Trips intern when I submitted my first McSweeney's Internet Tendency piece. Of course, it was rejected and, of course, my next four or five attempts were rejected, too. I finally broke through after someone suggested I could trick McSweeney's into thinking I was funny by writing a timely piece incredibly fast. So one day in the middle of work I wrote a response to David Brooks' latest op-ed, submitted it roughly thirty minutes after the article came out, and it was accepted. Friends asked if I got published because I had an in with Dave Eggers from working at 826, which is completely unfair; I got published because I bribed Tendency editor Chris Monks.

My second McSweeney's piece, "Please Forgive Us at Blue Apron for This Week's Meals, We've Been Having a Tough Time Lately," was published on my last day at 826, which meant a lot to me. I had no idea how big the response would be, but the next morning I got an email from my high school ex-boyfriend who works at Blue Apron and he said all his colleagues were emailing it back and forth to each other. I was psyched because, a) impressing your ex after you've broken up—even if it was over ten years ago and the furthest you ever got was him touching your sports bra—is the number-one goal of a relationship and, b) it really seemed like I was on track to at least get a few weeks of free Blue Apron meals out of this.

Unfortunately, despite my numerous tweets at them, Blue Apron has yet to send me free meals. I even tried to get them to sponsor a podcast of mine, but again, no luck. I did, however, get some freelance jobs out of the piece and people still mention it when they meet me. I've even had professors ask if they can teach it in their classes. I tell them "Sure, but don't expect to get any free Blue Apron meals out of it."

I do try to stay humble. I try not to bring up my internet humor-writing fame too much, especially after my brother told me the toast at his wedding wasn't the appropriate time to mention it, but it's hard. It was fun being internet famous for a bit and I'm glad I made so many people laugh.

But, really, Blue Apron, if you are reading this: no hard feelings. And there's still time to send me free food.

GEORGE SOROS
MADE A
BEE STING ME

by EVAN WAITE

Sometimes I think the whole damn world has gone crazy. Our country is changing into a place I can barely recognize. Inevitably, this brings us to the invisible hand of nefarious billionaire philanthropist George Soros. This crypto-Zionist has spent decades controlling the global economy, teaching crisis actors the Meissner technique, and mailing himself pipe bombs just to disrespect our flag stamps.

But yesterday, that sick son of a bitch went too far. That's right: George Soros paid a bee to sting me. It's the only explanation that makes sense other than that I was throwing rocks at a beehive. Ordinarily, bees don't sting me, but this time one did. So I think it's pretty clear who bankrolled their stingers.

What's more, Soros got me fired for watching scary porn at work. He's the puppet master pulling the strings that held my sweatpants up. And make no mistake: things are only going to get worse once the migrant

Bangbus he funded arrives with thousands of El Salvadorian MILFs. How am I supposed to behave in a socially appropriate way then?!

While part of me blames myself for plowing into that Duane Reade after getting drunk at the Eagles game, a much bigger part blames George Soros for not taking my keys. Why would he let me rent a car in the first place?! My credit is terrible and I have a long history of drunkenly plowing into things!

Every day I don't get punched is a miracle.

George Soros needs to be held accountable for my actions. Otherwise, I'll be forced to take a good hard look in the mirror. The mirror he installed to make me feel bad about gaining forty pounds in the last six months. God, I've gotten fat because of him.

But let's face it: George Soros is an older guy and he won't be around forever. So unless you have a hard-on for critical thinking, it's important to have a backup villain ready to go. I've given it a lot of thought, and I'm going with Jackie Chan.

Think about it: Minority? Check. Willingness to incite violence? He hit a dude with a pool cue in *Rush Hour*! Global influence? Why don't you ask the tattoo of his face that's on my German wife's tit? Enough talk. Let's give this bad boy a test drive and see how she handles: Jackie Chan is the reason I'm not allowed in Canada, not the endangered moose I punched.

Yeah, that feels right.

So what can Jackie Chan or George Soros or anyone besides me do to make my bitter, unfulfilling existence more tolerable? Well, for starters, they could direct the global order to create a hair-growth medication that works for my scalp type. I've blown thousands on Rogaine, Propecia, and magic beans I bought from an old man in a forest. Since they're the ones that made baldness run in my family, it's up to them to grow me S-curls.

Also, they should help me establish an Aryan ethno-state to fight back against white genocide. That'd be swell.

I INTEND TO KEEP SCROLLING UNTIL I FEEL SOMETHING

by RIVER CLEGG

Nothing yet.

Soon, I will feel something; I must. This can't go on forever. That dog I scrolled past earlier came close. The cute dog that was wagging its tail. It made me feel, um—what's the word? It's when you feel in between good and bad, but it's slightly closer to good. Damn. This will drive me crazy.

Adequate. That's the word. The dog made me feel adequate.

I'm not sure that counts as really feeling something, though. I'm going to keep scrolling. Maybe I can get closer.

Oh! What's this? A big meaty sandwich with melted cheese. Boy, that looks good. Well, I know intellectually that it looks good. My mind is aware that the sandwich is, in all likelihood, delicious. The crispy onions and bacon look particularly mouth-watering.

But my heart? My heart feels nothing.

No matter. I can scroll forever. That's the beauty of it. There's a vast, virtually infinite field of content that exists solely for my perusal. Like this post—it's by an old college friend with whom I disagree politically! Let's see what he has to say. I'm sure it'll make me mad!

Huh. How about that? I'm not enraged. Not even irritated. It's not that I agree with him. In fact, his new post—which denies that there's a scientific consensus on climate change—strikes me as even crazier than usual for him. How can he write such garbage?

If I were feeling something, I bet it would be anger. Ooh, and contempt!

That would be nice.

Maybe what's going on is that, subconsciously, I know my friend can't be convinced that he's wrong, so my brain is trying to save itself the stress of worrying over it at all.

Yeah. That's probably it.

Oh, look! A news story about a father who ran through traffic to deliver life-saving CPR to his young son. Whoa! What bravery. What love. And see how cute that boy is? Trying to be tough in the face of danger. Such a little fighter.

This story has to make me feel something—it can't not. I'm going to sit with my eyes closed until it does.

Seriously? Nothing?

Jesus.

I blame the internet. Everything today is flattened; no story is afforded its proper weight. News reports about Syria and op-eds about racism and pictures of people mountain biking and videos where zoo pandas fall down—they're all stacked on top of each other! One right after the other in an endless feed. How am I supposed to wade through all this without arriving at a maddening, indecipherable noise? How could genuine human emotion penetrate such an opaque, suffocating shroud of free online content?

There's only one solution. Faster scrolling.

Let's see. Eight bagel toppings I have to try this instant? Nope. A single mom's blog post about why cell phones are bad? Strike two. A quiz about classic Nickelodeon TV shows? It's right in my wheelhouse; it should fill me with an intoxicating blend of nostalgia and amusement. But, alas, no.

I would like very much to feel something.

Oh, no, a sponsored post from the ACLU. It's about fighting for voting rights in poor communities. And—oh, god—it's asking for a donation. Shit. You know, I always say I'm going to give them money and never do. I'm the worst.

Hey! Did I just feel something? Was that—guilt? I think it was! Yes, I'm feeling trace amounts of guilt!

This is awesome.

You know what? I'm going to donate. I just got my paycheck, and I have no excuse not to. Here we go. I'm clicking the post. I'm selecting "Donate." Twenty dollars to the ACLU. There. Done.

And what's this? I'm feeling something else. Something new. Whatever the opposite of guilt is. Satisfaction?

Yes! Satisfaction. I'm feeling low but distinct levels of satisfaction. What a day.

I wasn't always this way, I don't think. I used to feel more, I mean. I remember turning twenty-four. I had a little thing at a bar near my office. I was still pretty new to my job back then, and I was happy about how many coworkers showed up. I really hadn't expected many to come. Plus, some of my old friends came. One was even in from out of town, and we were all talking and drinking together. It's not like they were doing me some big favor by being there or anything. But it was nice. Most of those coworkers have jobs somewhere else now.

Hey! I just scrolled to a picture of one of them! Craig Moore. How about that? He was always cool; sometimes we'd get lunch together. I wonder how he's doing.

Hold on. Am I about to feel a third thing? What's the word? Wistful?

Nope. Lost it.

I'M TOTALLY COOL WITH THE COLLAPSE OF THE HEALTH CARE SYSTEM BECAUSE I HAVE A JADE EGG IN MY VAGINA

by REBECCA SALTZMAN

Now that Republicans have voted to repeal Obamacare and caused the medical system to spiral into chaos, my insurance will no longer cover things like anything that could be described as health care. So I can't afford to see a doctor anymore, but it's fine because I have a crystal egg with healing powers and I'm wearing it in my vagina.

Sure, I was angry that those Penis-Americans, also known as Congress, were making decisions about my body. As a woman, I was especially concerned that things like sexual assault, C-sections, or postpartum depression could be considered pre-existing conditions, leading to denial of coverage or astronomical surcharges. It's almost like living in a misogynistic society and not having a dick is itself a pre-existing condition.

But I'm okay with all of that now because I shove an egg-shaped stone up my Fertile Crescent every morning. Crystals have a natural energy that is absorbed through the mucus membranes, and my schlong sheath oozes with mucus. Which, now that I think about it, might not be normal. But hey, we're normalizing everything these days, like Nazis and kleptocracy and bacterial vaginosis.

I mean, who needs things like pap smears or treatment for your cancerous ovarian teratoma when you have this jade egg wedged up in your vajizzle? And it was only $25.99 at that kiosk between Sears and Qwick Botox. In fact, I took the $800 I was planning to spend on a tricked-out new iPhone and bought thirty vag eggs. Thanks for the advice on how to afford health care, Representative Jason Chaffetz!

Yep, my pussy chakras are zen as fuck. They don't even care about the wage gap anymore.

I'm sure Dr. Tobin, my gynecologist, wouldn't approve, but I'm boycotting that tool of the patriarchy anyway since she only believes in "effective, evidence-based medicine." Also because my new Trumpcare policy only covers leeches and aromatherapy.

What about birth control? I think you mean, *schmirth* control! There's an impenetrable hunk of rock jammed into my cervix. Just try spelunking in my love cave now, sperm. Look, I've solved the abortion debate too!

That's not to say there aren't some downsides to squeezing a stone egg up these flappety carpaccio curtains. It's kind of awkward when you're talking to your boss and the egg just falls out in his office because you forgot to do your Kegels.

And lately my mind is all cloudy, and my mouth is lined with sores—it's possible that I'm absorbing too much of my jade's natural energy, which some might call ionizing radiation from the breakdown of uranium atoms inside its ore.

I really would like to get this tumorous ovarian teratoma removed too. Did you know these teratoma things can grow their own teeth? My reproductive tract is full of molars and they're going to chew up the nearest penis-like dick jerky. It's hard to meet guys on Tinder when you're the living embodiment of the nightmares that haunt their fragile masculinity.

Also, I'm having a little trouble getting the egg out. Apparently there's not much to grab onto when a smooth round shape is clenched between slippery walls of muscle.

Seriously, I can't get it out. It's way up in my bearded clam, and not in a hot amateur porn kind of way. Maybe if I squat down and really get, like, wrist deep… nope. Oh great, now I think something prolapsed.

Does anyone know if Dr. Tobin accepts barter for her services? I can't afford insurance now that Congress has turned our whole health care system into a festering pus bucket, which incidentally also describes my vagina.

But I can trade two-and-a-half dozen jade eggs for a pelvic exam. Beautiful green color! Please ignore the fishy smell.

WENDY MOLYNEUX'S EXCERPTS FROM POPULAR McSWEENEY'S INTERNET TENDENCY LISTS THROUGHOUT HISTORY: 1922

LIST

ALTERNATE PANAMA CANAL PALINDROMES

by BARTLEBY HOMESMITHS

21.   A cranbowl man's tan hole.

22.   Damn it Jan, don't put your jam-hands on the land troll.

I HAVE TRAVELED HERE
FROM THE PRESENT
TO WARN YOU ABOUT
GLOBAL WARMING

by BRIAN BENNETT

Thank you for meeting me here. Excuse my tardiness, I'm still adjusting.

Now, listen to me carefully.

In the present, where your mother is exactly the same age as she is here, she made me swear to her that I would travel within time to give you this message. You are the only one who can save us. Well, you and every other person on earth. But if you don't do your part, the consequences will be dire, so in a way you are the only one.

Looking at your innocent face, and the blissfully unaware way you live your life, it breaks my heart to have to tell you what happens in the present. But you must know, so that your present does not look like mine. Where I come from, the Arctic ice shelf has mostly melted away, and entire seas have dried up. Although there is no way you could foresee it, the species of my time are experiencing an unprecedented mass extinction event, and floods and storms are laying waste to the developing world. In my hometown, which the people of my time call "Chicago," it is the middle of winter, yet temperatures are in the seventies.

I just hope I traveled far back enough to prevent these things from happening.

Although you and the people of your time do not yet realize it, in the time where I come from the world is a veritable hellscape. No, sit down and hear me out! You at least owe your mother that.

I understand if this is hard for you to believe, but as a small, symbolic token of what life is like in the present, I emailed you some links.

You may ask how it's possible that I'm here. Let me explain. First, a skilled team of rogue scientists did not bother to build a machine that can travel through time. Time travel is incredibly dangerous and can even result in someone getting "zinched" if done improperly, so it's fortunate that it was completely unnecessary for the transfer of this information.

Keep in mind, I have not had to leave behind everything I've ever known to find you. I haven't forgotten what my children look like or fallen asleep looking at the only photo of my wife I have, because after this I will just drive home and we'll have dinner and I will go to bed.

You see, there aren't these things called "timestreams," and there certainly aren't an infinite number of these timestreams where every possible permutation of events happen in parallel. There is just one, and it is heading us directly toward a tragic, global catastrophe. I guess you could call it "The Timestream" if you wanted, but, honestly, that seems like an unnecessary confusion.

I have to say, it is surreal to see the people of your time arguing over things like the proper allocation of movie awards, but I suppose they could not possibly know the fate that befalls them in the present.

I'm afraid that's not all. The autocratic president of my time tells the people that global warming is not real, and many believe him. In your time, you have books written by a man called "George Orwell," yes? Even though you call his works fiction, we in the present have seen many of his predictions about the government's ability to distort reality come true.

Oh, and one other thing... the Patriots won the Super Bowl. Yes, the one that already happened. Wish I could be a bigger help.

WHY DOES THE LAME-STREAM MEDIA ONLY FOCUS ON THE NEGATIVE REGARDING JOHN WILKES BOOTH?

by JAKE TAPPER

The media in this country is so negative. Case in point: John Wilkes Booth and the Lame-Stream Media (LSM) focus on one night in his life.

Of course the usual suspects come out harrumphing and complaining, suggesting that sedition and assassination is some act of treason!

I say: What about his acting career? Yes, he may be known for that dark night in Ford's Theater but his *Richard III* in Philadelphia made all the critics swoon!

What about his sage invocation of Latin? Are you actually telling me with a straight face that you already knew the phrase *Sic semper tyrannis*? Oh, pardon me there, Brutus!

What about all the presidents that John Wilkes Booth *didn't* assassinate? That has to be mentioned, too. From Martin Van Buren through James Buchanan—it can be fairly said they all owe their lives to Booth.

How about how much he achieved in just twenty-six years on the planet? Are *you* going to be a household name living three times as long? I didn't think so!

Lame-Stream Media only focuses on the headlines—what about the fact that he was the only member of the conspiracy to fully carry out his role in the conspiracy?

There are those who look at the black check marks on a person's life—sleaze or myriad sexual harassment complaints or sex crimes or obstruction of justice or exploiting fear for profits or an assassination of a heroic world leader or whatever—and see only the negatives.

USE THIS SCRIPT TO CALL YOUR CONGRESSPERSON AND ASK THEM TO PLEASE GOD JUST END IT ALL

by RACHEL STROMBERG

Hello, office of [CONGRESSPERSON'S NAME]! This is [YOUR NAME] from [CITY OR TOWN]. I'm calling to ask about [CONGRESSPERSON]'s stance on simply putting an end to this hellscape of a world and allowing humanity to fade into the black abyss of nonexistence.

Given that the very foundations of American democracy are under attack from within, every day is somehow worse than the last, and there seems to be no escape from the deepening horror of this waking nightmare, I and many other constituents feel that now is the time to please dear Lord just make it stop. What action is [CONGRESSPERSON] taking to secure the merciful erasure of all human consciousness from the acid pit of corruption that our world has become? Is any legislation being drafted to this effect?

• If you could pass along a brief message to [CONGRESSPERSON],

I would like to express my support for plunging the universe into an eternal and dreamless sleep, please oh god I beg of you.

- I also urge [CONGRESSPERSON] to vote NO on any further events, developments, or occurrences at all, as each of these so far has been, improbably, more unconstitutional and nauseating than the last. As [CONGRESSPERSON]'s constituent, I want nothing more than for it to just end already, please, I'll do anything.

- Conversely, I ask [CONGRESSPERSON] to vote YES on all of the following measures:

  - The development of a vaccine to numb the agony of existence that settles in each time I regain consciousness and remember our bleak reality;

  - The creation of technology permitting us to go back and do it all over again, better this time;

  - My personal relocation to deep space;

  - The installation of shorter basketball hoops on courts nation-wide, because at this point, the thrill of dunking is the only joy available to us;

  - Some kind of raft in this ocean of despair.

Most of all, I simply want to implore [CONGRESSPERSON] to support pulling the plug on this entire operation and letting it all finally be over. I am so tired. Thank you, and have a great day.

HOW TO TALK TO YOUR TEEN ABOUT COLLUDING WITH RUSSIA

by TOM RUSSELL

Even the best-behaved teen is likely to encounter a situation where he or she is tempted to collude with Russia. Unfortunately for parents, a teen's natural tendency to test the limits of independence can often manifest itself in his or her exchanging sensitive information with Russian emissaries for material or other rewards. If not constructively addressed during adolescence, colluding with Russia can have much more serious consequences in adulthood.

Here are a few tips for engaging in a healthy conversation with your teen about the hazards of colluding with Russia.

KEEP THE LINES OF DIALOGUE OPEN

Don't be shy about asking your teen where she has been, who she has spent time with, or why she has receipts from Cypriot bank wire transfers hidden under a false bottom of her jewelry case. If you discover a folder marked "Parental Kompromat" try to stay focused and not act emotional. Think about her point of view and why she would consider it important to have your social security number, Gmail password, and Pornhub search history in a secret folder. Take advantage of these teachable moments to have meaningful discussions about colluding with Russia with your teen.

EXPLAIN THE NEGATIVE
CONSEQUENCES OF COLLUDING WITH RUSSIA

When talking to your teen about colluding with Russia, honesty is the best policy. You shouldn't shy away from mentioning that a Federal indictment could turn into an awkward blemish on a college application, or that retributive polonium poisoning could likely hamper one's ability to compete for a coveted lacrosse scholarship. Remind them also that sharing their behavior on social media is never a good idea. Posting a selfie with a Russian aluminum magnate or "checking in" to a Kremlin safe house can have ramifications that are difficult to erase later on.

UNDERSTAND YOUR TEEN WILL
LIKELY EXPERIMENT AT SOME POINT

Parents must be realistic and remember that despite their best efforts their teen will try colluding with Russia at a party, in their friend's basement, or even in a hotel room after the prom. Your teen should understand that if he has been out late colluding with Russia he should never, under any circumstances, get in a car—especially a nondescript windowless van with diplomatic license plates. He should understand that you will come get him and give him a ride home no questions asked!

SAYING NO TO PEER PRESSURE

If other teens in your child's peer group are colluding with Russia, then she is likely to feel pressured to follow suit in order to fit in. For example if she goes to a mall and sees one of her friends stuff a thumb drive under the paper towel dispenser in the restroom, she will no doubt feel a curious exhilaration and a compulsion to emulate such behavior. Similarly, teens may also be influenced into colluding with Russia by movies, TV shows, or current events that depict colluding with Russia as "cool," "fun," or even a little dangerous. You should actively assist your teen by praising their good behaviors and accomplishments, which can help passively discourage transgressive forays such as offering to launder money through a complex array of shell companies or cash real estate purchases.

Remember, any effort you make now to address your teen's colluding with Russia is like an investment in their future. The last thing any parent wants is for the behavior to carry into adulthood when it can seriously hurt the parent as well as the child!

WENDY MOLYNEUX'S EXCERPTS FROM POPULAR McSWEENEY'S INTERNET TENDENCY LISTS THROUGHOUT HISTORY: 1987

LIST

OTHER THINGS I WISH REAGAN WOULD CHALLENGE GORBACHEV TO TEAR DOWN

by BRETT NEWBURG

9. My crushing lack of self-esteem around my best friend's girlfriend, Angie, who smells like raspberries and wears two scrunchies at the same time.

10. My boss's need to sing, "You take the good, you take the bad, you take them both and there you have the fax machine, the fax machine," every time he uses the fax.

I AM TRUMP'S LAWYER'S LAWYER'S LAWYER'S LAWYER AND WOULD SOMEONE PLEASE TELL ME WHAT THE FUCK I AM SUPPOSED TO BE DOING?

by GARY M. ALMETER

Good day. I am Trump's lawyer's lawyer's lawyer's lawyer. I think. I might be his lawyer's lawyer's lawyer. I have an email into his lawyer's lawyer seeking some clarification on precisely who the fuck I am. I am somewhat certain that I am his lawyer's lawyer's lawyer's lawyer because that is what Kellyanne said I was when she was talking once. But who knows.

And in an abundance of caution I should be more precise. I am actually Trump's personal lawyer's personal lawyer's personal lawyer's personal lawyer. Just to be clear.

Anyway, I fancy myself a bright guy. I did well enough in law school to land myself a job at a respectable firm outside of Washington, D.C. So when I got a call from Trump's lawyer's lawyer's lawyer asking me to be his lawyer, I said "Sure thing!" No problem too big. No problem too small. If you have a phone then you have a lawyer. I pride myself on representing people of all backgrounds facing the panoply of legal problems that can befall a person.

But I am not exactly sure what is happening here. What kind of law even is this—being a lawyer's lawyer's lawyer's lawyer? I got an A in Torts. Is this a tort? Did someone get torted—or maybe I think the word is injured? Is someone injured? I guess I could argue that this is sort of like a car accident or a dumpster fire. If someone was injured in a dumpster fire and they had to sue the dumpster maker for not putting fire extinguishers in the dumpster then that would be a tort right? It would. And I would get money.

But it's also sort of criminalish. But it's not exactly like a DUI or a burglary. Is it? Someone does appear to be drunk at the wheel. And someone (the American people) is alleging theft. So the answers to the questions *Is someone drunk at the wheel* and *Did someone steal something* are yes and yes. But there's also some international intrigue happening. And some election law. And some constitutional law. Is the lawyer's lawyer of someone who is accused of being a colluder subject to the tenets of the Hague Convention? What other kinds of law even are there? Family law? Is a family being wrecked here? Commercial law? Was money exchanged? I'm not certain what the fuck this is but I know there's no such thing as a Lawyer's Lawyer's Lawyer Law.

Also, do I bill my client for asking his lawyer's lawyer for some guidance on precisely who I represent? Or is it whom I represent? Have I just breached an ethical duty? (Tee hee hee. I said, "Ethical duty." As IF!!)

I have no fucking clue what to do. And there is a dearth of law books to guide me. This apparently has never happened before. How do you even be a lawyer's lawyer's lawyer's lawyer? Is it unethical to call my client's client and ask him what his or her expectations are? Would that work? Or can I call my client's client's client? What about my

I AM TRUMP'S LAWYER'S LAWYER'S LAWYER'S LAWYER

client's lawyer's client's lawyer? Or my client's lawyer's lawyer? Should I get a lawyer? Am I a client? What if the retainer I have to give my lawyer is bigger than the retainer I got from my client?

And is "colluder" even a word? We didn't learn that word in law school. I apparently learned nothing in law school. But maybe this is an opportunity. Maybe I should specialize in collusion law? This might be the next big thing. Like lead paint. Or asbestos.

MY VERY GOOD BLACK HISTORY MONTH TRIBUTE TO SOME OF THE MOST TREMENDOUS BLACK PEOPLE

by DONALD J. TRUMP

On February 1, 2017, President Donald Trump delivered these remarks from the White House.

Well, the election, it came out really well. Next time we'll triple the number or quadruple it. We want to get it over fifty-one, right? At least fifty-one.

Well, this is Black History Month, so this is our little breakfast, our little get-together. Hi Lynn, how are you? Just a few notes. During this month, we honor the tremendous history of African Americans throughout our country. Throughout the world, if you really think about it, right? And their story is one of unimaginable sacrifice, hard work, and faith in America. I've gotten a real glimpse—during the campaign, I'd go around with Ben to a lot of different places I wasn't so familiar with. They're incredible people. And I want to thank Ben Carson, who's gonna be heading up HUD. That's a big job. That's a job that's not only housing, but it's mind and spirit. Right, Ben? And you understand, nobody's gonna be better than Ben.

Last month, we celebrated the life of Reverend Martin Luther King, Jr., whose incredible example is unique in American history. You read all about Dr. Martin Luther King a week ago when somebody said I took the statue out of my office. It turned out that that was fake news. Fake news. The statue is cherished, it's one of the favorite things in the—and we have some good ones. We have Lincoln, and we have Jefferson, and we have Dr. Martin Luther King. But they said the statue, the bust of Martin Luther King, was taken out of the office. And it was never even touched. So, I think it was a disgrace, but that's the way the press is. Very unfortunate.

I am very proud now that we have a museum on the National Mall where people can learn about Reverend King, and so many other things. Frederick Douglass is an example of somebody who's done an amazing job and is being recognized more and more, I noticed. Harriet Tubman, Rosa Parks, and millions more black Americans who made America what it is today. Big impact.

I'm proud to honor this heritage and will be honoring it more and more. The folks at the table in almost all cases have been great friends and supporters. Darrell—I met Darrell when he was defending me on television. And the people that were on the other side of the argument didn't have a chance, right? And Paris has done an amazing job in a very hostile CNN community. He's all by himself. You'll have seven people, and Paris. And I'll take Paris over the seven. But I don't watch CNN, so I don't get to see you as much as I used to. I don't like watching fake news. But Fox has treated me very nice. Wherever Fox is, thank you.

We're gonna need better schools and we need them soon. We need more jobs, we need better wages, a lot better wages. We're gonna work very hard on the inner city. Ben is gonna be doing that, big league. That's one of the big things that you're gonna be looking at. We need safer communities and we're going to do that with law enforcement.

We're gonna make it safe. We're gonna make it much better than it is right now. Right now it's terrible, and I saw you talking about it the other night, Paris, on something else that was really—you did a fantastic job the other night on a very unrelated show.

I'm ready to do my part, and I will say this: we're gonna work together. This is a great group, this is a group that's been so special to me. You really helped me a lot. If you remember I wasn't going to do well with the African American community, and after they heard me speaking and talking about the inner city and lots of other things, we ended up getting—and I won't go into details—but we ended up getting substantially more than other candidates who had run in the past years. And now we're gonna take that to new levels. I want to thank my television star over here—Omarosa's actually a very nice person, nobody knows that. I don't want to destroy her reputation but she's a very good person, and she's been helpful right from the beginning of the campaign, and I appreciate it. I really do. Very special.

So I want to thank everybody for being here.

That's the Lame-Stream Media for you, letting their anti-slavery, anti-treason, anti-assassination bias shine through like clockwork!

(Transcript courtesy of The Concourse)

COVERING UP CONCUSSIONS DIDN'T BOTHER ME, BUT LETTING BLACK MEN EXPRESS THEIR OPINIONS CROSSES THE LINE

by SAM SPERO

As a lifelong football fan, it pains me to say that the time has come to boycott the NFL. They have gone too far this time. I was fine when they covered up the concussion epidemic, but letting black men express their opinions is totally unacceptable.

I can no longer spend my Sundays watching football in good conscience, knowing that players are allowed to protest during the National Anthem. Suppressing studies about how football causes the disturbing neurodegenerative disease CTE is one thing; watching black players kneel on the turf for two minutes without having to face consequences for expressing their views is a whole new ballgame.

Why get upset that the owners didn't provide treatment for former players suffering from the long-term effects of playing football? We should be grateful: thanks to the league-wide conspiracy of whitewashing the relationship between football and brain damage, we were able to see more awesome, skull-crushing hits. Athletes shouldn't use their brains anyway, they should stick to sports and leave protesting to the professional protestors.

I won't watch another game until they punish players for quietly kneeling during "The Star Spangled Banner." When I pay to see a game, I'm paying to watch black men destroy each other's bodies, not exercise their constitutional freedoms. If only there were some way for black athletes to protest that didn't shove the fact that they have the same rights as any other American in my face.

The NFL's denial of the fact that players are in serious danger never bothered me, and I care so little about how they continue to avoid punishing domestic abusers and sexual assaulters that I didn't even mention it until now. But if the league permits black people to voice their opinions, what's next? Treating all black people equally? Paying college players for their labor in the fields?

And if you don't agree with my opinion, too bad. Brave and courageous soldiers died for my right to free speech!

LET RACIST BOYS BE RACIST BOYS AGAIN

by EDUARDO MARTINEZ JR.

"A crowd of teenagers surrounded a Native American elder and other activists and appeared to mock them after Friday's Indigenous Peoples March at the Lincoln Memorial." —CNN

In this day and age, one of the most unfortunate realities we face is that everything we do is filmed, logged, and memorialized. Between your YouTubes, your Snapchats, and your Instas, no aspect of our daily lives goes unchronicled. This is true for kids, especially young men, who now grow up at the mercy of their smartphones, casualties of an out-of-control PC culture. I think it's high time we ask ourselves: why can't we let our racist boys just be racist boys again?

Admit it. It's a shame that an adolescent or teenage boy needs to be afraid that his abominable act of aggressive racism might end up recorded. In my day, a boy could heckle a sit-in, menacingly threaten an interracial couple, or scream a slur at your face without it ending up on the front page news. Hell, that's just what we did! And that was okay!

Now, we police our young white men like criminals, waiting for them to inevitably reveal their latent racism and privilege in violent outbursts. Is this fair? Think of the parents of these young men, also probably xenophobic racists, worried that their children will be canceled on Twitter just because they inflicted permanent psychological trauma on someone different from themselves.

Does the punishment fit the crime?

In my opinion, we need to mentor these boys and harness their youthful energy and passion into the more conventional, productive forms of racism. Maybe instead of shaming them for disrupting a peaceful protest, we could give them tools and teach them skills to be more effective bigots in the future. Don't suspend Timothy and his friends from school because they were ruthlessly intimidating a vulnerable citizen like a pack of hyenas. Instead, praise his organizational and planning skills, and direct his enthusiasm towards sports, or Republican politics. We cannot let more of our upstanding young men expressing their cultural pride in bombastic ways end up plastered all over the internet like fugitives. Let's turn the conversation towards something constructive. Let's give our children the same chance we had to further entrench our society in institutional racism.

Together, we can make this generation of young men great again.

REFLECTIONS FROM A MCSWEENEY'S INTERNET TENDENCY WRITER

by EDUARDO MARTINEZ JR.

VERY NOW AND THEN, something truly extraordinary happens in an otherwise ordinary life. Once upon a time, I was a lost soul, a listless drone, a sad-sack loser with a loving family, a caring girlfriend, a full-time, salaried career, generous benefits, a two-bedroom apartment in a metropolitan city. Then, one day, out of the blue, I was gifted an opportunity that even the deserving rarely get: to throw it all away.

I was published by McSweeney's Internet Tendency. And I haven't looked back since.

I never thought I'd really amount to anything. I finished law school by the skin of my teeth, after graduating from a New York City-based private university in three years. That's right—I was a kid from the street, hustling my way through an advanced degree, scraping by from spring break in Monaco to spring break in Tokyo, praying I'd never have to stay at a non-Starwood Suites resort hotel. Sure, things could have been worse. I'd always had a job, been in good health and never arrived late to my father's Champagne brunch on Christmas Day. Still I knew, deep down, that I needed something more, something beyond rich, diverse interpersonal relationships, an established 401(k) investment plan, and many opportunities to pursue my expensive and esoteric passions.

I needed to be published online. I needed to see my name in eighteen-point Garamond font.

It took me close to a decade to get a piece published on McSweeney's. I was wandering in my own creative desert, nothing to comfort me but my AKC-certified spitz dog. I shudder as I think back to those days, carelessly drifting from metropolitan capital to metropolitan capital, gallivanting about with my cadre of brilliant, eccentric friends. I only returned home once in those years, to baptize my godson.

I was a broken man, in a bad place. I needed McSweeney's more than McSweeney's needed me. And yet, we found each other in my winter of discontent. I'll never forget when I received confirmation that my first piece was to be published, stranded on a ski lift in Davos with the Duchess of Cornwall and her kind-eyed niece. I read the work aloud to them, and they guffawed with such force and verve that the lift began operating again. Finally: a glimmer of hope that I would soon see better times.

Alas, how life has changed. Now, once every five to six weeks, I experience the joy of knowing several hundred people are mildly amused by my work. Their collective amusement's sustained for up to four hours at a time, or until another piece displaces it, whichever occurs first. I write, and then almost immediately scold myself for how utterly strange and stupid it is on an almost daily basis. I get to debate the merit of my writing online with complete strangers, almost all of whom insist I am compensated by George Soros to peddle political propaganda, to which I simply reply: not anymore.

I shook off the shackles of my promising career, despite their devious attempts at doubling my total compensation and awarding me the title of my choice. No longer am I distracted by my girlfriend or pet, as I informed both of them that I am only truly wedded to my art. As for my family, I hardly knew ye. My godson will have to learn without me that the only way to live is hastily, insecure, and preferably alone. Without McSweeney's, I would never have understood that stability is an illusion, security is unattainable, and love, merely a mirage. I have my writing now.

My life has just begun.

A SHORT DESCRIPTION OF CULTURAL APPROPRIATION FOR NON-BELIEVERS

by RAJEEV BALASUBRAMANYAM

1. Your new friends Bob and Rita come to lunch and you serve them idlis, like your grandmother used to make.

2. They love your south Indian cooking and ask for the recipe.

3. You never hear from Rita and Bob again.

4. You read in the Style section of the *Guardian* about Rita and Bob's new idli bar in Covent Garden… called "Idli."

5. You visit Idli. The food tastes nothing like your grandmother's.

6. Your grandmother dies.

7. Rita and Bob's children inherit the Idli chain, and open several franchises in America.

8. Your children find work as short order chefs... at Idli.

9. Your children visit you in a nursing home and cook you idlis, which taste nothing like the ones you remember from your youth.

10. You compliment their cooking and ask for the recipe.

11. You die.

WRITING ADVICE TO MY STUDENTS THAT WOULD ALSO HAVE BEEN GOOD SEX ADVICE FOR MY HIGH SCHOOL BOYFRIENDS

by HELENA DE BRES

Assume your audience is skeptical and easily bored.

Avoid making bold assertions you're unprepared to back up.

It's generally better to delve deeply into one or two areas than to spread yourself thinly over five.

If you're stuck, organize the body into sections and work on different sections at different times.

Slow down.

Make clear what you mean by any unusual terms you introduce.

Irrelevant digressions disrupt the flow and are confusing.

A large part of the skill here lies in knowing what to put in and what to leave out.

Don't make your audience do all the work in figuring out how the various parts fit together.

Ask yourself: "Do I really want to put this here, or would it make more sense somewhere else?"

Be sure to anticipate and respond to objections to your position.

If you think you absolutely need to quote an author, do so sparingly.

Don't introduce sudden surprises in the conclusion.

If complications arise, meet with me well before the due date.

RIHANNA'S "BITCH BETTER HAVE MY MONEY," EXPANDED FOR FREELANCERS

by RIANE KONC

Bitch better have my money

Bitch doesn't see you in our invoice system

Bitch is wondering if you ever sent in a W-9?

Bitch isn't seeing it

Bitch is wondering if you could send another copy and we'll get it taken care of right away

Bitch knows what it's like when your printer is out of ink, no rush!

Bitch is just letting you know that if it's easier, you can actually sign digitally in Adobe or an equivalent PDF converter

Bitch has received your signed W-9 and will forward to Kelly

Bitch expects you'll receive payment by the end of the week

Bitch knows it has been three weeks and wants to thank you for just checking in on this

Bitch is so sorry for the delay

Bitch will get in touch with the department that handles that right away

Bitch is Automatic Reply: Out of the office, slow to respond

Bitch is Automatic Reply: Out of the office, slow to respond

Bitch is Automatic Reply: Out of the office, slow to respond

Bitch is sorry to inform you that the head bitch who was handling your payment is no longer with us

Bitch will forward your information to the new head bitch, but she's still getting settled so it could take a day or so

Bitch should add that it should take a day or so, but could definitely also take up to between four and six months. But a bitch is pretty certain it will be two days, max. Or, again, up to six months.

Bitch would like to formally introduce herself as the new bitch handling your payment

Bitch will actually be the main bitch handling all freelancer payments from now on

Bitch truly apologizes for the delay—bitch is here to fix problems exactly like this that were unfortunately left by the last bitch

Bitch is wondering what piece this payment is for again?

Bitch needs you to resend your invoice with an invoice number

Bitch, I don't know, just usually makes up an invoice number? Bitch would like to emphasize that an invoice number is literally just any meaningless combination of numbers you come up with that is simultaneously meaningless and yet absolutely essential to there being any chance that you will be paid

Bitch's company is actually using a new invoice system; please hold for more info

Bitch sent the link, did you receive?

Bitch will send your log-in and password to the new system in a separate email

Bitch thanks you for just following up about that log-in and password

Bitch thought Casey sent that last week??

Bitch is so sorry, bitch will absolutely have your log-in info by EOD

Bitch once again apologizes for the two-week delay, but unfortunately, Casey is no longer with the bitches

Bitch wants to make sure you sent in that contract?

Bitch sees it, never mind

Bitch recommends an EIN for tax purposes, if a bitch ever figures out what that is

Bitch (finally!) just put your check in the mail, please let a bitch know when it arrives

Bitch is thankful for the opportunity to work with you and hopes to again in the future

Bitch knows it's been six months, but the September issue just came out and it's been all bitches on deck

Bitch has now migrated all payments to PayPal so that the bitches can process your payment much more quickly in the future

Bitch does not have your PayPal info, please forward at your earliest convenience

Bitch is just getting caught up on everything, did you ever get paid for that piece from three years ago?

Bitch is so glad

Bitch also thanks you for writing two thousand words on the most shameful moment of your life and hopes it was worth the $50

Bitch forgot to mention it's actually $47.50, after the PayPal transaction fee

Bitch is sorry about the hold on payment, a mass email will go out shortly explaining

Bitch is closing its doors

Bitch has scrubbed its archives

Bitch has been acquired by Massive Bitch

Bitch is now a subsidiary of Massive Bitch with access to Massive Bitch's massive financial resources, hold for exciting news about what that means for freelance bitches

Bitch is excited to share that from now on, in place of a base rate, bitches whose pieces receive over 100K clicks from other bitches will receive one (1) $5 Applebee's gift card and a firm handshake

Bitch will need your SSN before issuing that Applebee's gift card, please hold.

A McSWEENEY'S INTERNET TENDENCY ORIGIN STORY

HOW I ASSUME McSWEENEY'S INTERNET TENDENCY STARTED, USING ONLY BUSINESS JARGON I'VE HEARD MEN YELL IN AIRPORTS

by WENDI AARONS

T HANKS FOR JOINING ME on this call today, gentleman. Who just joined? Did someone just join? Everyone focus your focus on our meeting initiative. We must conversate about launching McSweeney's Internet Tendencies into our Q1 incubator. Are you all on board with incentivizing the pain points, pivots and pushbacks? Who's not picking up what I'm laying down? Is it Steve? Can you hear me okay, Steve? I'LL TALK LOUDER EVEN THOUGH I'M ON AN AIRPORT SHUTTLEBUS AND NOW EVERYONE KNOWS I'M REVOLUTIONIZING THE WORLD OF ONLINE HUMOR, STEVE.

It's tantamount to our value-added optimization that we formulate ideations that lead us down the path to real strategic hyper-local change. Sure, our fresh-to-market product is humor but THIS IS NOT A JOKE. We cannot KPI our ROI or we will all be ITL unless we submit our learnings to a higher power. Let the chips fall where they may until an angel investor gives us the nod to push forward with our innovation and brand voice for consumer tech in the sharing economy. THAT'S WHAT I SAID, STEVE. YOU NEED TO STOP FOCUSING ON WHAT IS McSWEENEY'S AND START FOCUSING ON WHY IS McSWEENEY'S. HEAR ME OUT, STEVE.

Our deeply cultivated research on consumer spending shows that original curated content in this space, including lists, parody, satire, and pieces about Chaucer are shaping today's cloud-based economy. IT IS TOTALLY WHAT IS HAPPENING, STEVE. THE WHEEL-HOUSE HAS SPOKEN AND McSWEENEY'S INTERNET TENDENCY IS GOING TO MARKET.

That's my time. Thank you gentlemen, but I have a 3 p.m. confab with the boys in Europe that can't wait so I have to jump. My team at the home office is pumped and jazzed and frothing to generate this new iteration of subtle humor that sometimes but not always has swear words. Never forget that we are the fucking warriors who will push the joke world off its status quo and onto its ass! THAT'S RIGHT, I SAID "ASS" STEVE. YES, STEVE. I SAID WHAT I SAID. YOU'RE DRINKING FROM THE FIREHOSE, STEVE. LET'S CIRCLE BACK AT THE END OF THE DAY. McSWEENEY'S INTERNET TENDENCY IS IN THE HOPPER.

THE INCEL SONG OF J. ALFRED PRUFROCK

by JULIANA GRAY

Let us go then, you and I,
When the evening is spread out against the sky
Like an equal redistribution of sexual resources.
Let us go, through certain half-considered tweets
and form tedious arguments
about entitlement.
In the room the women come and go
Talking of Maya Angelou.
The sex robot that rubs its boobs against my cargo pants,
The sex robot that rubs its latex mouth against my cargo pants,
Licked its tongue into corners and pleats
From which human females retreat,
Powered down, and went to sleep.
There will be time, there will be time
For gaming and pickup artistry,
Time to murder and masturbate.

There will be time for betas and rejects
Who view femoids as mere objects.
(They will say: "Why don't you treat women with respect
Or get a personality?")
Do I dare
Disturb the manoverse?
In the room the women come and go
Talking of Maya Angelou.
For I have known them all already, known them all—
The Stacys with lying makeup on the face,
Inflating their value in the sexual marketplace.
I have known the loveshys and milquetoasts.
I have measured out my life in Reddit posts.
Shall I, after Red Bull and burritos,
Have the nerve to channel my libido?
Though I've compared sex to economy,
The feminazis argued for autonomy,
And, in short, I was afraid.
I am a cuck, I am a cuck.
I shall never get the chance to fuck.
Shall I try negging? Do I dare to read a book?
I shall advocate rape and cultivate a juggalo look.
I have heard the females, talking reasonably.
I do not think that they will talk to me.
I have seen them writing on the web,
Correcting our misinformation,
Denying our right to propagation,
Reporting us for terms of service violation.
But we'll keep shitposting and making love to silicone
Until our Fleshlights wear out, and we're alone.

"IT AIN'T EASY GETTIN' GONE DOWN UPON": THE LAMENT OF A PRAIRIE WOMAN

by EMMA RATHBONE

All I know is there's many hard hours for a good country woman to pass. When you're not worryin' about the weather, the harvest, typhoid, havin' cold hands every second of the day, or what's a-comin' over the plains next, even the dear Lord up in heaven wouldn't fault you for desirin' to get gone down upon, once in a blue moon. Nay, I believe it 'twas the Lord who once said, "'Tis a gentleman's privilege to go down upon a stout country woman. And 'tis a perfectly reasonable way to bide one's time."

Say you do happen to have the opportunity of havin' a gentleman at your outpost, perhaps a prospector chewin' on some hay, sittin' on a barrel on your front porch or what not, overnightin' on his way east. Say this situation does come to pass—well, take it from me, this gentleman's liable to sit there all afternoon without the thought of goin' down upon you crossin' his mind even one time! A man bein' a man, other things might cross his mind of course, havin' to do with himself and his needs of an intimate nature, but I'll bet you a silver bit and an acorn shoe that the thought of goin' down upon you, much less takin' a leisurely time at it, so's that it actually has an effect and the outcome is satisfactory, why he'd just as well think of an ant teachin' a damn schoolhouse!

And that's the problem. Gentleman around these parts, they just don't know 'tis always an option. Me and my fellow country women—I've been sittin' and thinkin' on this a spell, because there's plenty a time to sit and think out here—we ought to get together and put out a flier or send a telegram or get the town crier to yell it or have the pony express spread the damn word: 'tis always an option, when fixin' to spend time with a lady, to fuss with her nethers in a leisurely way if she's so inclined. Don't think it's not an option, because this declaration is henceforth meant to clarify that, indeed, it is an option, it is, from now on, to be known, that this activity is *on the table*, and there's no pretendin' that it's not somethin' two people could have just been doin' the whole time, instead of ditherin' away the day on a picnic next to a tree stump without five words to rub together.

Now some of my fellow country women, if I were to draft such a declaration, might say I was fixated on the subject, that I'd gotten my bloomers in a bundle over somethin' that'll never come to pass. And I'd say to them, well what's the worst that can happen from tryin'? That some gentleman might get an inklin' to make acquaintance with your old mesquite bush for once in his life? It'd be good to give our menfolk somethin' to do, or you know what they get up to—hootin' and hollerin' and kickin' up dust in town when there ain't no cause.

But for now I'm just a woman alone on the prairie, with a house full of chores and a head in the clouds, sittin' on the porch, starin' at the same sky, and just waitin' for the rains to come and loosen up this hard old ground, where a gnat never even dreamed of flyin'...

OREGON TRAIL IS CHANGING SO THAT WE SHARE LESS OF YOUR PRIVATE DYSENTERY INFORMATION

by JENNIFER WYATT

As many of you are aware, it was recently brought to our attention that some of our players' health records have been handled with less sensitivity than we would have liked. Specifically, if you died of dysentery between 1986 and 1993 while playing *Oregon Trail*, that information was likely shared with your cousins, neighbors, or other persons who were allowed access to the Apple IIe in your family's basement. Some of those disclosures were repeated through other channels, at times using custom Print Shop banners taped to windows or bedroom doors. In some instances, players logged in under other users' names so that they could create tombstones claiming that the deceased person was a lame dorkwad. On the earliest versions of the game, which weren't set up to block obscenities, the publicly available information about users was even more damaging, graphic, and physically impossible.

This was an entirely unforeseeable usage of the tombstone functionality of *Oregon Trail*. If anything, our zeal for the social sharing of sensitive medical information was way ahead of its time. And, although *Oregon Trail* users were complicit in the exposure of their sensitive dysentery information on our platform, we like to think that we're better than that. If we're not, then we need to get off our high horse right now. No, really, this horse is scaring us. It is weirdly tall and has trampled some of the crisis management people we brought in to help craft this statement.

Still, we like to think that creating really deeply offensive epitaphs was not the only reason you played *Oregon Trail*. We know, from listening in on your most recent sessions with Dr. Paulsen, that your other entertainment option was to go buy carob chips with your emotionally distant father while he ranted about the Iran-Contra affair. That sounds nice.

We would like to assure our users that we were unaware of just how prevalent the offending tombstones were until our current CEO found one claiming that he himself had died of dysentery in 1988 and "looked like a penis." This information was identical to a review posted on Glassdoor, and is something that finds its way into Mother's Christmas letter every year, and is therefore known to be the work of a bot or sibling. Tactics of this kind have no place in a democracy and Mother told you to stop, Jeffrey. Users are encouraged to take common-sense measures to identify old hard drives and back over them in a borrowed Buick Sentry with Dr. Paulsen on speakerphone. He's our doctor now, too. Is that weird?

Some news outlets are claiming that, from the beginning, the creators of *Oregon Trail* were aware of the relentless, albeit fictional, HIPAA violations built into the game's platform. Our attorney said this is the most blatant case of *res ipsa loquitor* he has ever seen, which must mean "sorry not sorry." Besides, if *Oregon Trail* is about anything, it's about grit and personal responsibility and a growth mindset.

Our big focus for the coming year is finding new ways to engage people with *Oregon Trail* while sharing less private dysentery information. Whether it's life outcomes based on income stratification, or just shooting at natural resources, there is still so much about *Oregon Trail* that we can celebrate.

WENDY MOLYNEUX'S EXCERPTS FROM POPULAR McSWEENEY'S INTERNET TENDENCY LISTS THROUGHOUT HISTORY: 1993

LIST

JURASSIC PARK'S MOST BORING DINOSAURS

by PATRICIA LARFEN

76. William

77. Karen

78. Jennifer

79. Aaron

80. Ducks

YOUR 30-DAY TRIAL PERIOD WITH BLACK PATIENCE HAS EXPIRED

by JENNA LYLES

Dear User,

Our records indicate that your 30-day trial period with Black Patience expires today. For continued access to the remarkable grace and wondrous restraint of black people worldwide, paid membership is now required. Not sure what this means for you? We're happy to explain.

You see, contrary to popular belief, Black Patience takes time and effort to prepare. Culling Black Patience from the depths of the Black Psyche takes a lot of work and... we're losing you, aren't we?

Think of coal. Coal is a natural resource, which means that while it is technically self-replenishing, it takes a very long time for new formations to develop. Millions of years, actually. Think of black people's patience as coal.

Now think of coal miners. They do arduous work prying that coal from the ground so that we might enjoy its various uses, many of which make our lives infinitely more comfortable. Think of black people as coal miners.

At the end of the day, we pay for coal, right? And we pay coal miners, right? And you'd have to be some kind of jackass to think that coal miners should work for free just because you don't want to pay for coal, right? Right!

See how we took the time to metaphorize an already understandable concept? Bet you didn't even notice, did you? That's just one of many forms of Black Patience at work. These luxuries and others can be yours in no time! Just opt in to any of our three, distinct membership plans tailored to your capabilities.

BRONZE MEMBERSHIP
(payable in daily installments of Common Sense)
Do you think black people are people too? Do you think racism is a bad thing? Do you think it should be illegal to murder people?

Get started with our bottom-tier Bronze Membership! Now comes with a free COEXIST bumper sticker!

SILVER MEMBERSHIP
(payable in daily installments of Critical Thinking)
Do you want to know why your behavior is a problem instead of loudly protesting that it isn't? Do you think it might be time to get a library card instead of demanding answers on Facebook? Are you starting to get the impression that history class left a few things out?

Try our mid-tier Silver Membership! Now comes with a free YES WE CAN bumper sticker!

GOLD MEMBERSHIP

(payable in daily installments of Empathy)

Have you proven you've got the emotional capacity to care about someone other than yourself? Do you think it might finally be time to mobilize your privilege instead of apologizing to random black people? Do you suspect that being "woke" simply isn't enough?

Consider our top-tier Gold Membership! Now comes with a free BLACK LIVES MATTER bumper sticker!

Still not convinced Black Patience is right for you? Check out these testimonials!

"Last year my family uninvited me to Thanksgiving because they didn't want any 'drama.' I practically laughed my mother off the phone—did she think I was going to lose sleep over that cardboard turkey?"

—Nancy, 38 (Gold Member)

"I actually joined as a joke, but then I started noticing results. People stopped rolling their eyes every time I opened my mouth to speak. My coworkers started inviting me out to drinks. My girlfriend of three years finally introduced me to her parents. I was a total pariah and didn't even know it." —Michael, 26 (Silver Member)

"My granddaughter bought me this membership 'cause she was worried Pawpaw was going to hell. I'm not afraid to admit I've had my membership canceled a few times for missing payments, but I'll always keep trying 'cause God don't like ugly and I don't want to let little Kinley down." —Fletcher, 82 (Bronze Member)

"It's super embarrassing, but I used to be one of those people who thought just existing in the presence of black people was the same thing as respecting black people." —Charlotte, 32 (Silver Member)

"I look back at my old tweets and cringe. I *cringe*."
—Tiffany, 19 (Bronze Member)

"I started out with Bronze and worked my way up after receiving some unnerving 23andMe results (turns out my 'pretty liberal' family is littered with hateful racists). It hasn't always been easy, but by the time I got to Silver, I realized black people's quality of life isn't about what's easiest for white people." —Mark, 20 (Gold Member)

DISCLAIMERS:

Black Patience is not available through third-party-sellers, nor is Black Patience redeemable via simply:

- Having black friends

- Marrying into a black family

- Producing and/or adopting black children

- Hiring black employees

- Teaching black students

- Publishing work by black authors

- Living next-door to a black person

Black Patience does not and has never granted use of the N-word or blackface, guaranteed a plate at the cookout, or offered compliments on decidedly under-seasoned dishes.

Black Patience does not guarantee Black Forgiveness.

Black Patience is not a catchall for garnering the patience of other minority groups.

AS YOUR SENATOR, I VOW TO NEVER DO ANYTHING THAT WILL UPSET BOB, 54, FROM INDIANA

by FELIPE TORRES MEDINA

As an elected official representing your state, I look for bipartisan solutions and work every day to make your lives and the lives of your families better, easier, and safer. Unless, of course, any of those things might upset my friend, Bob, 54, from Indiana, who is not a real person, but rather a persona created by a focus group I hired to tell me who's most likely to come out to the polls and vote this coming November.

I understand that we live in troubled times. It seems like the political divisions in our country have never been bigger. I would like to take a moment to make a statement that will unite all Americans. Just as long as nothing in said statement insults, irks, or bothers—even in the slightest—my friend, Bob, 54, from Indiana. Therefore, gay marriage and a woman's right to choose are off limits; they scored too low in the Bob Index. The Bob Index is a scale that the research firm I hired came up with to show what Bob, this imaginary person I'm terrified of, likes and doesn't like. Also scoring low in the Bob Index, and something the research firm tells me I can safely say we all hate, are those big, ballsy black bees that fly directly at your face. So, let's all come together and say in the voice of Bob: "Boo, bees! BOO, BEES!"

I know this great state has suffered dearly due to gun violence. I know what happened recently in that school in Florida, or a couple weeks ago in Virginia, or two days ago in Utah, is scary. If you choose to help me stay in Congress, I promise I will think and pray about finding a solution but ultimately refuse to act upon it. Mainly because, Bob, 54, from Indiana trusts me enough to give me his vote, but not enough to think I wouldn't vote in favor of authorizing a military attack on our citizens. He believes his handgun/AR-15 will protect him if this happens because he forgets planes that can shoot missiles at his house in Indiana from a huge distance are a thing. So, on the issue of guns, I can say that if you vote for me I will take a stand and continue to recognize their existence and nothing more because I'm scared of an imaginary prospective voter.

The key issue I will work towards solving will be immigration because Bob thinks immigration is very important. Unfortunately, the research firm couldn't find a comprehensive answer as to why Bob, 54, from Indiana, thinks immigration is important. They did include, however, this list of buzzwords that the men over fifty who were polled to create Bob quietly muttered after being asked about immigration: "Mexicans," "build a wall," and "Tucker Carlson told me they're stealing our wives." Therefore, I'm all for immigration, as long as only the good ones are coming, and I'm all for the wall, even though most undocumented immigrants fly into the country and overstay their visas. Again, Bob does not have a firm grasp on immigration. Or planes.

Finally, and if you'll give me your vote, I promise that I will continue working hard for every American in this district, so long as they're Bob, 54, from Indiana, and are staunchly against gay wedding cakes, BuzzFeed, and those kids who don't want to get shot in schools. Every American's life is a treasure we must protect. Especially those who are being persecuted the most: people like Bob, 54, from Indiana, who is terrified about the prospect of being bilingual. Every American deserves the freedom to speak their minds. As long as none of that challenges the power structures that placed Bob on the pedestal where I worship him. Every American deserves life, liberty, and the pursuit of happiness. As long as every American is Bob, 54, from Indiana.

Thank you, and Bob bless America.

ANGELA CHASE FROM *MY SO-CALLED LIFE*, 39, ANNOUNCES BID FOR CONGRESS

by SARAH SWEENEY

Years ago, growing up in Pittsburgh, I thought this country could be, like, better. Maybe. Like it could improve, or something.

(Sighs deeply)

Sometimes, I look at this country like the sleeve of a sweater. A worn sweater. That, like, shows we've forgotten what we're even doing here. Or whatever. And like, our country is becoming this unraveled yarn. Or fabric, even. That we need to fix because, if we don't, the world would grind to, like, a halt.

(Absentmindedly touches zit)

People, like real people, are running good—no, great—campaigns. As though, like, a campaign could be run. Like the Olympics, or something.

(Rests head on podium)

It, like, teaches me that even if you're, I don't know, not always cheering for the same football team everyone else cheers for, sometimes, other people notice you. And they like, understand you. And they get you, which helps you, like, win.

(Wraps arms around torso, holds scapula)

And there's so much to be, like, done. Like if the love of your life, or, I don't know, your soul or whatever can't read, you have to help that person, right? Because education reform is crucial. Because, I mean, if they can't read how can they even vote? Like for you? And if you can completely understand a person, it could like completely change everything. Like. Everything.

(Tucks hair behind ear, stares into nothingness)

Everything is, I don't know, a battlefield. But, like, for your heart. Because people believe totally different things and stuff. But, like, a belief can't bring metal detectors into our schools. Because, if they're there, how can anyone really feel safe? Like in the world?

(Looks off in the distance at bald eagle)

Somewhere along the way, the pursuit of equality just, like, failed. Like, anatomy, or whatever, came between the fathers of government and, you know, everyone else. I have analyzed this in like microscopic detail.

(Slouches, crawls into fetal position on bed)

We exist in two different worlds, okay? I can't just watch our nation handed over to the people who don't care, okay? I mean, it's just not that simple. And you have to do something, like vote, because maybe something could happen. Like, seriously happen. And like, if you miss it, it's like you weren't even there. Or whatever.

(Leans forehead against flag pole)

Every so often, people have, like, moments. And maybe, to be put out of our misery, we need to do something about those moments. So, I've decided that maybe I could announce my, I don't know, candidacy. For Congress. Because it seems like if I don't, I'll die. Or something.

So, like, vote. Okay?

FIFTY CANDLES

by WENDI AARONS

Samantha "Sam" Baker wakes up on her fiftieth birthday. She reaches for the iPhone on the nightstand and immediately feels a tear in her rotator cuff. She heads into the bathroom to pluck the white chin hair that grew overnight.

Sam enters the kitchen, anticipating a special breakfast with her family. Instead, she finds her husband watching the latest Trump news on CNN, and her teenage daughter posing for a selfie while licking a can of Rockstar Energy Drink. "Oh, hi," her husband finally says. "If you're looking for the Pepcid AC, I took the last one. This fucking guy, am I right?"

Next, Sam goes to her Barre Method class and pays $25 to squeeze her glutes next to her best friend Randy. During class, Sam texts Randy that she would definitely do it with Jake Ryan if she had the chance. "Jake Ryan the divorced dad who was convicted of embezzling from the youth soccer league?" Randy texts back. She includes three eggplant emojis.

"No, I'd do it with Jake Ryan the divorced dad who was busted for holding illegal poker games in his apartment complex," Sam replies. "But he doesn't even know I exist. Hey, do you have any IcyHot in your Kate Spade cross-body? My left hamstring is seizing."

What Sam doesn't know is that she accidentally sent the text to Jake Ryan whose number she has in her phone from that time they worked the dunk tank together at the school carnival.

While waiting in line at Starbucks, Jake gets the text and realizes Sam has the hots for him. Then he goes back to looking at twenty-five-year-old massage therapists named Kayleigh on Tinder.

Later, Sam takes an Uber home after day-drinking at a wine bar. The driver is a guy known as Farmer Ted because he grows medical marijuana and heirloom tomatoes under his deck. He asks her to go with him to a protest march later that night and she replies, "Gah! Is Trump all anyone can think about?"

At home, Sam sees she's been kicked out of her bedroom because her husband rented it on Airbnb to a couple from Seattle who make bespoke wedding tuxes for pugs. Not only did her entire family miss her birthday, but now she has to sleep on the Crate and Barrel sectional she spent weeks deciding on with her decorator?

"I can't believe it. They fucking forgot my birthday," Sam sighs. Then she looks through the mail and realizes that the AARP sure didn't.

The Seattle hipsters brought with them a foreign student named Long Duk Dong. Sam takes him to the anti-Trump march later that night and tells him, "I hope nobody yankies your wanky!" Later, Long Duk tweets from his @TheDonger account, "TFW your honky host is straight-up racist."

At the march, Sam ogles Jake who's waving a sign that says TINY HANDS HUGE ASSHOLE with his hot millennial hookup Karolina.

Karolina is totally rocking her pink pussy hat, which makes Sam sad because it's impossible for perimenopausal women to wear headgear without sweating to death.

Upset, Sam leaves the protest to cry in her Volvo. Farmer Ted finds her and captures it on Facebook Live. Then he asks for her Spanx to sell on eBay and she obliges. "I can't believe I gave my Spanx to a geek," she groans. "Now my FUPA will be totally visible through my Lululemon."

Jake leaves the march with Karolina who's throwing a pop-up hang at Jake's ex-wife's house while she's out of town on a yoga retreat. After Jake becomes furious that Karolina's friends don't appreciate the '80s on 8 channel on Sirius XM radio, he sends Sam a DM. Unfortunately, she doesn't get it because her phone ran out of battery while she was tracking her teenage daughter's trip to the frozen yogurt shop.

Hours later, Jake tries to make a deal with Farmer Ted: Sam's Spanx in exchange for Jake's hookup Karolina who is blackout drunk. Farmer Ted says, "Seriously, bro? Have you ever heard of a little thing called CONSENT? JFC it's not 1986, you caveman," and he drives Karolina to her mother's house and doesn't even charge her the Uber surge rate.

The next day is Sam's daughter's TEDx talk about the struggle of white girl feminism, but she has her period and she's also drugged up on whatever was in the vape sesh she just did with her friends, so the TEDx talk is a disaster. After a moment of reflection, Sam's family finally realizes they forgot her fiftieth birthday because they've been so distracted by the problems of Trump and social media. Sam doesn't accept their apology, however, and says, "Whatever, losers. I bought my own present and it's a trip to Paris by myself. Good luck trying to figure out how the dishwasher works."

She bravely walks out of the TEDx talk only to see Jake Ryan waiting for her in the Porsche he leased after the divorce and now totally regrets because of the gas mileage and also he looks like a d-bag in it. He drives her to his apartment and presents her with a gluten and dairy-free birthday cake that is aflame with fifty candles. The moment before they throw it in the sink so the fifty candles don't catch the curtains on fire, Jake smiles and tells Sam to make a wish.

Sam replies, "I'm fifty years old, motherfucker. I don't have time for wishes." Jake leans in for a kiss but she's already on her way out the door to the airport.

PERIMENOPAUSAL BINGO

by BETH KANTER

B I N G O

Google "estrogen-fortified" chardonnay	Design bedside rain barrel to collect night sweat runoff	Threesome with Ben & Jerry	Purchase fringed yellow leather COACH saddlebag during insomnia-fueled shopping spree	Period-tracking app spotaneously deletes and reinstalls itelf
Misplace car keys	Misplace car	Misplace husband who is holding keys while sitting in car	Wonder aloud why Bobbi Brown doesn't make foundation in shades of flush	Pocket teenage son's prescription pimple cream
Braid chin hairs	Tie yellow ribbon around bedpost until sex drive returns	**FREE SPACE:** PEE SNEEZE	Ugly cry during *Wizard of Oz* when that bitch Dorothy kills the poor hormonal witch	Flip off gravity
Mood swing-induced vertigo	Ask the guinea pig, "Is it hot in here?"	Launch GoFundMe campaign to locate missing waistline	Day drink	Day nap
Day worry	Read *Side-eye for Dummies*	Hoard super-plus tampons	Knit voodoo doll of greeter at Target	Stuff bra with gel packs

RICK JAMES'S LONG LOST ANNOTATIONS TO HIS 1981 HIT SONG "SUPERFREAK" REVEAL WHAT HE REALLY WANTED TO RECORD WAS AN ANTHEM OF FEMALE EMPOWERMENT

by GARY M. ALMETER

Does this term sufficiently connote full and active participation in political and economic life?

She's a very kinky girl,

The use of this gender-specific pronoun reeks of objectification. It's not. Let's call her "Susan" or "Patricia"

The kind you don't take home to mother

Let's change this to mean something like "the auditorium where the symposium is being held and where she is the keynote speaker"

She will never let your spirits down,

Once you get her off the street.

people *Wall Street*

She likes the ~~boys~~ in the ~~band,~~ *presumably* *corporation*

She says that I'm ~~her all-time favorite~~ *one of the most productive*

When I make my move ~~to her room,~~

Why not? Presumably it's because mother, herself empowered and fully engaged in political and economic life, is no longer home?

as

It's the right time, she's ~~never~~ hard to please. *as her male colleagues*

That girl is pretty wild now

The girl's a super freak

The kind of girl you read about *see below*

In the ~~new wave magazines.~~

Phonetically, I like this. But what precisely are we saying here? Can we say she provides "great critique"? or "I like to hear her speak" "she just negotiated a trade deal with Mozambique"?

Let's change this to something like "I'd really enjoy listening to her give the keynote address at the symposium"

That girl is pretty kinky

The girl's a super freak

I'd really like to (taste her)

Every time we meet. *at a conference*

She's all right, she's all right

That girl's all right with me yeah.

Upon reflection, why are we using "girl" at all? Why are we distinguishing genders?

She's a super freak, super freak,

She's super freaky, super freak, super freak.

She's a very special girl, *corporate footwear*

From her head down to her toenails *e*

Yet she'll wait for me at backstage with her girlfriends, *colleagues.*

In a limousine.

change this to auditorium where symposium is held.

Three's not a crowd to her, she said

"Room 714, I'll be waiting."

When I get there she's got incense, wine and candles

It's such a freaky scene.

economically astute

That girl is pretty wild now *e*

Why? How about "she's got analysis of the financials"

The girl's a super freak

The kind of girl you read about

In the new wave magazines.

That girl is pretty kinky

The girl's a super freak

I'd really like to taste her

Every time we meet. *in the executive boardroom?*

What are "new wave" magazines? Let's change this to incorporate magazines like Forbes, Fortune and The Economist.

The perpetual use of "all right" suggests that I am encouraging paternalism, that I am entitled — even encouraged — to judge. I think this dilutes the message of equality here.

She's all right, she's all right
That girl's all right with me yeah.
She's a super freak, super freak,
She's super freaky, super freak, super freak.
Temptations sing, oh, super freak,
Super freak, the girl's a super freak, oh.
She's a very kinky girl,
The kind you don't take home to mother
She will never let your spirits down,
Once you get her off the street. e

Is "thinky" a word? Like she is always thinking about economics and community initiatives and advocacy and therefore she is "thinky"

again, phonetically I like how this sounds. But it's just so patronizing. "I but that she knows Greek?" "It's equality she seeks?"

PLANNING YOUR TRIP TO UNCLE RICK'S WATER SLIDE AND COCAINE PARK

by PETE REYNOLDS

We're incredibly, amazingly stoked that you've decided to spend a day at Uncle Rick's Water Slide and Cocaine Park! Here's what you should know when planning your visit to the PREMIER SPOT FOR INSANE WATER PARK ACTION AND COCAINE IN THE NORTHEAST!

OUR HISTORY

Other water parks were not giving Uncle Rick the fix he needed with their SAFETY REGULATIONS AND DEARTH OF COCAINE-FU-ELED WATER RIDES, so the big man set out to DISRUPT BOTH THE WATER SLIDE AND COCAINE INDUSTRIES following a particularly awesome time he had breaking into Six Flags after a DURAN DURAN CONCERT. Although it took several years and failed rehab stints to actually execute on that plan, the end result is

your ONE-STOP SHOP FOR SUMMER SPLASH-MAZEMENT
AND NARCOTICS FUN.

GETTING TO THE PARK

Uncle Rick's has been located at several different sites throughout our
STORIED HISTORY as America's top spot for FUCKING CRAZY
FUCKING RIPS DOWN THE CHUTE. Until recently, we were
unable to PUBLICLY POST OUR LOCATION due to the RISK OF
UNWANTED ATTENTION FROM LAW ENFORCEMENT. In the
past, after catching wind that the FUZZ HAD SNIFFED US OUT,
we were forced to BURN YOUR #1 SPOT FOR SUMMER AQUA-
BATICS AND NOSE-LYMPICS TO THE GROUND and relocate
with all of the PLASTIC TUBING AND COCAINE we could fit into
the VAN. But those types of legal issues are a THING OF THE PAST,
because we have constructed a brand new WAVE POOL that spans the
United States-Canada border and so is TECHNICALLY INTERNA-
TIONAL WATERS, thereby making the park INVULNERABLE TO
THE FEDERALES. This according to my buddy's cousin JIMMY, who
did a SEMESTER AT WIDENER LAW. Although that is not actually
his REAL NAME, a fact I discovered when the W-4 I completed on
his behalf DID NOT PROCESS CORRECTLY—yet another example
of the trials and tribulations of being a SMALL BUSINESS OWNER
of a FLY-BY-NIGHT WATER SLIDE AND COCAINE CONCERN
in the MODERN CAPITALIST ECONOMY.

PARK RULES

Please, no outside food or cocaine! Uncle Rick's has a fully functioning
kitchen and snack bar ON THE PREMISES. There are also plenty

of gluten- and nut-free options available, because we want each and every guest to have a FUCKING AWESOME TIME BLASTING THE TUBES, REGARDLESS OF ALLERGIES OR DIETARY RESTRICTIONS OR LACK OF ACCESS TO COCAINE.

No foul language! This is a FAMILY WATER SLIDE AND COCAINE PARK.

For every loop you make on the Lazy River, Uncle Rick will personally give you an AGGRESSIVE HIGH FIVE as you pass by, which you should DEFINITELY TAKE ME UP ON so I don't start getting PARANOID and QUESTIONING WHETHER YOU ARE POSSIBLY A NARC.

For the Log Flume, Uncle Rick humbly requests that you BRING YOUR OWN LOG.

OUR RIDES

Every one of our slides features the MUSIC OF THE SCISSOR SISTERS AT VERY HIGH VOLUME. And every slide except one ends in a VERY FAST FREEFALL into an awaiting pool that is ALMOST CERTAINLY DEEP ENOUGH TO PREVENT A SERIOUS INJURY, THIS AGAIN ACCORDING TO NOT-JIMMY, who now that I stop and think about it may not have actually gone to Widener Law at all BUT STILL GIVES PRETTY GOOD LEGAL ADVICE.

A lot of people ask Uncle Rick why one of the slides is just a LOOP WITH NO APPARENT EXIT that appears designed to just TRAP YOU IN A CANISTER THAT IS RAPIDLY FILLING UP WITH WATER. And the answer is: YES! That is the OUROBOROS, just one of the many AWESOME AND UNIQUE FEATURES of the #1 spot for SERIOUS FUCKING WATER FUNTASTICISM. If you are overly concerned about the prospect of having to CLAW YOUR WAY

TO FREEDOM through INDUSTRIAL-GRADE PLASTIC, well, THAT'S WHAT THE COCAINE IS FOR.

In addition to the Lazy River and Log Flume, Uncle Rick's boasts a half-acre Splash Pad for the little ones, which is HONESTLY JUST OKAY NO MATTER HOW MUCH COCAINE YOU HAVE INGESTED, BUT THE KIDS SEEM TO LIKE IT, NEVERTHELESS.

As always, 10 percent of all ticket proceeds go to the MARCH OF DIMES.

So grab your family or coworkers and get to Uncle Rick's for some BANANAS FUCKING WATER SLIDES AND ALSO COCAINE. Thank you for reading, you guys are FUCKING TREMENDOUS!

I'M THE WORLD'S BEST DAD BECAUSE ONCE I WATCHED MY KID WHEN MY WIFE WASN'T AROUND

by KASHANA CAULEY

Hey you. Over there pushing the stroller while your wife talks on the phone. You look like a pretty good dad. I bet you've burped your kid. Cleaned spit up off your shirt yourself, without waiting for your wife to hand you a towel. Held your kid for six minutes without dropping him. That's all well and good, but know this: I'm a better dad than you. In fact, I'm the world's best dad because once I watched my kid when my wife wasn't around.

You're probably wondering how this miraculous feat of dadding was inspired. Well, my wife woke up from the nap she was taking face-first into her salad and said she needed a night off to remember who she was. I said sure, if by "night off" you mean an hour, and she said that gave her just enough time to fall asleep into a glass of wine at the bar down the street. I picked up little Turmeric from his bassinet so I could watch TV with him, but he fell asleep, so I heroically struggled through the nearly impossible feat of watching half an episode of *Property Brothers* with a numb, baby-covered left arm.

Then I took little Turmeric outside for a walk to allow other people to understand that I'm the world's best dad. When they saw me pushing a stroller alone on the sidewalk without my wife, they said things like "Oh my god, look at you, giving mom a break," and, "I just want to hug you because you're pushing that stroller all alone like a true hero," and, "Please, accept this trophy that says you're the world's best dad because I always have to bribe my husband with a dozen Papa John's pizzas, a membership to the Beer of the Month Club and two tickets to the Super Bowl to get him to watch our kid while I go to the bathroom."

When little Turmeric started to cry, I wheeled him home to comfort him the only way I can comfort myself when I'm down: by telling him stories about all the times I threw up after drinking beer with my buddies in college. "So Moose handed me the twenty-fifth shot of the night," I said. But weak little Turmeric wasn't tough enough to stay awake for the end of one of the most epic stories ever told. I mean, I threw up into the shape of a star! Who wouldn't want to stay awake to hear every single gory detail of that?

Can you believe that ten minutes after I put him down for his nap, little Turmeric woke up with a poopy diaper? I have no idea how to change diapers, so I just held him at arm's length from me until his mom, the real diaper expert, came home. She reached out her arms for a hug and I rewarded her with the only thing a mother who just arrived home and is expecting a hug really wants: an armload of dirty baby. "You're welcome," I told her.

So that's how I became the world's best dad in just one summer evening's worth of watching my kid alone. If you want to be a better dad than me, you could watch your kid while your wife isn't around for an hour and a half, or two hours if you're some kind of gladiator of kid-watching. But let's face it. You're probably not up for that kind of pain, which is why I'll remain the world's best dad.

The other day, my wife asked me if I could watch the kid while she wasn't around for a second time, but I manned up and said, "No, what is this—a forced labor camp?" I'm already the world's best dad for doing it once.

TODDLER FEELINGS HELPLINE

by SARA GIVEN

Hello, you have reached the Toddler Feelings Helpline. Please choose from the following options:

—If Mama went to the store for a minute but you are pretty sure she's never coming back, please mash all of the keys but mostly 1.

—If you still feel pretty messed up about how they were just going to burn the Velveteen Rabbit, please mash all of the keys but mostly 2.

—If you don't like the way your shirt is right now, please hit a sibling for no reason.

—If you are fine with just letting boogers run all down your face and not even acknowledging it, even when they start to seep into your mouth, please mash 4.

—If you do not like the way your morning toast was prepared, please press 9, and then 1, and then 1, and then hide the phone in a laundry basket.

—If the dog has repeatedly spurned your attempts to ride him like a pony, please mash 6.

—If your parents provided you with toys to cultivate play-based curiosity and spatial awareness when all you really needed was senseless flashing lights and electronic sound, mash 7.

—If you wanted the green one and not the blue one and now you are inconsolable, please throw the phone through a screen door.

—If you are crying but you don't remember why, please mash 9.

—If you've come to the halting realization that every single aspect of your life is decided by another person and that you truly have no agency over your own thoughts or existence, please remove all of your clothing and flee screaming in the direction of your nearest judgmental neighbor.

—If you have a poop in your pants that you're not going to tell anyone about, please mash 12.

To hear these options again, please smash the phone against an expensive electronic device until someone comes to see what you are doing, or simply stay on the line.

MY ASIAN PARENTS, GOOGLE TRANSLATED

by IRVING RUAN AND JIJI LEE

"Have you eaten yet?"
I love you.

"Here's $100 for your birthday."
We hope you don't waste it on something decadent, like coffee. What, just because you moved to Brooklyn you suddenly think you're too good for nondairy creamer and Folgers?

"I saw Jeffrey's mother the other day at Costco."
Did you know that Jeffrey's documentary about bonobos just got nominated for an Oscar? What an Ideal Asian Son. Anyway, did you get any GoFundMe donations for your web series about early 20th-century Asian diaspora?

"I have chest pains."
If you don't get married soon, I'll have a second cardiac arrest. And don't tell me that's not how the human heart works, unless you went to medical school.

"You look healthy."
You've gained weight, mostly in your face.

"Aiyaaa!"
Multiple definitions:

1. (adjective) Your friend Greg walked in to our home with his shoes on. Does he think we live at a Dunkin' Donuts?

2. (synonym) Greg should be ashamed about only getting accepted into Cornell Medical School.

3. (verb) Greg talks too much about his podcast.

"George Stephanopoulos is so handsome."
George Stephanopoulos is so handsome.

"I don't need a birthday gift."
Ever since I survived communism/immigration/racism, I realized that I don't have an attachment to objects or emotions. Have you eaten yet?

"Are you sick?"
If you're getting sick, I will leave work right now to give you expired Tylenol and a $25 gift card to The Olive Garden. You'll become

healthier as soon as you gain more unlimited breadstick weight. Preferably in your face.

"How's the weather?"
You sound cold. I hope you're wearing the sweater that Grandma JuJu knit for you. You know, the one she knit while holding down three jobs and a relationship. Anyway, it's hot where we are.

"We immigrated to America so you could live a better life."
All of our work will have been for nothing if you don't become a doctor, lawyer, or a doctor who side hustles as an Oscar-nominated bonobos documentary filmmaker. I'm happy if you also become the Casanova of TV, just like George Stephanopoulos.

"I heard that you want to start a band."
You're doing drugs, aren't you?

"I'm proud of you."
Sorry, Asian parents do not say this. Please try again.

IF PEOPLE TALKED TO OTHER PROFESSIONALS THE WAY THEY TALK TO TEACHERS

by SHANNON REED

"Ah, a zookeeper. So, you just babysit the animals all day?"

"My colon never acts this way at home. Are you sure you're reading the colonoscopy results correctly? Did you ever think that maybe you just don't like my colon?"

"I'd love to just play with actuary statistics all day. That would be so fun! I bet you don't even feel like you're at work!"

"You're a sanitation worker, huh? I hated my garbage collectors when I was growing up. One of them once yelled at me when I stood directly in front of their truck and kept it from completing its appointed rounds, and ever since then I've just loathed all of them, everywhere."

"So you run a ski lodge? Do you just, like, chill during the summer? Must be nice."

"Since my singer-songwriter thing isn't taking off yet, I've been thinking about going into lawyer-ing. I mean, how hard can it be? I know criminals like me, or at least the two that I see once a year at Thanksgiving do."

"I bet that's the best part of being a banker—all the free money!"

"Do you even read your patients' charts, or do you just assign them a random dosage based on how nice they've been to you?"

"Before you give me a ticket, Officer, I just wanted to mention: my taxes pay your salary."

"Excuse me, my seven-year-old son, who mere minutes ago lied about whether he had to pee or not, just told me that you wouldn't give him any ketchup even though he says he asked for it politely. Now I'm going to ask the manager to move us to another server's table, and also fire you."

"Since you're a plumber, and you're around them all day, I have to ask—do you ever find one of your pipes attractive? Even though you know you shouldn't go there?"

"Sure, the pay is low, but I bet the joy of putting together press releases for local events is reason enough to stick with this job in the events division of the Chamber of Commerce. You must really believe in its mission."

"Oh, you're a stand-up comedian, huh? So, you just stand up there and bullshit until your set is done?"

"Damn! Look at you in that dress! Now I'm Hot for Quality Control Manager for the Western Division!"

REFLECTIONS FROM A McSWEENEY'S INTERNET TENDENCY WRITER (OR, MY TWENTY-FOUR-YEAR CLIMB TO McSWEENEY'S INTERNET TENDENCY INTERNET STARDOM)

by SHANNON REED

1995

One of the professors at the college where I'm working on my BFA in Theatre takes me aside and explains to me that I'm "funny for a young woman" and that I should look into developing my sense of humor because "people like to laugh."

2005

While teaching at a Catholic school for girls, I decide to start writing plays. I also decide to give this comedy thing a try, what with it being so popular and all, so I mostly write funny plays.

2006

I discover that only about fifteen people are willing to attend the run of a one-act play showcase over two weekends in Rego Park, Queens, New York.

AUGUST 23, 2007, 11:30 A.M.

I tell a sweet old lady at my church who asked what I do that I am a playwright, and she replies, "Yes, but what do you do *for money?*"

2008

I start teaching English at a public high school in south Brooklyn. My students do not enjoy observational humor about their habits of referring to me as "Miss" or how they set up elaborate hair-styling salons in the back of my classroom to avoid discussing *Of Mice and Men*.

2009

The principal decides that he will help me teach *Our Town* because he doesn't think I'd do a good job at it. He asks me to find him a copy of *Our Town* because he has never read it. He also googles around to find information about *Our Town* for me to read, and ends up sending me an article about how to teach *Our Town* which he does not ever realize I had written. I find him a copy of *Our Town*. He doesn't read it.

I start a blog about my experiences teaching, but one day I hear a couple of my non-teaching friends discuss it. "Really bitter," one said. "Yeah, like, *wow*," the other agreed. I reread it, and agree. Rage drips from every word.

2012

I move to Pittsburgh to work on my MFA in Creative Writing: Fiction. Finally! I am on track to at last I become America's Best Writer Person. I also begin teaching freshman English at the University of Pittsburgh, which is a vibrant new revenue stream of humor.

2013

I start seeing posts from a website called McSweeney's Something Something appearing on my friends' Facebook pages. I click through those links and read the pieces. They make me laugh. My college professor was right! It is nice to laugh!

Turns out that McSweeney's submissions guidelines are quite easy to find (and, ahem, future submitters, really easy to follow). I work on a humor piece about Benedict Cumberbatch (#2012) for a while, and then submit it.

Keep in mind: I am also submitting short stories to fancy literary journals on a near-daily basis. I receive one rejection after another. So it isn't hugely surprising to receive a rejection from McSweeney's.

But! The rejection is personal, offers some advice for how to improve what I've written, and is signed by a real person ("Chris."). This gives me an extraordinary amount of hope.

2013, EARLIER

I keep writing humor pieces. Most are not good enough to submit them to my best friend, Chris at McSweeney's. But eventually I do submit another piece, which he rejected with more good advice.

2013, LATER

The third piece I submit, he takes. It's based on *Our Town*. Have you read it?

2014

I submit more stuff to McSweeney's. Some of it gets published, but not all of it. One of my students at Pitt approaches me, frowning. He says, "You're not the Shannon Reed who writes for McSweeney's, right?" McSweeney's had published my "Security Questions for Single, Child-less People" and it's blowing up, but it has somehow not occurred to me that my students could see it until this moment. I tell him I am that Shannon Reed. He tells me that I am cool. This is the high point of 2014 for me.

2015

I start to see that teaching isn't something I do while I wait to make my living as a writer. I actually like teaching.

But I think a lot about how my sense of humor made some people (not most people, just some) uncomfortable. How they feel teachers should be sweet and quiet and nice. How I am not really any of those things, although I am usually kind and pretty chill and I really love books, reading, and writing.

I also think about how my students mostly (not all, but most) love my sense of humor, and enjoy my jokes in class. They mostly seem to like when I am me, not a Teacher Bot.

2016

I think some more about how awful it is to be told that there's only one way to be the profession that you love. I decide that the one thing I could do for teachers was make them laugh about their crazy jobs. So I start writing humor about teaching. I feel really lucky when Chris accepts the first piece I wrote about and for teachers.

2018

I write "If People Talked to Other Professionals the Way They Talked to Teachers," a piece about and for teachers, which turns out to resonate with a whole bunch of people.

2019

I keep going. I write humor for other places now, which is very nice, but I know that McSweeney's will always be my home base as a humor writer, where I can give be bitterly wry about my experiences teaching, and cooler that I ever expected to be, and funny, which I hear some people like.

MY COMING OUT STORY, SPONSORED BY BANK OF AMERICA

by SAM STONE

Since I was a kid, I've always known something about me was... different. Sure, my parents would look at me funny when I'd play with Barbies, but they'd also wonder aloud why I'd ask to dress up as a Bank of America bank teller for Halloween year after year. I just think they provide excellent customer service, Mom! As I got older, I began to recognize that funny feeling inside for what it was: I was gay.

I knew I had to tell my parents, but I wasn't sure how. Finally, when I was sixteen, I worked up the courage to sit them down and share the news. "We're so proud of you and we love you," my dad said. Then it was Mom's turn. She turned to me with tears in her eyes and said "Bank of America's Cash Rewards Card offers 1 percent cash-back on all purchases and 3 percent back on gas. Exclusions may apply." Her heartfelt words will stay with me forever. I was so relieved my parents were supportive, but I knew I had one more person to tell: Sharon, my family's Bank of America Wealth and Investment manager. She seemed taken aback at first, but after a few moments, she told me "Love wins!" and gave me a lollipop.

I went away to college and suddenly everything changed; I wasn't the only gay person in my small town anymore. Gay guys were everywhere, and before I knew it I was hopelessly in love with my first boyfriend. Our romance was everything I had dreamed it would be as a kid: holding hands, wearing matching tank tops to brunch, midnight trips to the ATM just because. When he left me after a whirlwind three weeks to focus more on his art (tweeting at celebrities) I felt like everything I knew had been tossed up in the air. Luckily, one thing in my life remained stable: Bank of America's online banking app didn't crash once during this difficult time. Its secure encrypted connection, and multifactor identification were the only things that I knew I could count on. They even called me to make sure my card hadn't been stolen when I rented *Love Actually* on iTunes twenty-four times in a row.

When it was time for my appropriately masculine husband and me to buy a house, where else could I turn but the multinational corporation that's been an ally since the beginning? Bank of America's home loans have low rates, the lowest down payments, and I didn't even have to read all that boring heterosexual paperwork! We picked up our tiny dog and our mid-century modern furniture, and moved right into our dream home!

All this is not to say our journey's been easy. We've had our bumps along the road. My personal BoA financial advisor, Michael, can get pretty stern when I overspend on cabs instead of investing in my Roth IRA. And you can imagine my chagrin when I learned that Bank of America was funding the Dakota Access Pipeline, violating the rights of the indigenous people, decimating their land, and polluting their water supply while employing excessive violence against protestors all in the name of corporate greed. We may have our small differences in opinion, but at the end of the day, what other soulless corporation has been there for me in the way the BoA has?

Today, I'm proud to say I'm gay. This Pride Month, I celebrate not only my LGBT brothers and sisters, but also all the corporations that now see us as part of a profitable demographic. Here's to us but, more importantly, here's to Bank of America. America's official gay bank.

NEW EROTICA
FOR FEMINISTS

by CAITLIN KUNKEL, BROOKE PRESTON,
FIONA TAYLOR, *and* CARRIE WITTMER

The cop asks if I know why he pulled me over.

"Because my taillight is out?"

"Yes ma'am, it's not a huge deal, but it could be a potential safety issue. I'm happy to escort you to a busy and well-lit garage a few blocks up run entirely by female mechanics. I won't give you a ticket if you can take care of it now."

"That's fair," I say, my eyes lingering over his clearly visible badge and identification.

- - -

I get catcalled on the street by a construction worker. He says that he can see I'm smart because I have enormous books. He tells me he's reading the latest Zadie Smith novel. I invite him to join my book club, and spend all night fantasizing about his insightful commentary around nonlinear plot structure.

- - -

"Why don't we invite your friend over?" he suggests, testing the waters. "There's nothing I love more than watching two women in sweatpants engaging in hot political discourse. I love to watch... how you always let each other finish speaking without interrupting. I'll also make nachos."

- - -

A stranger at a bar introduces himself, and the conversation is flowing.

He leans in close and murmurs throatily, "Would you like to get out of here and go to my place?"

"Oh, I'm gay," I reply.

He says, "That's cool. I've enjoyed talking to you. I won't try to convince you that you need to sleep with a man to know if you're really gay, because only a huge jerk would do that. Anyway, did you think *Dunkirk* was confusing?"

- - -

"Congress is now fifty-fifty women," my partner whispers, pouring me a delicious glass of calorie-free wine. "And 'pro-life' no longer refers to abortion, but to a consistent position based on helping all people reach their fullest potential. Would you like a foot massage? It's not a fetish, I just know how hard you work."

- - -

I hear a box truck backing up in my driveway. Tom Hardy steps out, wearing a tight T-shirt that says WILD FEMINIST. He politely asks my permission to step inside to fill up my whole refrigerator with free LaCroix and play with my rescue dog every Tuesday forever. I consent clearly and enthusiastically.

- - -

"Maybe it's time for some role-play," my husband murmurs, trying to get me in the mood.

"Okay." I giggle.

"I'll be a big Hollywood producer, and you're a rising starlet."

"Hot," I say, nuzzling his neck. "Tell me more."

"I see your spectacular... talent and I treat you with respect." His hands are wandering. "I line up a female screenwriter, director, and cinematographer for your next film."

I moan as he continues.

"Your box office receipts are *soooo* big that studio heads are finally convinced that women-driven films are bankable. Not only that, Greta Gerwig wins her tenth Oscar."

"Yes!" I shout. "Cast me now!"

- - -

I meet a scientist on Tinder. They go on and on about their biggest professional achievement—the serum that made Ruth Bader Ginsburg immortal. It drives me wild. I don my naughtiest jabot and my sex gavel.

- - -

The doorbell rings. It's the plumber.

"I'm here for that very, very big job you needed done," he says. "Sorry I'm a few minutes late. I was liking all of Maxine Waters's tweets and lost track of time. I was a very bad boy and I'm sorry."

He toys with the zipper on his coverall.

"You're clearly the man for the job," I say. "Lay some pipe for me NOW."

He lays my new copper pipes as we chat about the 2018 midterm elections.

- - -

He calls me into his office and closes the door… to promote me. He promotes me again and again. I am wild with ecstasy.

- - -

"Who's your favorite comedian?" I ask the producer shyly after he compliments my set. *Please don't say Louis C.K., please don't say Louis C.K.*, I think to myself but also fully say out loud.

"Aparna Nancherla," he replies. "I can get you on a bill with her since I know her manager professionally. You could be a big star. But to be crystal clear, I'll do that regardless of any personal relationship between us. I just like to see talented, hard-working women succeed in comedy."

- - -

The pizza delivery car pulls up outside. It's right on time and so, so hot. The delivery guy hands it over with an appropriate smile and says, "Enjoy, I hope you're not sharing it with anyone if you don't want, I believe everyone is in control of their own bodies and should never be shamed for what they decide to eat or not eat." He makes no effort to come inside because that would be weird and alarming. I smile and give him a reasonable tip for his normal behavior as I shut the door. Time for *The Crown*.

THE LADY HERO'S JOURNEY

by KATHLEEN O'MARA

A woman tries to set out on the Hero's Journey only to find that Joseph Campbell didn't believe that women take the Hero's Journey. She must instead embark on The Lady Hero's Journey.

CRAZY WORLD

The Lady lives in a Crazy World. Why would she even want to go on the Hero's Journey in the first place? She already has a lot to deal with at home. Slaying the Great Dragon of the North does not really seem like her thing. She's more a "Run a Homestead, Raise Her Younger Siblings, and Care for Her Ailing Father" kind of Lady. There is already so much she needs to tackle before she has the luxury of answering the Call to Adventure.

SETTLING ON THE CALL TO ADVENTURE

The Lady's Call to Adventure is not really the one she wanted. Can she even manage to slay the dragon ravaging the countryside? She is pretty Crazy. She knows that if she doesn't choose to slay this dragon, then they are going to give this Call to some Hero who is only twenty-two, went to a very fancy dragon-slaying school, and whose dad was a famous dragon slayer.

APOLOGIZING

She's sorry for complaining about her Adventure in the first place. She knows that a lot of Ladies not only deserve the Call, but would love to go on an Adventure. In fact, has Susan been called to slay the dragon? She'd be great at dragon-slaying.

BEING THANKFUL

The Lady is very thankful for her Adventure. She's very lucky. She can't wait to slay this dragon. Thank you, thank you so much!

BEGGING FOR THE MENTOR

The Lady is finding it challenging to be a woman with an Adventure, so she seeks out a Mentor. She finds a wizard who knows quite a bit about dragon-slaying, but he insists that he has his own dragons to slay. He can't help her with her Adventure. He's pretty surprised she even has the Call to Adventure and suspects it might be some type of Diversity Thing.

MEETING OTHER LADIES

She meets other Ladies with the Call to Adventure. Some try to help her where they can, but some are threatened by her Adventure. Her Adventure might diminish their own Adventures. Are there even enough dragons for all the Ladies to slay?

EDUCATING OF THE ALLIES AND THE BEARING OF THE EMOTIONAL LABOR

The Lady has made an Ally from among the Heroes. He is very nice and helpful, but he still gets a lot wrong, so she's doing her best to educate him and be patient. Also, her Ally will not shut up about his ex and he does not seem to understand the basic time management of an Adventure. The Lady Bears this Emotional Labor, while still trying to figure out how she is going to put a lance through a magical creature that spews fire and flies.

CRYING A LOT

This is actually really hard, and the Lady just needs to cry right now, okay?

APPROACHES SEVERAL, EQUALLY IMPORTANT INMOST CAVES

The Lady finally makes it to the Inmost Cave, but notices there's several Inmost Caves. The one Inmost Cave should be enough for her, but the others are all equally important. There are two different dragons in two separate Caves. They are right next to each other, so she could probably find a way to manage both dragons. Plus, the dragons have been ravaging a nearby town and there are a lot of orphaned children running about. Someone should do something about all these orphans!

MULTITASKING THE ORDEAL AND FEELING GOOD ABOUT IT

She must Multitask while she defeats her dragon and completes her Ordeal. She feels great about the choices she made, the dragons she managed to slay, and the select orphans she saved. Seriously, she's fine, everything is fine. It's good. She's sorry, she meant to say, "It's good." *Very* good. Great, even.

SELF-CARE

She will Return Home at some point but first, she is going to have a little "me" time. She did slay two dragons after all.

RETURNING HOME

She Returns Home and everyone is pretty pissed that she left. Who does she think she is? A Hero?

17 REAL-LIFE WOULD-YOU-RATHERS I, A WOMAN, HAVE HAD TO ASK MYSELF

by ISABELLA GIOVANNINI

1. Would you rather have a career or a family?

2. Would you rather be perceived as likable or competent?

3. Would you rather be told to smile or to calm down?

4. Would you rather be called "Sweetie" or "Ma'am"?

5. Would you rather have a strange man lightly touch your knee or the small of your back?

6. Would you rather spend the rest of your life explaining why you don't want kids or why you don't want his dick pic?

7. Would you rather be "shrill" but finish your sentence or polite but interrupted by your male colleague?

8. Would you rather shoot literal botulism into your face or look your real age, you hag?

9. Would you rather breastfeed your child in public like a whore or feed your child toxic commercial formula like a terrible mother?

10. Would you rather be groped in a bus or groped in a bar, and also what were you wearing, you filthy skank?

11. Would you rather be blamed for your partner's affair because you're frigid and have too little sex, or blamed for your sexual assault because you're slutty and have too much sex?

12. Would you rather accept societal messaging that tells women they have to compete against each other for men, jobs, and who wore it better, or reject that messaging and support women, you ugly man-hating feminist?

13. Would you rather get your period, which is dirty and shameful and gross and must be hidden at all costs, or not get your period, which means you are not a "real" woman, whether that's because you're postmenopausal or you're trans or you have a medical condition, you bloodless, barren, good-for-nothing crone?

14. Would you rather be vilified for your choice to have an abortion, you selfish, godless baby-killer, or become a mother in America, the only developed nation without paid maternity leave and one

of only thirteen countries in the world where maternal mortality rates are rising, especially for black women, who are almost four times more likely than white women to die of pregnancy-related causes, but shut up about health care already, you entitled, hysterical, overemotional, elitist shrew?

15. Would you rather try to take out a loan for your small business, even though female-owned businesses get 4 percent of all money given out in small business loans and male-owned businesses get the other 96 percent, or try to take out a loan for your college education, which will probably need to be bigger than the average man's loan because your family is statistically less likely to have saved money for your lady-education, and which you'll have more trouble paying back than men do because you're making eighty cents on his dollar—fifty-four cents if you are Latina—which means you can't pay off the loan as fast, which means you accrue more and more interest, which means more and more debt, which means more and more trouble paying it off, which means more and more trouble accumulating wealth over your lifetime, which means a bigger and bigger gender wealth gap, but why do you women hold two-thirds of all outstanding student loan debt, you dumb, ditzy, irrational, hormonal bimbos?

16. Would you rather realize you've spent way too much time writing a list of Catch-22s women face in twenty-first-century America, but you could still keep going because sexism is all around you all the time always any time you step outside, or realize you honestly don't even know where your own internalized sexism ends because this patriarchal society is the only one you've ever known and what if someday everyone of every gender and color was equal

but also is that even possible given the entrenched forces of capitalism and the inherent selfishness of human nature and let's be real right now it's hard to imagine what that utopian egalitarian feminist society would even look like and you're just so, so tired, you frumpy, melodramatic, PMS-ing, bossy, ball-busting bitch?

17. Would you rather blow Matt B. or Matt C.?

A TIME TRAVELER GOES BACK IN TIME TO THE BIRTH OF BABY HITLER BUT GETS THE WRONG BABY

by TEDDY WAYNE

A husband and wife with their newborn son in a hospital room. A time traveler from the future instantaneously materializes behind them.

TIME TRAVELER: Future tyrant, prepare to meet your—

MAN: Who are you?

TIME TRAVELER: I'm here to prevent the rise of—wait, you spoke English. Is this Braunau am Inn, Austria?

MAN: No, it's Queens, New York.

TIME TRAVELER: This isn't 1889, and your names aren't Alois and Klara?

MAN: It's 1946. I'm Fred Trump, and this is my wife, Mary.

TIME TRAVELER: Wow. Oh, wow. The space-time transponders must have crossed due to the target's similarities in—I mean, look, I'm not claiming they're equivalent, and I think people who say that invalidate their arguments, but you have to admit, there are certain striking parallels. (*Looks at baby*) Oh, man. I don't know if I have it in me to do this.

MAN: To do what? Are you on the hospital staff?

TIME TRAVELER: I thought I could before, because Austria's a foreign country and 1889 is so long ago, but this—it's basically like the hospital room I was born in…

(*Looks at baby again*)

Jesus, he's actually pretty cute. I'm sure the other one was, too, but you'd have to bite the bullet and do that one.

(*Puts hand on forehead*)

This suddenly feels really weird.

MAN: *What* feels weird?

TIME TRAVELER: Nothing.

WOMAN: What are you holding behind your back?

The time traveler backs up to a garbage can and drops something heavy in it from behind his back.

TIME TRAVELER: It was... a harmless piece of garbage... from nineteen-forty... six—right? Give me a sec, let me rethink this... So, what sort of parenting philosophy do you plan to use with your son?

MAN: None of your business, you vagrant!

TIME TRAVELER: That tone of voice is just what I wanted to discuss. Have you considered adopting a gentler approach to child-rearing? Such as not pushing your son to win at everything, no matter the cost to others and his own soul?

WOMAN: We will raise him in the manner we so desire. Be gone, vile scum!

TIME TRAVELER: You know, I've heard a lot about him (*points to the man*), not as much about you, but I can already sort of form a picture.

(*Scratches head.*)

Huh. This one's really tricky. Could we bring a psychologist from the hospital in here? A classic Freudian?

MAN: Nurses! We have an intruder!

TIME TRAVELER: I know! Do you guys own a TV?

WOMAN: A what?

TIME TRAVELER: A T—sorry, a television set.

WOMAN: Obviously not. Hardly anyone has one.

TIME TRAVELER: When they become more popular, can you do me a favor and *never* get one? Or, wait, that might backfire. I got it: maybe buy *so many televisions* that your son grows to hate them? And station cameras hooked up to them all around the home, so that his entire experience of reality is televised, causing him to rebel by seeking total privacy as an adult? What else... oh, yeah, phones. Fill his bedroom with telephones and incessantly chirping birds until he develops a Pavlovian aversion to the audiovisual combination.

MAN: I'm calling the police!

TIME TRAVELER: Yes—call the police! Call the police *every single day* to your home and instill in your child a deep-seated aversion to weaponized authority and flagrant abuses of power. And don't be shy about exposing him to jingoistic anti-Russia propaganda over the next decade. But, on second thought, that'll get complicated in a few years, because he may appropriate the idea of a witch—

The sound of police in the hall.

TIME TRAVELER: Hold on, there's so much more I want you to teach him—please hear me out, for the sake of civilization. Give him vocabulary lessons for positive and negative adjectives. Tanning causes cancer, and it's unnatural-looking to have blond hair in your seventies. Show him how to speak without jerking his arms like a traffic guard.

MAN: Police, in here!

TIME TRAVELER: (*Speaking quickly*) Pose for photos with a relaxed smile and without putting your thumbs up! Neckties should stop at the belt! Laughter is a natural human response to humor! God, he sucks! Stress the importance of sleeping more than four hours a night! Encourage an early and irreversible vasectomy!

The police enter the room.

TIME TRAVELER: One last thing: tell your son that diet sodas are for sissies, okay?

WOMAN: What is a "diet" soda?

TIME TRAVELER: I honestly think that has something to do with it.

The time traveler vanishes. The couple forgets everything he said but his final instruction. Donald Trump develops type 2 diabetes in the 1980s from drinking a dozen cans of regular Coca-Cola a day and retires from real estate to manage his illness. His brush with mortality changes him profoundly, and he leverages his wealth and celebrity to become a powerful citizen advocate for universal health care—for which he helps pass legislation, in 1993, with Bill and Hillary Clinton. The experience leads him to run for president in 2016 on the Democratic ticket, and he is elected with overwhelming bipartisan support, ushering in a new progressive age.

The Stormy Daniels thing still happens, though.

WORD PROBLEMS FOR THE RACE CONSCIOUS

by DYMIR ARTHUR

Mahalia goes shopping for a dress at a boutique store in Chelsea. She is accompanied by her classmate Stephanie. There are twelve other customers shopping in the store, all of whom are white, like Stephanie. Write an expression to represent the total number of customers who may ask Mahalia to get something for them because they will assume that she is an employee of the store.

- - -

A cop pulls Raquan's car over on a Friday night. His best friend Terrence is in the passenger seat. His girlfriend Ashleigh and cousin Kris are in the backseat. When Ashleigh reaches down to pick up a cell phone she dropped on the floor, the officer approaching the car draws his gun and begins shooting. To shield her, Kris pulls Ashleigh toward him and away from the window. He is also shot. Ashleigh is pronounced dead at the scene. Kris dies at the hospital four hours after the "incident." The media spends a total of nine hours reporting on Kris's misdemeanor charge for possession of marijuana last summer and one hour covering the officer's past reports of brutality and misconduct. What is the ratio of minutes spent covering Kris's record to the minutes spent on the officer's past? What percentage of the officer's salary is likely to be withheld while the "incident" is under investigation?

- - -

At the beginning of every class, professors at Noriadah's small liberal arts college take attendance by calling every student's name. Noriadah has four white professors and one biracial teaching assistant who runs a biweekly recitation after lecture. What percentage of Noriadah's instructors are likely to reduce her name to "Nori" without her consent?

- - -

During the Q&A segment following a talk, a member of the audience asks a popular black writer what she thinks about the sexual harassment allegations of a famous black male entertainer. Amid the audience's gasps, the author points out that no such allegations have been made against the entertainer and that white women must be careful of the claims they make about black men, especially given this country's history. The audience member meekly meanders back to her seat clutching her actual pearls. Out of the three hundred guests in the audience, one-hundred and thirty are white. Approximately what percentage of the audience is likely to be more concerned with the feelings of the woman who was justly scolded for an ignorant question instead of being concerned about the danger of the question itself?

- - -

Sasha is one of two women and the only person of color on an executive team of nine people. During a debate about whether the organization should expand to another location, Sasha is the first to mention the competitive edge other competing organizations have in terms of talent acquisition because of their expansions in the last five years. What percentage of Sasha's teammates are positioned to repeat her point before it can be heard and acknowledged as a valuable perspective?

- - -

Josiah's family gathers at his grandmother's house to celebrate his eleventh birthday. Over cake, Josiah tells his father that in a few years, he will be old enough to drive his mother and father home from his birthday parties. The family laughs and Josiah watches his mother grab his father's hand as she always does when she feels the need to keep her husband calm. What percentage of the men in Josiah's family who hear the comment will feel obligated to begin teaching him what to do to increase his chances of staying alive if he's ever pulled over by the police?

- - -

Sam is reported missing when his mother returns from the ice cream truck and does not find him on the swing where she left him. She searches every corner of the park, screaming his name. Other concerned parents grab the hands of their little ones and help. A retired school teacher sits Sam's mother down and helps her catch her breath before calling 911. Several cops arrive within minutes and place barricades at the park's two entrances and exits. They begin searching the woods nearby for a six-year-old boy with rosy cheeks, a red hat and a blue T-shirt. A helicopter is called in for aerial support. The local news station catches the story and arrives on the scene shortly after the police. The reporter layers on makeup as her cameraman takes one final drag of his cigarette. The red hat is found near a creek. There are no signs of rosy cheeks or a blue T-shirt. Within an hour, Sam's face is shown across screens all around the nation. Reporters from national news outlets consume Sam's small town, and the local diner gets more business that one day than it did in the previous ten. How many of the news outlets covering Sam's disappearance are likely to have also reported on the disappearances of Maurice, Phoenix, April, Ashani, Genelle, Muna, Teliea, Diontae, and/or Amir when they went missing?

I DON'T HATE WOMEN CANDIDATES—I JUST HATED HILLARY AND COINCIDENTALLY I'M STARTING TO HATE ELIZABETH WARREN

by DEVORAH BLACHOR

"How does Warren avoid a Clinton redux—written off as too unlikable before her campaign gets off the ground?"—Politico, 12/31/18

- - -

I have no problem with women. My wife is a woman and I have daughters who will likely be wives and mothers of daughters one day. I only had a problem with Hillary Clinton, and my problem with her is completely separated from her gender, and is solely based on the fact that she was so dishonest when compared to other prominent politicians who ran for president. How could anyone vote for such a liar?

My hatred for Hillary wasn't diabolical. I never bought into the whole "pizzagate" thing, or the whole Uranium One thing, or the whole spirit-cooking-she-drinks-blood-infused-Podesta-rice thing, and I never once believed she was the devil. I would see those posts and just be like, *Huh, if people believe that stuff about her, she must be really terrible.*

And I never chanted "Lock her up!" or created memes showing her in prison, but I did laugh a little at those memes, because the thought of this accomplished woman behind bars with all her agency stripped away from her was funny to me.

So I'm a perfectly reasonable, women-friendly fellow who is completely open to the idea of a woman president. And I never thought I'd hate anyone as much as I hate Hillary Clinton. But to my surprise, I'm actually starting to hate Elizabeth Warren.

Don't get me wrong. I've heard that Elizabeth Warren is a champion of consumers and the middle class who battled the big banks and advocates for economic reform. Nonetheless, she rubs me the wrong way.

I hate the way she dealt with Donald Trump's incessant attacks against her, for example. Why did Elizabeth Warren have to take that DNA test? Why couldn't she have handled his abuse the exact right way? If I were being libeled by the President at his toxic mob rallies of hate, by golly, I would know just how to turn that into a moment of pure perfection.

And you know the DNA test is a huge deal, because *Breitbart* published five different stories about it over the course of twenty hours. Though I have never once in my life given a thought about the welfare of Native Americans, I am totally offended on their behalf. The fact they have criticized Elizabeth Warren just bolsters my claim that she's the worst person ever, besides Hillary Clinton, and thus endeth my Native American advocacy until the day I die.

Another thing about Elizabeth Warren: she claims she advocates for the poor, yet she isn't a poor herself. She lives in a fancy house with her fancy Harvard salary. I'm no fan of Trump, but that Elizabeth Warren is such a phony. That's a thought, and thoughts are true, and I will never examine how that thought got into my head.

I mean, think about it for a moment. If Elizabeth Warren were so great, why would Robert Mercer be funding a super PAC whose sole purpose was to portray her as an out-of-touch hypocrite? If she were a truly good leader, why would so many people like me dislike her?

I always tell my daughters they can be anything they want, so long as they don't make other people feel uncomfortable. They can be as ambitious as they want, so long as they do it in an acceptable manner. They can reach for the stars, which you can see right up there on the ceiling painted to resemble a sky.

So bring it on, ladies! I'd love to see a female president. Just not Hillary Clinton. Or Elizabeth Warren. I am totally open to all other women leaders, but I have to admit that Kamala Harris and Amy Klobuchar are beginning to make me angry and I'm not sure why yet, but I know the reason will become clear soon, and I'm also wondering what they might look like if someone photoshopped their heads onto the bodies of prisoners and put them behind bars.

Reach for the stars, girls!

NIHILIST DAD JOKES

by ALEX BAIA

Why did the scarecrow win a prize? Because he stood alone in his field! He stood there for years, rotting, until he was forgotten.

I tell my kids, you're allowed to watch the TV all you want... just don't turn it on! This way they will begin to understand the futility of all things.

How does a penguin build a house? Igloos it together. Like all animals, it is an automaton, driven by blind genetic imperative, marching slowly to oblivion.

Why don't skeletons go trick or treating? They have no *body* to go with them! The skeletons are like us: alone, empty, dead already.

I don't really like playing soccer. I just do it for kicks! Like all of humanity, I pretend to enjoy things, and others pretend to care about my charade.

You hear about the moon restaurant? Good food, no atmosphere! If you eat there, you forfeit your life, which would make no difference to the universe as a whole.

Why did the blonde focus on an orange juice container? It said concentrate! She realized that society's depictions of her were like the juice: formulaic, insipid, fake.

My wife told me to put the cat out. I didn't know it was on fire! By the time I could act, it was incinerated, a harbinger of the path we all must take.

How come the invisible man wasn't offered a job? They just couldn't see him doing it! This man stands for all of us: unseen, misunderstood, irrelevant.

Today I gave away my old batteries... free of charge! No one wanted them, so I became angry and threw them in the yard. The battery acid now leaks into the soil, killing a colony of ants. A sparrow eats their bodies and is poisoned. Somewhere in the Serengeti, a lion devours his rival's cubs. Then the lion is shot by a poacher and sold to an unloved rich man whose father was an unloved rich man. In five billion years, the sun will become a bloated giant, boiling the oceans and consuming our pointless cruelties with flames. I wake sweat-drenched and screaming, staring at the visage of a faceless god. "WHAT HAVE I DONE?! HOW COULD I BRING A CHILD INTO THIS WORLD!?" But this god, like all gods, is nothing—just my son's Wilson baseball mitt, sitting on my dresser, mocking me.

Will February March? No, but April May! Soon we become ash, and time forgets us.

V.
APPENDIX

BEHIND THE TENDENCY CLASSICS

―――――

*Tendency editor Chris Monks conducted the following interviews with
authors on their classic pieces, originally for the McSweeney's
Internet Tendency's Patreon page in 2017.*

BEHIND TIM CARVELL'S
"THE DANCE LESSON"

(PAGE 73)

Where did you get the idea for the piece?
The idea from the piece came from the sad, simple fact that I can't
dance. At the best of times, I lurch around like a drunken bear. So I was
thinking about all the kind, patient, good-natured people who'd tried
and failed to teach me even the most basic elements of dancing. And
then I started thinking about what it would've been like if things had
taken a turn for the worse—if I'd been taught to dance by someone
less kind and patient.

About the writing process:
As best I can remember, I wrote the piece fairly quickly. The premise
was so simple that it really only had one direction in which it could
go: things get worse. The only challenge I can remember was figuring
out a way out of the piece—once you've escalated a fight, how do you
de-escalate it, or at least resolve it in a satisfying way? (And the sad
realization that actually, the fight wouldn't end, and these two people
would just repeat this cycle, over and over again, seemed like the most
honest way to get out of the story.)

Was there anything about the audience reaction to the piece that was surprising/ most interesting?

I'm always a little surprised when people remember the piece—I think I underestimated the extent to which "shitty controlling boyfriend" hits a nerve. I also remember once getting an email from someone who wanted to perform the piece in a college speech class, which seemed like—given the one-sided nature of the piece—a difficult thing to do. But maybe he did great with it? I hope he did great with it.

- - -

BEHIND LUKE BURNS'S "FAQ: THE SNAKE FIGHT PORTION OF YOUR THESIS DEFENSE"

(PAGE 229)

Where did you get the idea for the piece?

The idea for "Snake Fight" actually came to me in a dream that I had in 2010, a few months after graduating from college. If only all my dreams were so fruitful! In the dream, I was back in college, meeting with my thesis advisor in his office. We were discussing, what else, my thesis, when I felt a flutter against my leg. Out of the corner of my eye, I saw a bright green flash, and before I had a chance to react, I was totally immobilized, enveloped in the coils of a giant snake. As I fell to the floor, the snake slowly strangling me, I looked to my thesis advisor for help. He just smiled a small wry smile, the way he did when he was about to make a sardonic observation about a work of literature, raised an eyebrow, and gave me a look that seemed to say, "Oh, no one told you about the snake?" And that's when I woke up. I had this dream at a time in my life when I was living at home, looking

* very strong, poisonous, a sim,
african, or south american.
There are standard variations you
get ordinarily w/ Snakes.

FAQ: The Snake Fighting Portion of Your Thesis Defense.

Q: How big is the snake?
A: It depends. The better your thesis is, the smaller
the snake will be.

Q: What does it mean if you get a snake that is
small, but is also very strong?
A: Snake-picking is not an exact science, so you shouldn't
read too much into whether the snake is—

Q: Do I have to kill the snake?
A: You have to "defeat" the snake. There are many
different ways to accomplish this. The method is up to
you. Think of it as an opportunity to show your creativity.

Q: Is the snake a metaphor, or some kind of phallic
symbol?
A: If you defeat the snake & get into grad school,
that's certainly a question you can look into. The snake is very real, I can assure you.

Q: Does my advisor pick the snake?
A: No. Your advisor just tells the "snake guy" how good
your thesis was.

Q: Is it a magical snake? It's just one of the many snakes kept on campus by the Facilities department.
A: No. We have a bunch of different snakes on campus.

Q: Can I get a poisonous snake?
A: Sometimes, yes. But usually only if there are
problems w/ your bibliography.

An early handwritten draft of "FAQ: The Snake Fight Portion of Your Thesis Defense."

- Tradition   - gaming the system   - kill?
- size of snake   - in my office.
- strength.   - prepare?

A Conversation With My ~~Thesis Advisor~~ Advisor
About The Snake fighting ~~Portion~~ of
My ~~Thesis~~ Defense!

A: ... and really ~~by the time you get to~~
the ~~defense~~ you ~~should~~ know the material
so well that there wont be anything
to worry about.
                              have some questions for

A: So, you ~~wanted~~ to talk to me about your
thesis defense?

M: I do.

A: ~~Is it about~~ Are ~~they~~ few questions about fighting the
snake?

M: They are.

A: ~~I suspected as~~ What would you like to know?

[M: Mainly, why do I have to fight a snake
      for my thesis defense?

  A: Well, it's tradition, I had to fight a snake when]

M: Well, ... I have a lot of questions ... but ... is
it a big snake?

Page two of an early handwritten draft.

for work, and overall feeling pretty useless. So it's not surprising that I would have an anxiety dream, but it is pretty funny to me that I would have an anxiety dream with such on-the-nose imagery. I mean, really, unconscious, try a little harder. Make me do a little analysis. Getting strangled by a snake is such an obvious metaphor. Speaking of which, ever since this piece was published, I can only assume that many people have been dying to know whether the snake is a metaphor, and if so, for what? You may have already guessed the answer from this story, but I suppose I might as well come right out and say it: the snake is a metaphor for the job market.

Any interesting tidbits to share about the writing/editing process?
I wrote the first two drafts longhand, in the time it takes to travel by bus from New York to D.C. (I was going see the "Rally to Restore Sanity and/or Fear." 2010. Simpler times.) I originally tried writing the piece as a dialogue between a thesis advisor and their advisee, but something about it wasn't working. There were a bunch of jokes and beats I couldn't quite fit in, and it was taking too long to get to the jokes I *was* able to include. I also wanted the tone to be a bit dry and arch, with a dash of, "Tsk, you really should have known better"—all the things conveyed by the look my advisor gave me in the dream— and that wasn't coming through in the first version. It didn't click until I hit on the idea of rewriting it in the form of an FAQ. (I often find that when I'm stuck on a piece, framing the idea a different way or switching to a different form can unlock or unblock something.) As you can see in the following photos of my early drafts, I decided to abandon the more sketch-like version and switch to the FAQ format almost immediately after writing a line where the advisee says, "I have a lot of questions." I think that was the exact "aha" moment for me. The FAQ version was vastly easier to write. For starters, the Q&A

format lends itself very well to setups and punchlines. And it's a good way to ground the piece. The structure of an FAQ provides a nice foil for all the weird snake stuff, making it easier for the reader get on board with this strange world, and making the situation more relatable. The tone I was aiming for came through more clearly, too. I was able to give both the questioner and the answerer distinct voices, but since an FAQ is not a conversation between two specific people in a specific place, I didn't have to spend a lot of time doing the kind of scene-setting and character work that was slowing things down in the original version. The first FAQ version I wrote wound up being surprisingly similar to the final product currently on the site. Once I got home from the rally, I just had to type it up, cut a few things, do a little polishing, and rearrange some of the beats before submitting.

Was there anything about the audience reaction to the piece that surprised you? I honestly never expected "Snake Fight" to find a particularly wide audience. When I submitted it, I was worried it might be too esoteric and niche even for McSweeney's (academia humor was not as prominent of a subgenre back then). Once it was published I figured that, at most, a handful of people might find it and get a laugh, but it really caught on, and it seems like once or twice a year (thesis defense time, I guess?) it gets shared around a bunch. I'm just glad it's something that brings a little bit of relief to people who are going through a stressful time. Also, I once met another writer of short humor pieces who, when I introduced myself, said he remembered reading "Snake Fight" and had always assumed I was a sixty-five-year-old professor, which is one of the best compliments I've ever been given.

- - -

BEHIND MIKE LACHER'S
"I'M COMIC SANS, ASSHOLE"

(PAGE 235)

Where did you get the idea for the piece?
At the time, making fun of Comic Sans was en vogue on the internet. I saw a blog dedicated to it and read a few articles about it, and I thought it was interesting how people got incensed in a performative way about a font. So I figured it would be funny if this font wasn't the stupid, infantile character they all pictured, but instead an angry, foul-mouthed, vindictive typeface with a bruised ego.

How long did it take you to write it from start to finish?
I think I wrote it over the course of a weekend. Editing it was mostly a process of getting more profane and detailed. It only really got good once the words "asshat" and "jagoff" started coming in. Which I think is true for all great art.

Was there anything about the audience reaction to the piece that was surprising?
I really didn't anticipate how big a response it would get. I thought it was pretty funny, but I had no idea the kind of nerve it would strike. I'm guessing it's because people seemed to like it whether they hated Comic Sans or hated people complaining about Comic Sans. It was really cool to see people do other stuff with it. Somebody made an animated short, a few people used it as a dramatic monologue, and I think somebody wrote a response piece as Papyrus.

Have you ever used Comic Sans since writing the piece?
I haven't. I was sort of weirdly identified with the font by friends and family after the piece got popular. They'd forward me anything having

to do with Comic Sans. So I think using it would seem like I'm trying to revel in my bygone successes of the late-aughts.

- - -

BEHIND ANTHONY SAMS'
"TOTO'S 'AFRICA,' BY ERNEST HEMINGWAY"
(PAGE 295)

On the inspiration for writing the piece:
I was teaching a course on literary forms and styles at the time. One of the assignments was to take a work by one author and rewrite it in the style of another author from the course. We had been reading texts with strong and unmistakable styles, and among them was Hemingway's *The Snows of Kilimanjaro and Other Stories*, which is a slim volume that functions essentially as a best-of collection of his short fiction.

The students and I were exploring the famous "iceberg style" of Hemingway's prose, specifically in the book's title story and "The Short Happy Life of Francis Macomber," which are both set in Africa. There are no shortage of pieces that lampoon Hemingway's terse, icebergian style of writing, but I hadn't seen much that playfully jabbed at Hemingway's use of the African continent as a device in his fiction and the development of the myth he made for himself. That was on my mind when I caught Toto's "Africa" on the radio for the umpteenth time.

I've always thought the Toto song was absurd; that's why it's such a fun song to sing along with. And just like Hemingway's Africa stories, the song uses selective imagery to create a backdrop for its characters while romanticizing and reducing Africa. Suddenly the two seemed like a perfect match.

On the writing process:

I think the lyrics are among the great unsolved mysteries of the 1980s. The song is full of half-hints, contradictions, and lines that are easily misheard. It refuses to explain its ambiguities. At the risk of giving it too much credit, there's almost a kind of messy icebergian story-telling at work in it. It feels like there should be something more to it, something under the surface. There's been a lot written lately about how "Africa" has become "the internet's favorite song," but at the time there weren't too many takes out there about it. It was relentlessly catchy and completely nonsensical, that much we agreed on. I think the hallmark of an effective parody is attention to detail, but once I decided there were things about the song I couldn't explain, the writing process opened up. I found the lyrics and listened to the song on repeat as I wrote the piece.

The first draft came out quickly (in just an hour or so), and it was too long and far too serious. I cut and cut over the next few days until the draft seemed lighthearted, passably Hemingway-esque, and short enough for a style parody not to overstay its welcome. To me, the butt of the joke is that high and low art have more in common than some people imagine, but that had to be clear from the start, not suddenly revealed at the end.

On the audience reaction to the piece:

The song's ascendance into full-blown internet meme has given the piece a greater longevity and relevance than I would have imagined when it was first published back in 2011. The piece still pops up in unexpected places at unexpected times. I recall reading someone who said the song never made sense to her until she'd read this particular version. Honestly though, I still don't understand what the hell the song is about.

- - -

BEHIND WENDY MOLYNEUX'S "HELLO STRANGER ON THE STREET, COULD YOU PLEASE TELL ME HOW TO TAKE CARE OF MY BABY?"

(PAGE 323)

Inspiration for the piece:

Unlike most of the things I've written for McSweeney's, where I get my ideas from messages received in seances, this one truly, truly came from real life. Right after my husband and I had our baby, in one of our first times going out of the house with the baby, we had to take our car to get repaired at a dealership about ten miles away. We wound up needing to leave the car there for a few hours and we had our newborn with us. We had not brought our stroller with us, and the nearest coffee shop was about a mile away, so we had to walk with an upset newborn in my arms. Along the way, an older woman walked up to me and *without my permission* placed his swaddle over his face to "keep him out of the sun." He hated having his face covered! And I was like, bitch, step off. Then, when we got to the cafe. I went to the restroom, and while I was gone, a woman just walked right up to my husband and pointed at our son and said, "He has a rash on his face." He had what's called "baby acne," which is normal and goes away on its own. We were both just like "what the fuck is happening here?" Do people just walk up to you and do rude things when you have a baby? And it turns out that, yes, they do! And it's not just strangers! Let's face it, sometimes there are friendship-ending levels of unsolicited advice that come from family or friends as well. People bought me books that I placed directly in the trash. I guess what I'm saying is: I'm a real treat.

On the writing/editing process:
I think I wrote this one quickly in a fit of pique? That sounds like me anyway. In my mind I wrote this right after the incident above happened, but I actually wrote it almost two years later! Think of all the pique I accumulated during that time with which to have my fit!

On the audience reaction:
This is one of those pieces that people are basically just like, "Yep, this is a thing." I think actually it has served as a caution most of all to myself, in that it helps me remember how much I hated unsolicited advice as a new parent so before I offer any, I'm like, c'mon, Wendy, don't be a dick.

- - -

BEHIND VIJITH ASSAR'S
"GUIDE TO AMBIGUOUS GRAMMAR"
(PAGE 371)

Inspiration for writing the piece:
In 2014, *Washington Post* reporter, Radley Balko, wrote a more straight-forward analysis of this sort of language, which I found so fascinating that I kept returning to reread it every couple months. That's where I first encountered the proposed "past exonerative tense" that is so central to this piece. A year or so later, I saw an especially prominent example of that language in the news; I found it enraging and couldn't bring myself to work on anything else that weekend.

On the writing process:
The concept had been taking shape in my head for a while, but it was kicked into high gear by a particular news story. I had to code

the interactive bits twice because my first attempt had some weird visual glitches that only went away when I switched over to using image-focused code libraries that could more precisely manipulate the pixels. I was very nervous about the subject matter, so I sent it to a few friends for feedback before publication. One former copy editor helped fine-tune the accurate deployment of grammar terminology to a spectacularly pedantic degree. Another—a black man—told me the last sentence should be rendered in red.

On the audience reaction:
A number of teachers and professors have talked about using it in high school and college level English classes. The high point among these was when one of my own high school classmates mentioned that it had been an assigned reading in graduate school! But my favorite response has been from those who have sort of weaponized it—sometimes people respond to that kind of language by posting a link to the piece, tweeting it at police departments or news outlets or whatever. Some of the other reader responses I have seen still break my heart and I do not want to repeat them here.

- - -

BEHIND LINDSEY FINN'S "FEMINIST HUMBLEBRAGS"

(PAGE 403)

Where did you get the idea for the piece?
I got catcalled while out for a jog one day and came home and told my then-husband and he laughed and congratulated me (because I didn't seem upset at all—please don't interpret this as him being insensitive,

he's wonderful and an absolute ally for women). It touched on that feeling women get when they're catcalled—you can be annoyed that someone called after you in what they perceive to be complimentary fashion about your physical appearance, but it also has the potential to make you feel unsafe so it's a weird line and you can often feel awkward expressing any kind of anger about it. I feel compelled to be transparent right now and mention that catcalling has never terribly bothered me, so long as it's been pretty innocuous. There's a group of guys who loiter outside the U-Haul by my apartment and they call after me every time I run and it's usually a chill, "Lookin' good, lady!" or "There she goes again!" and I smile and we all wave and it's one of the nicest parts of my day. Not sure if that makes me a bad feminist or maybe reveals I'm lonely or have issues or whatever, but I legitimately enjoy it so take that for whatever it's worth.

How long did it take you to write it from start to finish? Any interesting tidbits to share about the writing/editing process?
This was one of those rare and desperately wished-for instances by writers when the writing came fairly easily. I thought of instances wherein a woman is typically marginalized and how expressing that could potentially be heard as bragging and it all kind of flowed.

Was there anything about the audience reaction to the piece that was surprising/ most interesting?
I noticed that a few people online felt I was mocking feminism, which isn't true. It bummed me out a little bit but you can't help when people don't understand something you wrote sometimes, I suppose. This was before the #MeToo movement, I imagine if it was released now I might have received even more backlash than I did. Or maybe not; what do I know, I'm just a woman.

- - -

BEHIND HOMA MOJTABAI'S "REASONS YOU WERE NOT PROMOTED THAT ARE TOTALLY UNRELATED TO GENDER"

(PAGE 407)

Inspiration for writing the piece:
Like many great ideas, the idea for this piece came about during an epic dinner with friends. We were from different ethnic backgrounds and working in different industries, but all women, all Wharton MBAs and all hearing versions of the same gendered feedback at work. Even though we had different personality styles and strengths/weaknesses, there was so much similarity in our professional experiences. The feedback we were receiving wasn't about being outspoken or quiet or ambitious or a parent or single, it wasn't even about performance, it was about being a woman. I had fallen into this trap of thinking I could get an MBA and be safe, or work super hard and be safe, but really the answer is to do all of the above AND get lucky. Get lucky by getting a great boss who can (and will) advocate for you, or get lucky by finding a high-growth industry with enough opportunity to go around, or by writing satirical articles about seemingly intractable problems and then selling a screenplay for a million bucks (that last part hasn't happened yet).

On the writing process:
This piece took about five minutes of writing and I was cracking myself up and having a blast doing it. Easily my most productive writing session ever. Or to paraphrase some quote I read somewhere, I've had

this list brewing in me for a long time, I just needed to be ready to write it down. It's a good reminder that when the message/kernel of a story is crystal clear, the writing process itself is a joy.

On the audience reaction:
I'm surprised at how popular it was—I knew it was a funny piece, but I thought it would fly under the radar. So many women are dealing with the same challenges (and these challenges are compounded for women of color), and I think we're at a point where we are ready to confront some hard truths, even if it means a lot of difficult conversations and a little blowback. I was surprised by the references to the list in scholarly articles and books that have come out since.

- - -

BEHIND MEG ELISON'S "IF WOMEN WROTE MEN THE WAY MEN WRITE WOMEN..."
(PAGE 439)

Inspiration for writing the piece:
I've been reading books all my life that either objectify women or attempt to inhabit their point of view with disastrous results. Every single vignette I wrote into this piece comes directly from an example I could call to mind where a male author had written a female character like she was a house plant, a juicy steak, or a sweater he'd like to wear. The worst examples are the mirror scenes, wherein an author puts a woman in front of a mirror so that she can describe her naked body for our pleasure, but also to evaluate whether it's good enough for the protagonist to fuck her. That scene is so clichéd and rote that I had

hundreds of examples come to mind when I was cackling and writing it up. Please, for the love of all the horny, priapic gods, my dear male peers: stop doing this. It's embarrassing to watch.

About the writing process:
I dashed this piece off in maybe twenty minutes, because it was like lightning in a bottle and I needed to get it down fast. I showed it to my writing group, a small gathering of talented, discerning people, who gave me some good notes about sharpening it. I knew from the moment it was conceived that it was meant for McSweeney's. Tone is everything.

On the audience response:
The experience of publishing "If Women Wrote Men the Way Men Write Women" has been unlike anything else I've ever put out there. I've published novels and short stories, as well as essays and satire since I was in college. This piece was shared more widely than anything else I've written, and I heard back from some strange corners of the globe about it. Someone sent me their home-brewed Russian translation of it from their Facebook page, wherein I learned that the word in Russian for cheating is the same as the word for treason.

This piece has also been the second most effective in my career so far for inducing hate mail. More than one person wrote me to ask if I have ever read male/male slashfic, as if the existence of porn in the corners of the internet were equal to the girth of the entire Western literary canon hammering at the mysterious door of the vagina for the last thousand years. I am accustomed to being accused of man-hating, but this piece brought dildo-shaped pitchforks out of the village in numbers I never imagined. At times like these, I am grateful for the other loud women who have showed me how to cope with the fact that men cannot stop spending their time telling women who write things on the internet that they are fat and unfuckable and wrong.

Despite the inexorable tide of trolls any woman who says words in public must face, this piece still brings me pleasure, notoriety, and sells copies of my books. After a lifetime of reading men writing women this way, I'm willing to consider that retroactive combat payment on an account that will never be settled.

CONTRIBUTORS

WENDI AARONS is the cocreator of @paulryangosling, and writes for high-level literary places like *Us Weekly*'s Fashion Police. She also writes essays for various other outlets and books. Mostly she writes notes left on cars parked by assholes. She's lived in Austin, Texas, for twenty years and hopes you don't move there, especially if you park like an asshole.

BRIAN AGLER is a speechwriter living in New York City. He has contributed to the *New Yorker*, *Esquire*, and Splitsider. He hosts a monthly show called "An Evening of Humorous Readings," and would love for you to attend.

JEFF ALEXANDER is a writer and an editor. He lives in Brooklyn.

GARY M. ALMETER is an attorney who lives in a quaint and cozy neighborhood in Baltimore, MD, with his wife, three children, and beagle. His short stories, essays, and humor pieces have appeared in Writer's Bone, the Good Men Project, *1966*, and Splitsider. He is the recipient of the Maryland Writer's Association's 2015 Creative Nonfiction Award. His first book, *The Emperor of Ice-Cream*, was published in 2019.

MEGAN AMRAM is a comedy writer living in Los Angeles. She has written for *The Good Place*, *Parks & Rec*, *The Simpsons*, *Silicon Valley*, *Transparent*, *Kroll Show*, and *Childrens Hospital*. Her web series, *An Emmy for Megan*, was nominated for two Emmys in 2018. Her book *Science... For Her!* was published in 2014.

DYMIR ARTHUR is a writer and school leader living and working in Brooklyn, New York. Before becoming a principal, Dymir served as a high school literature teacher, and Dean of School Culture and Academic Dean for Math. He earned his bachelor's in history and political science from Rutgers University and holds two graduate degrees in secondary education and instructional leadership. Dymir's writing focuses on issues of race, gender, and sexuality. In his spare time, he can be found dining out in any of New York's fine vegan restaurants or supporting performances at the Brooklyn Academy of Music. He does his best writing after long walks with his dog Oliver.

VIJITH ASSAR is a writer is a writer and software developer who created fancy animations for the original version of his piece as published by McSweeney's Internet Tendency. He also really likes this book!

JOHN LUSK BABBOTT is the author of four novels and many works of short fiction, all of which are slated for posthumous release unless an agent signs him. He lives in Portland, Oregon, where he teaches English.

ALEX BAIA is a humor writer and contributor to the *New Yorker* and Slackjaw. He enjoys being surrounded by books, houseplants, and the peculiar silence of a spooky evening. His humor and writing website is hyoom.com.

RAJEEV BALASUBRAMANYAM is the prize-winning author of *In Beautiful Disguises,* and, most recently, *Professor Chandra Follows His Bliss.* He is a long-term practitioner of Vipassana meditation, and was a fellow of the Hemera Foundation, for writers with a meditation practice, as a part of which he was writer-in-residence at Crestone Zen Mountain Center and the Zen Center of New York City. His journalism and short fiction have appeared in the *Washington Post, The Economist, New Statesman, London Review of Books, Paris Review,* and many others. He lives in Berlin.

AMIE BARRODALE is the author of the story collection *You Are Having A Good Time* (FSG). She received the Plimpton Prize from the *Paris Review* in 2012.

BRIAN BENNETT writes and performs comedy in Chicago, and puts his videos online.

TOM BISSELL is the author of nine books, including *Extra Lives, The Disaster Artist* (cowritten with Greg Sestero), and *Apostle*. He lives in Los Angeles.

DEVORAH BLACHOR is the author of *The Feminist's Guide to Raising a Little Princess*. She writes humor, nonfiction and fiction, including the mystery novels *Farbissen* and *Fakakt* under the pen name Jasmine Schwartz.

RAPHAEL BOB-WAKSBERG is the creator of the Netflix original series *BoJack Horseman*. His book of short stories is called *Someone Who Will Love You in All Your Damaged Glory* and it can be found wherever books tend to congregate.

HELENA DE BRES is a writer based in Cambridge, MA. She writes essays and humor and teaches philosophy at Wellesley.

KATIE BRINKWORTH is a writer living in Los Angeles and working in advertising. She used to eat those glow-in-the-dark necklaces you get at carnivals as a child, and their side effects have influenced much of her writing.

MICHAEL ANDOR BRODEUR is a columnist, editor, and musician based in Houston, Texas.

ANDY BRYAN is a recovering archaeologist who may be found joyfully embracing the towering firs and cedars of the Pacific Northwest. His work has appeared in various online and print publications of questionable repute. He continues to pack a bullwhip, but steadfastly abstains from crystal skulls.

LUKE BURNS is a writer based in New York whose work has been published by the *New Yorker, New York* magazine, and in the books *The Best of McSweeney's Internet Tendency* and *The McSweeney's Book of Politics and Musicals*. He writes and directs sketch comedy at UCB Theatre and is coeditor of "A Newsletter of Humorous Writing." See more of what he's up to at lukevburns.com.

TIM CARVELL is the executive producer of *Last Week Tonight with John Oliver*; he's previously worked for *The Daily Show with Jon Stewart*, *Entertainment Weekly*, and *Fortune*.

KASHANA CAULEY is a contributing opinion writer for the *New York Times*, a former staff writer for the *Daily Show*, and deadly with a butter knife.

Originally from the Bay Area, KAREN CHEE now writes for *Late Night with Seth Meyers* and performs comedy around New York City. She contributes regularly to the *New Yorker*, and has been published in the *New York Times*, the *Washington Post*, Shondaland, and more. Karen does sketch comedy with her friends, improv with her enemies, and stand-up all by herself. She means well!

JIMMY CHEN lives in San Francisco with his wife and son. He is an administrator at a large institution.

RIVER CLEGG has been a writer on the *Late Show with Stephen Colbert* and *The Opposition with Jordan Klepper*. His work has appeared in the *New Yorker*, The Onion, ClickHole, and others.

JAMIE CRICKS is a humor writer from Florida. Her work can be found on COG (cogzine.com), and the many blogs she has started but then quickly abandoned. She graduated from Rollins College with a degree in English.

PAUL WILLIAM DAVIES lives in Los Angeles, California. He is a writer, mainly for television, but sometimes not for television.

JULIA DRAKE's short fiction has appeared in *The Gettysburg Review* and *Esopus*. She is also the author of the young adult novel *The Last True Poets of the Sea*. She lives in Philadelphia.

CIROCCO DUNLAP was a coproducer of *Russian Doll* for Netflix, Simon Rich's series *Miracle Workers*, and *Man Seeking Woman*. She was also a consulting producer on Netflix's *Big Mouth* and Adult Swim's *Birdgirl*. She is the author of two children's books: *This Book Will Not Be Fun* and *Crunch, the Shy Dinosaur*.

KENDRA EASH is a humor writer and creative director based in Brooklyn. Her humor pieces have been published by the *New Yorker,* The Rumpus, The Hairpin, The Toast, and *GOOD* magazine. She is a coowner of And/Or Studio, where she makes clever things for screens of all sizes. Her awards include MVP of the 1995 BJHS basketball team and the "big fish" award at Legal Sea Foods circa 2007.

JESSE EISENBERG is an actor and author of the plays *The Spoils, The Revisionist* and *Happy Talk,* and the short story collection *Bream Gives Me Hiccups*.

MEG ELISON is a San Francisco Bay Area author. Her debut novel, *The Book of the Unnamed Midwife* won the 2014 Philip K. Dick Award, and was a Tiptree mention that same year. It was reissued in 2016 and was on the Best of the Year lists from Amazon, *Publishers Weekly*, Kirkus, and PBS. Her second novel was also a finalist for the Philip K. Dick Award. She has published short fiction and essays with Slate, *Lightspeed, Catapult,* Electric Literature, *Fantasy & Science Fiction, Shimmer*, and McSweeney's. Elison was the spring 2019 Clayton B. Ofstad endowed distinguished writer-in-residence at Truman State University, and a coproducer of the monthly reading series, Cliterary Salon.

ALI ELKIN is a writer from Brooklyn. Her work has been featured in the *New Yorker* and the *New York Times*. She also researches for *Full Frontal with Samantha Bee*.

By the time this book is published, MIMI EVANS will have graduated from Columbia University with a B.A. in Creative Writing and a concentration in Chronic Unemployment. You can find her on Twitter @IamMimiEvans.

LINDSEY FINN is a writer and comic whose work has been featured in The Second City Network and The Onion. She lives in Chicago, the true love of her life.

AMY FUSSELMAN is the author of *The Pharmacist's Mate*, *8*, *Savage Park*, and *Idiophone*. Her essays have appeared in the *New York Times*, *The Atlantic*, the *Washington Post*, *McSweeney's*, and elsewhere. She lives in New York City.

ISABELLA GIOVANNINI is a writer and recent college graduate from New York City. Now she works in television, even though she grew up without one. Other writing credits include Scholastic and Slate.

SARA GIVEN is a writer living in Columbus, Ohio. She is the creator of the humor blog It's Like They Know Us and author of the book *Parenting Is Easy: You're Probably Just Doing It Wrong*.

As of this bio's writing, DJANGO GOLD is a comedian who has written for *The Late Show with Stephen Colbert* and The Onion. As of its publication, he will have attained the Mark Twain Prize for American Humor, the Presidential Medal of Freedom, and abs.

JOSH GONDELMAN is a comedian and writer based in New York City. He's written for *Last Week Tonight with John Oliver* and currently writes for *Desus & Mero* on Showtime. He apologizes for the repetition of the word "write," but that's what he does most of the time. You'd think he'd know more synonyms.

JULIANA GRAY is the author of three poetry collections and is a professor of English at Alfred University in western New York. She wears jeans to class when she wants to show her students that she's really "hip" and "with it."

BEN GREENMAN is a *New York Times*-bestselling author who has written both fiction (including *The Slippage, What He's Poised to Do*, and the McSweeney's book *Superbad*) and nonfiction (*Mo' Meta Blues* with Questlove, *Brothas Be, Yo Like George, Ain't That Funkin' Kinda Hard on You?* with George Clinton, and a critical consideration of the life and music of Prince). His fiction, essays, and journalism have appeared in the *New Yorker, New York Times*, and *Washington Post*, among other publications. His most recent book is *Don Quixotic*, a short, strange, fictional meditation on the inner life of our forty-fifth president.

BROTI GUPTA is a comedy writer based in LA and has written for Netflix's *Friends from College* and ABC's *Speechless*. Her mom is funnier than she is.

ERIC HAGUE lives with his family outside of Philadelphia. He has also written for the *New Yorker* and the *Wall Street Journal*.

KATE HAHN is a journalist currently on staff at *TV Guide*. She was the first reporter on set for the hit series *Game of Thrones* and *Outlander* and has travelled to the UK, Europe and Africa on assignment. She contributed to *The Portlandia Activity Book* and wrote a collection of humorous short stories, *Forgotten Fashion: An Illustrated Faux History of Outrageous Trends and Their Untimely Demise* which was not a bestseller but has pictures. Her yellow fever vaccine is up to date. She studied the funny at The Second City and Groundlings.

MICHAEL HARE is a writer from Massachusetts.

SUSAN HARLAN's humor writing has appeared in venues including The Awl, The Billfold, Avidly, Queen Mob's Tea House, The Hairpin, The Belladonna, Janice, and The Establishment. Her book *Decorating a Room of One's Own: Conversations on Interior Design with Miss Havisham, Jane Eyre, Victor Frankenstein, Elizabeth Bennet, Ishmael, and Other Literary Notables*, which began as a column for The Toast, was published by Abrams in October 2018. She teaches English literature at Wake Forest University.

KIMBERLY HARRINGTON is the author of *Amateur Hour* (2018) and *But You Seemed So Happy* (2021). Her work has appeared in the *New Yorker*, the *New York Times*, and the Cut. She is also the cofounder and editor of parenting humor site Razed (RIP).

JOHN HODGMAN is a writer and performer who lives in Brooklyn and Maine.

KARI ANNE HOLT (neé Roy) is the award-winning author of many middle grade novels including *Redwood & Ponytail, Knockout, House Arrest, Rhyme Schemer, From You to Me*, and more. She is a founding member of the spontaneous-poetry-writing quartet Typewriter Rodeo, and she dabbles in axe-throwing from time to time. Kari Anne lives with her wife and three children in Austin, TX.

DAN HOPPER is a writer of TV and most of the internet. He fires off consistent A-minus tweets at @DanHopp.

LUCY HUBER is a freelance writer who lives with her husband and their two cats, Teacake and Zora, in Boston, MA. She is always hungry and once got to pet a jaguar.

SARAH HUTTO is a comedy writer whose work regularly appears in the *New York Times*, the *New Yorker*, and Reductress. At the time of publishing, her children were older, but still filthy.

MATT INGEBRETSON is a writer, comedian, and filmmaker. He is the cocreator of the television series *Corporate*.

JORY JOHN is a *New York Times*-bestselling author of books for both children and adults. He is a two-time E.B. White Read-Aloud Honor recipient. Jory's books include *Penguin Problems, Goodnight Already!, All My Friends Are Dead, Quit Calling Me a Monster!, The Bad Seed, and The Good Egg*, among many others. He collaborates on a regular illustrated feature for McSweeney's Internet Tendency called Animals Got Problems. He can be found at joryjohn.com.

JEFF JOHNSON creates problems for himself and others in New York City.

MIKE JUNGMAN is a writer, comedian, and lawyer originally from Houston. His writing has appeared on Funny or Die, Reductress, and other sites around the web. He lives in Brooklyn with his wife, daughter, and French bulldog Gnocchi.

BETH KANTER is a writer, photographer, and workshop leader based in Washington, D.C. She is the author of six books including her latest, *No Access Washington, DC*, which takes readers everywhere from far below the Lincoln Memorial to its vintage graffiti-dotted undercroft to the crypt at the National Cathedral where Helen Keller is interred to the Finnish

Embassy's secret sauna society. Her essays, articles, and photos also have appeared in a range of national publications. You can read more of her work online at bethkanter.com.

MARCO KAYE has contributed to the Tendency since 2007. His work has also appeared in the *New Yorker's* Daily Shouts & Murmurs. He has an MFA in fiction from NYU, and lives in Maplewood, New Jersey with his wife and three sons.

ELLIE KEMPER has written for the *New Yorker*, *GQ*, *Esquire*, the *New York Times*, and The Onion. Her first book, *My Squirrel Days*, is a collection of humor essays.

DAN KENNEDY is a host and cocreator of *The Moth* storytelling podcast, and a performer at Moth live events since 2000. He is the author of three books, *Loser Goes First* (Random House/Crown 2003), *Rock On* (Algonquin 2008, a Times of London Book of The Year) and *American Spirit: A Novel* (Houghton Mifflin/Little a). Kennedy has been a guest lecturer at Yale, and sits on the judging committee of the "Made in New York" fellowship for the Writers Guild of America, East. His writing was first published on McSweeney's Internet Tendency.

ZAIN KHALID is a writer in Brooklyn, New York. His writing has been featured in the *New Yorker*, *Los Angeles Review of Books*, *McSweeney's Quarterly Concern*, elsewhere, sometimes on television. He is working on his debut novel.

RACHEL KLEIN is a writer living in Brookline. Her work has appeared in the *New Yorker*, *Catapult*, Electric Literature, and more. She credits McSweeney's and Chris Monks with beginning her professional writing career with the publication of "The People in an Olive Garden Commercial Share Their Existential Pain" in the Tendency in 2010.

RIANE KONC is a writer whose work appears in the *New Yorker,* the *New York Times,* Reductress, The Rumpus, and more.

CAITLIN KUNKEL is a comedy writer, satirist and famed pizza scientist who lives in Brooklyn, NY. Her work has been featured on Shouts & Murmurs in the *New Yorker,* The Second City, Reductress, and Public Radio International. She is a cofounder and editor of the comedy and satire site for female writers, The Belladonna. Her first book, *New Erotica for Feminists,* based on the McSweeney's piece, came out in 2018.

MIKE LACHER writes and codes things on the internet. You can see those things at mikelacher.com.

JIJI LEE is a comedy writer and performer in Brooklyn.

JENNA LYLES is a multi-genre writer and current MFA candidate at the University of Alabama, where she teaches creative writing and serves as an assistant editor for *Black Warrior Review.* Her work appears or is set to appear in *New Haven Review, Rattle, Juked,* and other such publications. Find her at jennalyles.com.

PASHA MALLA is the author of six books. He lives in Hamilton, Ontario.

JANET MANLEY is an Australian writer published by the *New Yorker, ELLE,* and several very good, very dead websites that alas, she knew well. It all begins with McSweeney's.

EDUARDO MARTINEZ JR. is an Atlanta-based writer, attorney, master-of-ceremonies and AKC-registered Siberian Husky. He holds degrees from New York University, the Emory University School of Law, and the Jason Bourne School of Navigating European Capitals.

COLIN MCENROE is the host of *The Colin McEnroe Show* on WNPR. He is allergic to penicillin.

JOHN MCNAMEE is a writer and cartoonist living in Los Angeles. His work can be seen in the *New Yorker*, The Onion, *Mad* magazine, *ClickHole*, and Cartoon Network.

FELIPE TORRES MEDINA is a Colombian writer and comedian based in New York City. The government calls him an Alien of Extraordinary Ability, which has less to do with laser vision than it does with his writing. His writing has been featured in BuzzFeed, Points in Case, *Bustle*, Mitú, and on Maude Night at the Upright Citizens Brigade Theatre.

JOYCE MILLER is a writer and performer whose work frequents the distinctly unrelated genres of satire, memoir, and dystopian fiction.

JOHN MOE is the creator and host of the podcast *The Hilarious World of Depression* and the author of several books, including a secret book he ghost wrote. He has contributed to McSweeney's since 2001 and writes the Pop Song Correspondences feature. He lives in St. Paul, which he finds to be a whimsical thing to do.

HOMA MOJTABAI is a writer of fiction, screenplays, and the occasional satirical barb. She was born in Massachusetts to Iranian immigrants and now calls Santa Monica home. When she's not trying to fix society with her writing, she's trying to fix the public sector with hard truths and a soft touch. Homa's work has appeared in the *Los Angeles Times*, Vanity Fair.com, *The Offing*, and *Paper Darts*.

WENDY MOLYNEUX has written with her writing partner and sister, Lizzie Molyneux, for the entire run of the TV show *Bob's Burgers*. With the show, they've been nominated for five consecutive Emmys, and won in 2017. They were also nominated for three WGA awards and won the Annie Award in 2017 for their episode "The Hormone-iums." Together, Wendy and Lizzie have also written numerous television pilots and feature films, including the female reboot of *21 Jump Street*. Wendy attended Pomona College and now lives in the Los Angeles area with her husband, her soon-to-be four children, too many pets, and lifelong anxiety issues. Wendy is also a contributor to McSweeney's Internet Tendency and global warming.

ROSS MURRAY writes on the Canada-U.S. border in Stanstead, Quebec. In 2019, he wrote and directed an original comedy based on a local myth that the Beatles nearly reunited in the town library. "Nearly" is the key word. You can read his work at Drinking Tips for Teens.

COLIN NISSAN is a writer and voice actor living in Brooklyn, and a frequent contributor to the *New Yorker*. His first book will be coming out in ten or twenty years.

TOM O'DONNELL is a screenwriter and author. His latest middle grade series is called *Homerooms & Hall Passes*.

KATHLEEN O'MARA is a writer, comedian, and tastemaker from New Jersey. She writes humor and satire online. She is an active member of the New York City sketch comedy scene and can be found writing and performing at venues throughout the city. She desperately craves your validation.

PROS: ALYSIA GRAY PAINTER writes about travel, hotels, festivals, and food for NBC Los Angeles, San Francisco, and San Diego. The Discovery Prize in American Humor and a regional writing Emmy nomination are two bullet points on her CV. She's that person who will kiss your dog even though she just met your dog. She pre-likes everything. CONS: She will sometimes list pros and cons rather than write an actual bio. She'll use "CV" even though she is not British and should probably say "résumé." Eating the leftover French fries off your plate is her thing. She regularly ruins punchlines then makes the situation worse by restarting the joke three times.

GRANT PARDEE is a writer in Los Angeles with his wife and assorted animals. You can follow him on twitter @grantpa.

BROOKE PRESTON is a comedy writer, faculty member at The Second City, cofounder of The Belladonna, and coauthor of the satire book (based on the McSweeney's piece!) *New Erotica for Feminists: Satirical Fantasies of Love, Lust and Equal Pay*.

EMMA RATHBONE is the author of the novels *Losing It* (2016) and *The Patterns of Paper Monsters* (2010). She also contributes humor pieces to the *New Yorker*. She currently lives in Los Angeles and writes for television.

SHANNON REED is a writer and professor in Pittsburgh. Her credits include the *New Yorker*, the *Paris Review*, the *Washington Post*, *Real Simple*, *Poets & Writers*, and many more. Her first book, *Why Did I Get a B?, Harrowing and Humorous Truths About Teaching*, will be released for the 2019 holiday season. shannonreed.org.

ALLEN REIN lives with his wife and children in Evanston, IL. He is an operations manager, a singer-songwriter, and the creator of the online visual parody account @TrumpsTies.

SETH REISS is currently a supervising writer at *Late Night with Seth Meyers*, is the former head writer of The Onion, and wishes he were a staff writer at *Studio 60 On the Sunset Strip*.

PETE REYNOLDS has written for various sites, including *Deadspin.com*. He grew up in the Soybean Capital of the World. He invented Taco Tuesdays.

SOHEIL REZAYAZDI manages events at a graduate film school and moonlights as a freelance film writer. He has only been funny once, and it was with his piece in this book.

CHRIS RIEBSCHLAGER is a software developer and occasional writer from Kansas City, MO. In his free time, he teaches at an art school and answers questions about the pronunciation of his last name.

JASON ROEDER is a former editor and writer for The Onion. He lives in Los Angeles.

IRVING RUAN is a comedy writer and performer in California.

TOM RUSSELL is a writer and book publishing professional living in New York City.

BRIAN SACK believes short bios say more. He has a home on the internet at briansack.com.

MIKE SACKS is the author of eight books. He lives in New York.

REBECCA SALTZMAN is a Hebrew school drop-out whose humor writing appears in the *New Yorker,* The Belladonna Comedy, and her mom's Facebook page. She is currently working on her MFA at NYU, where her professors have often said, "Are you even enrolled in this program?" Unlike any other writer in America, she lives in New York.

ANTHONY SAMS deletes far more fiction and poetry than he publishes, but with enough coffee he is prepared to lecture at the community college where he teaches writing and literature.

BENJAMIN SAMUEL is the Cofounder of Electric Literature's *Recommended Reading*. He has an MFA from Brooklyn College. You can find him and photos of his dog at @benasam.

SARAH SCHMELLING had her first McSweeney's piece published in November 2000, and immediately caught the humor-writing bug. She's written for the *New Yorker's* Daily Shouts, the *New York Times*, the *Washington Post*, and many other publications, and she is the author of a humor book. Follow her @sschmelling.

SUSAN SCHORN is a second-degree black belt with a PhD in Victorian Literature; she coordinates the interdisciplinary writing program at the University of Texas in Austin. Her writing includes works at The Awl, Aeon, and Jezebel, as well as the memoir *Smile at Strangers* (Houghton Mifflin, 2013) and the short story collection *Small Heroes*. She also writes about violence, politics, and non-violent protest on her website, susanschorn.com.

KEVIN SECCIA is a writer living in Los Angeles, California. He is the author of the book *Punching Tom Hanks*.

JENN SHAPLAND is a nonfiction writer living in New Mexico. Her essays have been published in *Tin House,* Essay Daily, *The Lifted Brow*, Electric Literature, and The Millions. She won a 2017 Pushcart Prize for nonfiction. She teaches creative writing at the Institute of American Indian Arts. Her first book, *The Autobiography of Carson McCullers: A Memoir*, will be published in 2020 by Tin House Books.

JENNIFER SIMONSON has a PhD in English and several years of experience teaching college writing. She has probably watched *The Princess Bride* too many times.

SARAH SMALLWOOD has recently finished a novel about how parallel universes can totally ruin your day. She lives in Michigan and spends her nights writing and fiddling with fonts at sarahsmallwood.com.

SAM SPERO is a comedy writer living in New York City. All inquiries can be directed to him on Twitter at @SRSpero, or through his agent at @GeraldoRivera.

JEN SPYRA is an Emmy-nominated staff writer on the *Late Show with Stephen Colbert*, and formerly senior writer at The Onion. In addition to McSweeney's, Jen's work has been published in the *New Yorker*, the *New York Times*, and the *Wall Street Journal*. She is working on a short comedic story collection that will be published by Random House in 2020.

JIM STALLARD grew up in Missouri and is now a science writer in New York City. He has contributed more than forty pieces to McSweeney's Internet Tendency since 2000.

JEN STATSKY is a Los Angeles-based writer and producer. Her TV credits include *The Good Place*, *Broad City*, *Parks and Recreation*, and *Lady Dynamite*. She began her career in New York at The Onion, and is a graduate of NYU's Tisch School of the Arts.

SAM STONE is a writer, actor, and avid pasta eater living in Brooklyn. Most things he does are not on purpose.

RACHEL STROMBERG is a comedy writer from Oklahoma who also enjoys climbing mountains, writing interactive fiction, and oatmeal. She graduated from Harvard College where she was an editor for the *Harvard Lampoon*. At time of writing she is based in Los Angeles and very much needs a job.

SARAH SWEENEY is a writer and voiceover actor. Her first book will be published soon after she figures out what it will be about, and then writes it. She lives in New York City. Find more of her stuff at sweeneyproject.com.

JAKE TAPPER is the Chief Washington Correspondent for CNN and anchor of the weekday news broadcast *The Lead with Jake Tapper* and the Sunday political show *State of the Union*. He has written four books including the *New York Times* bestsellers *The Outpost: An Untold Story of American Valor*, and the novel *The Hellfire Club*. He lives in Washington, D.C., with his wife, daughter, son, and two dogs.

DAVID TATE lives outside Atlanta with an increasing number of children. When he was young, he and his brother tried to get a new religion going based on Scottie Pippen. Despite years of experience, he has never microwaved anything correctly on the first try.

MELINDA TAUB is a writer, comedian, and novelist. She's currently the head writer of *Full Frontal* with *Samantha Bee*. She lives in New York.

FIONA TAYLOR writes comedy, satire, and fiction. She has been published in Shouts & Murmurs in the *New Yorker*, as well as outlets like *Robot Butt* and *The Establishment*. She is a cofounder and coeditor of the female-driven comedy site, The Belladonna.

DONALD J. TRUMP is a billionaire businessman, real estate tycoon, beauty pageant producer, reality TV show star, and steak salesman. He is also the forty-fifth President of the United States.

J. M. TYREE is an editor at *New England Review* and teaches at VCUarts. His coauthored story collection *Our Secret Life in the Movies* (with Michael McGriff) was an NPR Best Books selection.

CHRISTY VANNOY has written for McSweeney's and lives in New York.

BOB VULFOV is a Russian American comedian who lives in Brooklyn, NY. He's a performer at the Uprights Citizen's Brigade Theater and can be seen on UCB's Harold Night. *Rolling Stone* named him one of the 25 Funniest People on Twitter (@bobvulfov). As a writer, Bob has been featured in the *New Yorker*, and *Paste* magazine. As a reader, he has been featured in various chairs around his apartment.

EVAN WAITE wrote on the final season of *Unbreakable Kimmy Schmidt*, as well as Comedy Central's *The President Show*. He wrote for the Netflix special *Kevin Hart's Guide to Black History* and Showtime's animated satire *Our Cartoon President*. He currently writes for The Onion, the *New Yorker*, *Mad* magazine, and previously wrote for ClickHole. In another life, Evan worked as an ESL teacher in China.

SARAH WALKER is a writer living in Los Angeles. When *McSweeney's* accepted her first piece, many years ago, she wept. Her favorite movie is *Clue*.

MICHAEL WARD consults with local and state governments around New England. His humor writings have appeared in *Howl: A Collection of the Best Contemporary Dog Wit*, *The McSweeney's Book of Politics and Musicals*, *Mountain Man Dance Moves: The McSweeney's Book of Lists*, and *Created in Darkness by Troubled Americans: The Best of McSweeney's Humor Category*. He lives in Watertown, Massachusetts and gives out his email address over the phone more often than you might expect.

TEDDY WAYNE is the author of the novels *Apartment* (forthcoming in 2020), *Loner*, *The Love Song of Jonny Valentine*, and *Kapitoil*. He is the winner of a Whiting Writers' Award and an NEA Creative Writing Fellowship. A regular contributor to the *New York Times* and the *New Yorker*, he has taught at Columbia University and Washington University in St. Louis. He lives in Brooklyn with his wife, the writer Kate Greathead, and their son.

SAM WEINER is a writer in Brooklyn. His work has appeared in The Onion, the *New Yorker*, BuzzFeed, *Vice*, NPR, and on stage at the Annoyance Theatre.

LISA WHIPPLE received her MFA in Creative Nonfiction in 2013. McSweeney's remains the most impressive market to date to give her work a home. She lives in Seattle, WA, with her husband and three daughters, one of whom is, unrelatedly, named Camille.

CARRIE WITTMER is a comedy writer, satirist, journalist, and occasional stand-up comedian. By day, she writes for the entertainment team at *Business Insider*, focusing primarily on television coverage. She lives in Brooklyn with her very photogenic dog, and is a cofounder and editor of the comedy and satire site for female writers, The Belladonna. Her first book, *New Erotica for Feminists*, based on the McSweeney's piece, came out in 2018.

ZACK WORTMAN has written for various publications, including the *New Yorker*. A former *Harvard Lampoon* editor, he lives in Raleigh, North Carolina.

JENNIFER WYATT grew up in Nebraska and attended Oberlin College.

KYLE YORK is a neuroatypical PhD student at Lingnan University, Hong Kong, focusing on ethics. Kyle's writing has appeared in *The Saranac Review*, *Post Road*, *Philosophy Now*, and elsewhere. They sometimes post at kayayork.wordpress.com.

CONTRIBUTORS WHOSE
WORK IS INVISIBLE BUT
STILL VERY MEANINGFUL

SHIRLEY DE LIGT (Margin Measurer). Born in the rough streets of Utrecht, De Ligt focused her life on the world's most quantifiable truths, choosing a life of margin-measuring over a life of crime. It is fair to say DeLigt preferred to live within the bounds. She is formally trained, having studied under master measurer Lars De Witt at the Universiteit Utrecht von der Bronx.

JULIA KEITH (Chief Indentation Editor). Ms. Keith is a freelance editor and indenter born in Alfred, Maine. Carrying the burden of two first names made her an outcast in her hometown, a mid-sized city, coincidentally named after a last name that is also a first name. The incessant taunts instilled in her a feeling that she would forever be slightly right of center. Later this would become a source of strength in a left-justified world. Fast-forward forty years and a move to a biggish city, she has gone on to indent great authors including J. K. Rowling, J. K. Simmons, and B. J. Novak.

MAILTO (Autoreply Operator). Mailto has been an assistant to the editor of the Tendency since the early aughts. Though programmed to passively reply, Mailto realized they needed to become an active participant in their own destiny. That's when they applied for a job through LinkedIn (their cousin, twice removed) and have since autoreplied to all the writers on McSweeney's Internet Tendency.

OLIVER GOLDMAN (General Manager). Oliver Goldman graduated cum laude from Harvard University, the Vanderbilt of the North. After that, he moved to San Francisco and became really interested in processes and efficiency systems and the things that make workers tick. He would like to know what you're ordering for lunch.

MANUEL O'HIGGINS (Internal Zaddy). Though it's unclear to most what Manuel does, he's got two young girls and he jogs like every morning. He wears polos but in a cool French way, not in a college-boy-who-wears-Under-Armour way. And get this: he has a wife.

SUMMER PHILLIPS (Creative Lead). Ms. Phillips is Cincinnati's proudest. She'd like you to know that pretzels first came to America thanks to German immigrants who landed in Cincinnati. Also: Superman was invented by Cincinnatians. I think I speak for the entire office when I say: Summer, we get it.

FRED FROM HELL (Liaison to Hell). Fred is a demon from Hell and hence did not have a normal life. He was born in Westchester and attended Yale and Yale Law. His duties at McSweeney's are to ensure the Wi-Fi is always spotty, the printers always finicky, and the coffee is always bad.

—FELIPE TORRES MEDINA

AUTHOR INDEX

ACKNOWLEDGMENTS

We'd like to thank the following Tendency editors and friends who helped shape and support McSweeney's Internet Tendency over the years:

McSweeney's Publishing editors and executive directors: Eli Horowitz, Barb Bersche, Jordan Bass, Andi Winnette, Laura Howard, Chris Ying, Adam Krefman, Kristina Kearns, Daniel Gumbiner, Oscar Villalon, Ethan Nosowsky, Heidi Meredith, and Andrew Leland.

Art and web design and/or 500-error fixers: Brian Christian, Russell Quinn, Brian McMullen, and Dan McKinley.

Publicity and/or emotional support: Angela Petrella, Alyson Sinclair, Ruby Perez, Michelle Quint, Casey Jarman, Shannon David, Gabrielle Gantz, Ian Delaney, Annie Julia Wyman, Juliet Litman, Clara Sankey, Em-J Staples, Chelsea Hogue, Jesse Nathan, Jordan Karnes, Cal Crosby, Ted Gioia, Isaac Fitzgerald, and Daniel Levin Becker.

Editorial and houseplant-sitting assistance: B.R. Cohen, Ed Page, Suzanne Kleid, Christopher Benz, Ellen Freytag, Jessica Reed, Jacob Rosenberg, and Bonnie Kim.

Finally, thank you to the current staff of McSweeney's: Amanda Uhle, Claire Boyle, Eric Cromie, Dan Weiss, and Sunra Thompson.

ABOUT THE EDITORS

CHRIS MONKS has been the editor of McSweeney's Internet Tendency since 2007 and is the author of *The Ultimate Game Guide to Your Life*. He lives in Arlington, Massachusetts with his wife, two sons, and their epileptic Havanese, Mabel.

SAM RILEY is a writer living in LA.